T0333001

The Road to Freedom

The Road to Freedom

Economics and the Good Society

JOSEPH E. STIGLITZ

ALLEN LANE
an imprint of
PENGUIN BOOKS

ALLEN LANE

UK | USA | Canada | Ireland | Australia
India | New Zealand | South Africa

Allen Lane is part of the Penguin Random House group of companies
whose addresses can be found at global.penguinrandomhouse.com

First published in the USA by W. W. Norton 2024
First published in Great Britain by Allen Lane 2024
004

Copyright © Joseph E. Stiglitz, 2024

The moral right of the author has been asserted

Printed and bound in Great Britain by Clays Ltd, Elcograf S.p.A.

The authorized representative in the EEA is Penguin Random House Ireland,
Morrison Chambers, 32 Nassau Street, Dublin D02 YH68

A CIP catalogue record for this book is available from the British Library

ISBN: 978–0–241–68788–8

TABLE OF CONTENTS

PART III
WHAT KIND OF ECONOMY PROMOTES A GOOD, JUST, AND FREE SOCIETY?

The Road to Freedom

PREFACE

Freedom is a core human value. But many of freedom's advocates seldom ask what the idea really means. Freedom for whom? What happens when one person's freedom comes at the expense of another's? The Oxford philosopher Isaiah Berlin[1] put it well when he said, "Freedom for the wolves has often meant death to the sheep."[2]

How are we to balance political and economic freedoms? What is the meaning of the right to vote for someone who's starving? What about the freedom to live up to one's potential, which may only be possible if we tax the rich and deprive them of the freedom to spend as they want?

The Right in the United States[3] seized on the rhetoric of freedom several decades ago, claiming it as their own just as they claimed patriotism and the American flag as their own. Freedom is an important value that we do and ought to cherish, but it is more complex and more nuanced than the Right's invocation. The current conservative reading of what freedom means is superficial, misguided, and ideologically motivated. The Right claims to be the defender of freedom, but I'll show that the way they define the word and pursue it has led to the opposite result, vastly reducing the freedoms of most citizens.

A good initial and central place in which these shortcomings can be identified is the conflation of free markets with economic freedom, and economic freedom with political freedom. A few quotes from Republican leaders convey the spirit of what I have in mind.

As the US economy was on the verge of a meltdown in 2008 after decades of financial deregulation, and the government was about to undertake the most massive bailout of the private sector in the history of the planet, George W. Bush, who served as president when the financial crisis occurred, put what was at issue as follows:

> While reforms in the financial sector are essential, the long-term solution to today's problems is sustained economic growth. And the surest path to that growth is free markets and free people.[4]

Before Bush, Ronald Reagan, whose presidency (1981–1989) was widely viewed as a turning point toward the right and a full-throated embrace of free markets, had enumerated an Economic Bill of Rights.[5] He regretted that the Constitution hadn't gone far enough in guaranteeing these rights, focusing instead on political rights. As he explained:

> Inextricably linked to these political freedoms are protections for the economic freedoms. . . . While the Constitution sets our political freedoms in greater detail, these economic freedoms are part and parcel of it. . . . There are four essential economic freedoms. They are what links life inseparably to liberty, what enables an individual to control his own destiny, what makes self-government and personal independence part of the American experience.[6]

The four freedoms are (1) freedom to work, (2) freedom to enjoy the fruits of one's labor, (3) freedom to own and control one's property, and (4) *the freedom to participate in a free market—to contract freely for goods and services and to achieve one's full potential without government limits on opportunity, economic independence, and growth.* (italics mine)

While the colonialists rebelling against the British adopted the slogan "Taxation without representation is tyranny," their twenty-first-century descendants seem to have concluded that taxation *with* representation is also tyranny. Ron Paul, a long-serving Texas Republican who ran for president as the Libertarian Party candidate in 1988, put it baldly: "We need to understand that the more government spends, the more freedom is lost."[7]

Rick Santorum, a Republican senator (1995–2007) who vied to be the Republican presidential candidate in 2012 and almost succeeded, put it the other way around: "The less money we take, the more freedom you have."[8]

And Ted Cruz, the conservative Texas senator and erstwhile 2016 presidential candidate, famously named the parts of the government that he thought most encroached on freedom: "I have identified the *Five for Freedom*: During my first year as president, I will fight to abolish the IRS, the Department of Education, the Department of Energy, the Department of Commerce, and the Department of Housing and Urban Development."[9]

These conceptions of freedom stand in marked contrast to the ideals articulated by President Franklin Delano Roosevelt, who, in his State of the Union address to Congress on January 6, 1941, laid out a vision of freedom that moved beyond traditional civil liberties, which he confined to only the first two in his "Four Freedoms" speech:

> The first is freedom of speech, and expression—everywhere in the world. The second is freedom of every person to worship God in his own way—everywhere in the world.

Recognizing that these were not enough, he added two more. People needed:

> . . . freedom from want—which, translated into world terms, means economic understandings which will secure to every nation a healthy peacetime life for its inhabitants—everywhere in the world.

and

> . . . freedom from fear—which, translated into world terms, means a world-wide reduction of armaments to such a point and in such a thorough fashion that no nation will be in a position to commit an act of physical aggression against any neighbor—anywhere in the world.

A person facing extremes of want and fear is not free. Neither is someone whose ability to have a full life, aspiring to use all of her capabilities, is restrained because she was born into poverty. Growing up in Gary, Indiana, the once-thriving steel town on the southern shores of Lake Michigan, I saw firsthand this lack of economic freedom for African Americans, who had escaped oppression in the South in the Great Migration, and for the children of so many of the immigrants who had come from Europe to work in the mills. Several of my classmates shared their life experiences with me at our fifty-fifth high school reunion in 2015. When they graduated from high school, they said, they had planned to get a job at the mill just like their fathers. But with another economic downturn hitting they had *no choice*—no freedom—but to join the military. And when their service in the Vietnam War ended, they again had few choices, at least as they saw it. Deindustrialization was taking away manufacturing jobs, leaving mainly opportunities that made use of their military training, such as the police force.

Both as a policymaker in Washington and as an adviser and commentator on economic events, I saw freedom in a different light than Bush, Reagan, and others on the Right. From Reagan to Clinton, presidential administrations expanded the freedom of the banks. Financial deregulation and *liberalization* meant freeing the banks to do as they pleased, or at least allowed them to do more of what they wanted.[10] The very word "liberalization" connoted "freeing." Bankers used that new freedom in ways that enhanced their profits but carried huge risks for society. When the 2008 financial crisis hit, we discovered the cost. Many Americans lost their freedom from fear and want as the very real prospect grew that millions of workers and retirees would lose their jobs and homes. We as a society lost our freedom—we had *no choice* but to spend taxpayers' money to bail out the banks. If we hadn't, the entire financial system—and the economy—would have collapsed.

During my years serving as President Bill Clinton's adviser (the last two years as chair of the Council of Economic Advisers, 1995–1997), I strongly opposed deregulation of finance, in part because I understood that "freeing" the financial sector would make us all less free in the end. Following my departure in 1997, Congress passed two bills, one deregulating the banks and the other committing the government not to regulate derivatives—steps beyond what even Reagan had done. Deregulation/liberalization set the stage for the 2008 financial debacle. Reagan and Clinton had given freedom to the wolves (the bankers) at the expense of the sheep (workers, ordinary investors, and homeowners).

Freedom in America's historical context

For Americans steeped in the idea that their country was founded on the principles of freedom, the term is especially evocative. So, it's important that we think carefully about what the word meant *then* and, two centuries later, what it means *now*. There were ambiguities and inconsistencies at the founding, and the underlying conceptual problems have only become clearer since. Freedom *then* didn't mean freedom for everyone. It didn't mean freedom for the enslaved. Women and others without property were not guaranteed equal rights and didn't get them. Women faced taxation without representation—it would take 140 years for the country to face up to that inconsistency. Puerto Rico was conquered by force from the Spanish, and its citizens still face taxation without representation.

It has long been evident that there are connections between economic and political freedoms. The debate about which freedom should be given primacy was central to the Cold War. The West argued that political freedoms (clearly in short supply in the Communist world) were more important; the Communists argued that without some basic economic rights, political rights meant little. But could a nation have one set of rights without the other? Economists such as John Stuart Mill, Milton Friedman, and Friedrich Hayek have weighed into this debate[11] and addressed the question of what kind of economic and political system best delivers these twin freedoms and enhances individual and societal well-being. This book looks at the same questions from a twenty-first-century perspective, arriving at answers markedly different from Friedman's and Hayek's in the middle of the last century.

The concept of trade-offs sits at the center of economics, and this idea offers another reason that economists have much to add to discussions of freedom. As will become clear, I believe there are few, if any, absolutes in this arena. Economics provides tools to think about the nature of the trade-offs that should be central to discussions about freedom and how trade-offs should be addressed.

Moreover, once we get beneath the Right's superficial allegiance to freedom, we uncover a host of conundrums, including the key insight that mild coercion—forcing someone to do something that he of his own volition would not do—can, in some instances, enhance everyone's freedom, even the freedom of those being coerced. As I will demonstrate, economics provides an explanation for the many important instances in which collective action—doing together what individuals could not do on their own—is desirable. But often, collective action is not possible without a modicum of coercion because of what are called free-rider problems, which we will consider later.

Freedom from a twenty-first-century perspective

Ultimately, I will show that the true advocates of deep, meaningful freedom are aligned with the progressive movement both in the US and abroad. They and the center-left parties that represent them need to reclaim the freedom agenda. For Americans, particularly, that entails a reconsideration of the country's history and founding myths.

The first objective of this book is to provide a coherent and straightforward explication of freedom from the perspective of twenty-first-century economics, as John Stuart Mill did in the middle of the nineteenth century in his classic book *On Liberty* (1859). The world has changed in the more than a century and a half since, and so has our understanding of the economy and of society. What is debated today in the halls of power is different from what was on the political agenda long ago. Then, memories of state oppression of religion (in particular by the British government, with some migration to the US motivated by this oppression) were still alive, and it was this legacy as much as anything else that shaped people's views. Today, we grapple with climate change, guns, pollution, the right to abortion, and the freedom to express gender identity. More broadly, we debate the role of social coercion and the coercive reactions against it. Our present-day challenges require a rethinking of basic concepts, including freedom. Indeed, Mill himself said that freedoms need to be rethought as the economy and society change.

While I believe economists have much to add to our understanding of the meaning of freedom and its relationship to our economic and social system, the peculiar and specific lens through which they typically see the world is also limiting; there is much more to the subject that is not well captured within the distinct perspectives that economists bring, and at various places in the text I call attention to these limitations.[12, 13]

Economic systems and freedom

Understanding the *meaning* of freedom is a prelude to my ultimate objective: to describe an economic and political system that delivers not only on efficiency, equity, and sustainability but also on moral values. In this discussion, the most important of those moral values is freedom, but freedom conceived as having *inherent ties* to notions of equity, justice, and well-being. It's this broadened notion of freedom that has been given short shrift by certain strands in economic thinking.

Hayek and Friedman were the most notable mid-twentieth-century defenders of unfettered capitalism. "Unfettered markets"—markets without rules and regulations—is an oxymoron, because without rules and regulations enforced by government there could and would be little trade. Cheating would be rampant, trust low. A world without any restraints would be a jungle in which only power mattered, determining who got what and who did what. It wouldn't be a market at all. Contracts agreeing to receive a good today in return for payment later couldn't exist, because there would be no enforcement mechanism. But there is a big difference between saying that a well-functioning society needs to have some contract enforcement and saying that *any* contract should be enforced.

Hayek and Friedman argued that capitalism as they interpreted it was the best system in terms of efficiency, and that without free markets and free enterprise we could not and would not have individual freedom. They believed that markets on their own would somehow remain competitive. Remarkably, they had already forgotten—or ignored—the experiences of monopolization and concentration of economic power that had led to competition laws (in the US, the Sherman Antitrust Act in 1890 and the Clayton Antitrust Act a quarter century later, in 1914). As government intervention grew in response to the Great Depression, which throughout much of the world left one out of four or more workers unemployed and destitute, Hayek worried that we were on the road to serfdom, as he put it in his 1944 book of that title;[14] that is, on the road to a society in which individuals would become subservient to the state.

I come to a radically different conclusion. It was because of democratic demands that democratic governments, such as the US, responded to the Great Depression through *collective action*. The failure of government to respond adequately to soaring unemployment in Germany led to the rise of Hitler. Today, it is *neoliberalism*—the belief in unregulated, unfettered markets[15]—that has led to massive inequalities and provided fertile ground for populists. Neoliberalism's crimes include freeing financial markets to precipitate the largest financial crisis in three-quarters of a century; freeing trade to accelerate deindustrialization; and freeing corporations to exploit consumers, workers, and the environment alike. Contrary to what Friedman suggested in his book *Capitalism and Freedom*, first published in 1962,[16] this form of capitalism does *not* enhance freedom in our society. Instead, it has led to the freedom of a few at the expense of the many. Freedom for the wolves; death for the sheep.

Similar issues play out internationally, revealing interesting and important relationships between the notion of rules and the ideal of freedom. It is not that globalization proceeds without rules, but those rules grant freedoms and impose constraints in ways that generate the same differential fate for wolves and sheep everywhere—it is just that the wolves and sheep are distributed over different regions and nations of the world. Embedded in so-called free trade agreements are rules that constrain the freedom of developing countries and emerging markets and the people who live in them, even as they expand multinational corporations' freedom to exploit.

This entire discussion takes us beyond a simple inquiry into the meaning of freedom. We delve into questions that are at the foundation of a modern economy: the moral legitimacy of property rights and the distribution of income and wealth generated by the economy. The Right often talks about the "sanctity of contracts," but I'll argue that there are many contracts that are immoral, in a deep sense, and should be forbidden and not enforced through courts of law. From our current perspective, the founders of the American Republic had a flawed view of the meaning of fundamental concepts like property and liberty. They recognized the property rights of slaveowners—indeed much of the "property" of the South were enslaved people—but they did not recognize the rights of the enslaved to enjoy the fruits of their labor. Even as they talked about freedom from British rule, enslavers denied freedom to large numbers of those living in the South. Undoubtedly, today's views will also be found wanting in a hundred years' time.

The great Italian intellectual Antonio Gramsci (1891–1937) was almost surely correct when he described our societal ideology as providing the underpinnings to both the functioning of society and the maintenance of the power of the elites. The ideology helps legitimize institutions and rules that grant more freedom to some and less to others—including the freedom to make the rules. The changes in America's belief systems that have occurred since the Constitution should make us keenly aware of this. What seemed legitimate, almost unquestioned, at the time seems horrendous today. That makes understanding the processes by which ideologies are formed and transmitted within society crucial, and here, too, Gramsci's insights about the hegemony of the elites are relevant. The way that influence is exercised is, of course, different in the twenty-first century than it was during his lifetime. Part II of this book takes up the way commonly accepted beliefs about the meaning of freedom are shaped.

Words matter

Modern behavioral economics has explained that "framing" matters, and that means the words we use matter. A bonus for doing the right thing is perceived as different from a penalty for doing the wrong thing, even though in classical economics the two can be equivalent and can induce the same actions.

The language of freedom, as it now plays out, has constrained our ability to reason soundly about what kind of economic, political, and social system best enhances the well-being of society—including what kind of system is most likely to deliver *meaningful* freedom and well-being to the largest number of people. The language of coercion and freedom has become an emotive part of our political vocabulary. Freedom is good; coercion is bad. Indeed, there is a prevailing, simplistic reasoning that sees freedom and coercion as mere antitheses of each other. In one case, an individual has the freedom to wear a mask or not, to get a vaccine or not, to contribute financially to the defense of the country or not, or to give money to the poor or not. The state has the power to take away these freedoms. It may compel or coerce me to wear a mask, get a vaccine, pay taxes to fund a defense force, or support people with lower incomes.

The same dichotomy exists at the level of the nation-state in its relation to other nation-states. States may feel forced into doing what they don't want to do, either by threat of military action or through threats of economic actions that would impact their economy so severely they believe they have no choice.

In many contexts, however, the word "coercion" doesn't seem helpful. All individuals (and all states) face constraints. One might say I am coerced into living within my budget, but one could just as well say that I am not entitled to live beyond my budget, or that no one else can be coerced to give me resources beyond those that my budget allows me to enjoy. Few would use the vocabulary of coercion to describe the constraint of living within one's means. We can simply think of a tighter budget constraint as one of many *noncoercive* ways in which a person's freedom to act is reduced. But an individual's budget constraint is, in a sense, socially determined. In a market economy, it is the result of economic forces that are shaped by socially determined rules, as I will explain in greater detail below.

Thus, the simplistic use of the word "freedom" by the Right has impaired a critical societal freedom: the freedom to choose an economic system that could, in fact, enhance freedom for most citizens. In that sense, I hope that the discussion in this book creates space for a wider debate—that it is *liberating*.

My intellectual journey

Readers of my earlier work will notice that this book builds on ideas that have long preoccupied me. My academic career began by showing theoretically that long-standing presumptions that competitive markets are efficient were simply wrong, especially when information was imperfect, which it always is. But my stints in the Clinton administration and at the World Bank convinced me that the deficiencies in our economy (and in prevailing approaches to economics) were more profound. In my earlier work, I described what globalization, financialization, and monopolization were doing to our economy, and their roles in increasing inequality, slowing growth, and reducing opportunity.

I also became convinced that the problems in our economy and society were not inevitable; they were not the result of any laws of nature or economics. They were, in a sense, a matter of choice, a result of the rules and regulations that had governed our economy. These had been shaped in recent decades by neoliberalism, and it was neoliberalism that was at fault.

But there is a second strand of my work relevant to this book. It began with my concern for natural resources and the environment that I related in papers written many years ago. It was obvious that there were critical market failures in protecting the environment and managing natural resources. I sought to better understand both the nature of these failures and what could be done about them. I served as a lead author of the 1995 *Intergovernmental Report on Climate Change*, the first such report to take on board economic analyses.[17]

Simultaneously, at the Council of Economic Advisers I was spearheading an effort to revise our system of national accounts to reflect what was going on with our natural resources and environment—to construct a "green GDP." We received enthusiastic cooperation from the Department of Commerce, which constructs such accounts. We knew we were onto something important when several members of Congress threatened to have our budgets slashed if we continued to pursue these efforts. My work was temporarily stymied, but a few years later France's president Nicolas Sarkozy asked me to co-chair an international Commission on the Measurement of Economic Performance and Social Progress, along with Nobel Prize–winning economist Amartya Sen and economist Jean-Paul Fitoussi. Our subsequent report, called *Mismeasuring Our Lives: Why GDP Doesn't Add Up*, was influential in motivating a movement sometimes referred to as Beyond GDP and the creation of an alliance of countries called the Wellbeing Economy Government Alliance, committed to putting well-being, broadly construed, at the center of their agendas.[18] The central tenet of the movement and the alliance is that what matters is not only material goods and services, as measured by GDP, but also overall individual and societal well-being, which includes many things that traditional GDP leaves out, including possibly an assessment of the state of freedom.

This book is very much in that spirit. Even more important than the inefficiencies and instabilities to which neoliberalism gives rise are the corrosive inequalities it generates, the way it engenders self-ishness and dishonesty, and the narrowing of vision and values that inevitably follows. We value freedom as individuals and as a society, and any analysis of what constitutes a good society must incorporate how that society promotes freedom, including the sensitivity that people have about how their actions might constrain the freedom of others. Among the critical failures of neoliberalism, I will explain, is that it curtails the freedom of the many while it expands the freedom of the few.

This book brings together, builds on, and extends my other work. It is not enough to recognize the origins and nature of the failures of neoliberalism and understand that we need to go beyond GDP. We need to understand that there are better alternative economic systems and see what they might look like. We must also ask what a good society is and figure out how to get there. In the following pages, more than providing clean answers, I ask questions and introduce a framework for thinking about the issues, including how to weigh different freedoms.

The challenges to—and attacks on—democracy and freedom have never been greater in my lifetime. I hope this book contributes to a deeper understanding of the meaning of freedom and strengthens the democratic debate over what kind of economic, political, and social system will contribute to the freedom of the most citizens. We are a nation born from the conviction that people must be free. We cannot allow one side to commandeer the very definition of freedom in economic and political terms and put it to their use.

We won't and can't win this existential fight for freedom and democracy unless we have a clearer idea of what we want. What is it we are fighting for? How is it that the Right has long muddled thinking on these concepts? Their confusion serves their purposes well, as they engage in a set of political battles that, were they to win, would lead to the antithesis of meaningful freedom.

CHAPTER I

Introduction

Freedom in Danger

Freedom is in danger. By most accounts, the number of people around the world living in free and democratic societies has been in decline. Freedom House, a nonprofit organization in the US that compiles an annual assessment of trends in freedom, said in its 2022 report that there had been sixteen consecutive years of declining freedoms. Today, 80 percent of the world's population lives in countries that Freedom House describes as authoritarian or as only partially free—that is, lacking a key ingredient of a free society such as an independent press. Even the European Union, committed as it is to democracy and human rights, has not been spared. Hungary has been governed since May 29, 2010, by Viktor Orbán, who has declared himself in favor of "illiberal democracy" and taken strong steps against a free press and independence in education. On the other side of the Atlantic, Donald Trump has clear authoritarian tendencies, interfering with the peaceful transfer of power after he resoundingly lost the 2020 election. Yet despite multiple indictments and civil suits ranging from fraud to rape, he remains a strong candidate for the presidency as this book goes to press and is likely to be nominated by the Republican Party.

We are in a global, intellectual, and political war to protect and preserve freedom. Do democracies and free societies deliver what citizens want and care about and can they do it better than authoritarian regimes? This is a battle for the hearts and minds of people everywhere. I firmly believe that democracies and free societies can provide for their citizens far more effectively than authoritarian systems. However, in several key areas, most notably in economics, our free societies are failing. But—and this is important—these failures are not inevitable and are partially because the Right's incorrect conception of freedom has led us down the wrong path. There are other paths that deliver more of the goods and services they want, with more of the security that they want, but that also provide more freedom for more people.[1]

This book approaches the questions of freedom from the perspective and language of economists, so it focuses, at least at first, on what might be called economic freedom, as opposed to what is usually referred to as political freedoms (although I argue later that really, these are inseparable).

Freedom in a world of interdependence

To reconsider the meaning of freedom, we must begin by recognizing our interdependence. As poet John Donne famously put it in 1624, "No man is an island entire of itself." This is especially true in our modern, urban, interconnected society, far different from the agrarian society of the preindustrial era, in which many people lived in single-family houses, sometimes at great distances from one another. In dense urban communities, what one person does affects others, from honking horns to cleaning up the sidewalk after a pet. And in our industrial world, with cars and factories and industrial farming, the pollution from each person or company gradually contributes to an overload of greenhouse gases in the atmosphere, leading to global warming that affects us all.

A refrain throughout this book is that *one person's freedom can often amount to another's unfreedom;* or, put another way, *the enhancement of one person's freedom often comes at the expense of another's.* As Cicero said some two thousand years ago, "We are slaves of the law so that we may be able to be free."[2] Only through collective action, through government, can we achieve a balance of freedoms. Well-designed government actions, including regulations that restrain behavior in some ways, can be in a fundamental sense liberating, or at least can be for a large proportion of the population. In a sane, modern society, governments and freedom need not be at odds.

Of course, the boundaries of freedom have always been questioned and are inevitably ambiguous. Should there be *no* restraints on freedom of expression, even for child pornography? Private property represents a restraint—one person has the right to use and dispose of an asset, but others don't. But property rights have to be defined, especially when it comes to newer forms of property like intellectual property. Even the US Constitution recognized eminent domain, the right of the government to take away property, with just compensation. And the circumstances under which this can be done are evolving, court case by court case.

Much of this debate concerns the balance between freedom from coercion from the state versus freedom from being harmed by others. But there is an important positive sense of freedom that I have already noted: freedom to live up to one's potential. People who are living on the edge have, in some sense, no freedom. They do what they must to survive. But to give them the resources they need to live decent lives, let alone to live up to their potential, requires taxing the whole community.[3] Many on the Right would claim that such taxation—even with representation—is tyranny because they have lost the right to spend this money as they please. In the same vein, they see laws requiring employers to pay minimum wages—or a livable wage—as taking away the employers' freedom to pay whatever they can get away with. This freedom is even given an elegant name: freedom to contract.

My ultimate objective in this book is to understand what kind of an economic, political, and social system is most likely to enhance the freedoms of most citizens, including by appropriately drawing the right boundaries on freedoms, constructing the right rules and regulations, and making the right trade-offs. The answer I provide runs counter to more than a century of writings by conservatives. It is not the minimalist state advocated by libertarians,[4] or even the highly constricted state envisioned by neoliberalism. Rather, the answer is something along the lines of a rejuvenated European social democracy or a new American Progressive Capitalism, a twenty-first-century version of social democracy or of the Scandinavian welfare state.

Of course, behind these different economic systems—neoliberal capitalism on the one hand and progressive capitalism on the other—are different theories about individual behavior and how societies function, and theorists who explain why their preferred system works better than others. The next chapter takes up these alternative theories and theorists.

The Complexities of Freedom Illustrated by America

The complexities of the notion of freedom are well illustrated by the discussions about freedom in the United States.

Americans grow up on an elixir of freedom. The founding of the country was an act of freedom—wresting political control from British overlords thousands of miles away. Every schoolchild learns the Virginian Patrick Henry's cry, "Give me liberty, or give me death!" and on countless public occasions Americans sing their national anthem with the words "the land of the free and the home of the brave." The first ten amendments to the Constitution, the Bill of Rights, ensure that the state will not encroach on individuals' fundamental freedoms.

But recent years have not been kind to this telling of the American story. There was freedom for some but the antithesis of freedom for enslaved peoples. For others, the indigenous peoples of the continent, there was outright genocide. Evidently, the freedom the country's patriots championed was not freedom for all, or some generalized sense of freedom, but rather freedom *for themselves.* In particular, it was political freedom from the rule of the British king and from the taxes on tea that he had imposed.

It is hard, at least from our vantage point, to see how a society seemingly so deeply committed to freedom allowed slavery to continue. Apologists sometimes suggest that we need to look at the world through the mores of the time; but even then, there was an understanding of the moral outrage of slavery.[5]

From this perspective, the American revolution was less about freedom than about who exercised political power, about whether there was to be home rule with government by local elites or remote rule by a parliament seated in London, many of whose members were increasingly skeptical of slavery. Britain eventually abolished slavery in 1833, a third of a century earlier than the US. (The central role of slavery was even clearer in Texas, which "rebelled" against Mexico and then joined the US as a slave state in the very year that Mexico banned slavery.)

But as Ronald Reagan was making his pronouncements on the centrality of freedom, he was supporting efforts to undermine the democratic freedoms of others. His CIA was involved in military coups in a host of countries including Greece and Chile—the latter entailing the loss of the most fundamental freedom for tens of thousands of people: the freedom to live.

More recently, the January 6, 2021, insurrection was an attack to upend the most important aspect of a democracy—the peaceful transition of power. When much of the Republican Party turned into what looked like a cult, claiming against all evidence that the election had been stolen, it became clear that the country's democracy was in peril and, with it, the freedoms that Americans have cherished for so long. Yet many participants in the insurrection claimed that they were *defending* freedom.

If there is any hope for this divided nation to come together, we need to better understand these concepts.

Central Themes and Questions

I've already explained that the central message of this book is that the concept of "freedom" is more complex than suggested by the Right's simplistic use of the word. I'd like to pause here to explain my use of the term "the Right." I employ it to loosely refer to the multiple groups—some calling themselves conservatives; others, libertarians; still others identifying themselves as "right of center" politically—that have many different viewpoints but share the belief that the role of the federal government and collective action should be limited. Unlike some anarchists, these groups do believe in the state. They believe that property rights need to be enforced. Most believe (often strongly) in spending money for defense. And some would support other limited federal actions, such as public support in the event of a crisis like a devastating earthquake or hurricane. This book explains why a more extensive role for the state is necessary and looks at this more expansive role, especially through the lens of freedom.

We'll see that reflecting on the meaning of freedom makes us think more deeply about many key aspects of society we often take for granted—for instance, the kinds of contracts that should be enforced. It makes us think about the meaning of tolerance and its boundaries. How tolerant should we be of those who are intolerant? I won't be able to provide answers to all the hard questions that arise, but I hope to at least clarify what is at issue and help frame a way to consider them.

Because some of the issues are so complex, I worry about losing sight of the forest for the trees. So, in the next few pages I want to sketch the landscape, describing some of the central ideas and questions that are critical to a deeper understanding of freedom. I organize the discussion around the three parts into which the book is divided.

The first part looks at freedom and coercion through a traditional economist's lens, in which individuals' beliefs and desires are taken as fixed, unchanging in time and unaffected by others. The second part incorporates insights from modern behavioral economics, which recognizes that beliefs and behaviors *can* be shaped, a particularly salient view today given the use of mis- and disinformation to construct and push views often untethered from facts or logic.[6] It also takes up the constraining effect of social coercion. The third part takes the ideas developed in parts I and II to help us understand what makes for a good society, and what kinds of government and international architecture are most likely to deliver it.

Key Principles: More Traditional Perspectives

Meaningful freedom: Freedom to act

An economist's notion of economic freedom begins with a simple idea: A person's freedom is about what she can do and what she can choose. This perspective might seem close to Milton Friedman's, reflected in the title of his bestselling book *Free to Choose* (published in 1980 and written with his wife, Rose). But Friedman forgot an elementary fact. Someone with very limited income has little freedom to choose. What matters is a person's *opportunity set*—the set of options she has available.[7] From an economist's perspective, this is the only thing that matters. Her opportunity set determines, indeed defines, her *freedom to act*.[8] Any reduction in the scope of actions she can undertake is a loss of freedom.[9]

The language used to describe an expansion or contraction of the opportunity set makes no difference.[10, 11] It makes no difference whether one induces someone to behave in a particular way by *incentivizing* him through rewards or *punishing* him through fines, even though we champion the former as "noncoercive" (praising economic systems that design clever incentive systems that induce the desired behavior) and castigate the latter as "coercive."

When you understand economic freedom as freedom to act, it immediately reframes many of the central issues surrounding economic policy and freedom. Libertarians and other conservatives see the ability to spend one's income as one wants as a defining characteristic of economic freedom.[12] They see constraints on that as coercion, with taxation the most coercive restraint. But this perspective gives primacy to markets and market-determined prices. I provide a critique of that position. There may be economic arguments concerning the level and design of taxation, but I show there is little to no moral primacy to be given to people's market incomes—the incomes they derive in our market economy, whether from wages, dividends, capital gains, or other sources—and hence little to no moral reason not to tax those incomes.

Freedom from want and fear and freedom to live up to one's potential

People who are barely surviving have extremely limited freedom. All their time and energy go into earning enough money to pay for groceries, shelter, and transportation to jobs. Just as there is no moral legitimacy to the incomes of people at the top of the economic ladder, there is none for people at the bottom. It is not that they have necessarily done anything to make them deserve the poverty they face. A good society would do something about the deprivations, or reductions in freedom, for people with low incomes.

It is not surprising that people who live in the poorest countries emphasize economic rights, the right to medical care, housing, education, and freedom from hunger. They are concerned about the loss of freedom not just from an oppressive government but also from economic, social, and political systems that have left large portions of the population destitute. One can frame these as *negative* freedoms: what is lost when individuals can't live up to their potential. Or, one can frame them as *positive* freedoms: what is gained by good economic and social systems, which is the freedom to live up to one's potential, a freedom associated with opportunity and access to education, health care, and enough food.

The Right claims that governments have unnecessarily restricted freedom through taxation, which constrains the budgets of the rich and thereby (in our formulation) reduces their freedom. Even in this claim, they are only partially correct because the societal benefits of the expenditures financed by these taxes, the investments in infrastructure and technology, for instance, may expand their opportunity sets (their freedom) in more meaningful ways. But even if they were correct in their assessment of the effect on the rich, they miss the broader societal impact on freedoms. Progressive taxation, with the proceeds redistributed to the less well-off through social programs or education, expands the opportunity set of the poor, their freedom, even while it may simultaneously constrain the opportunity set of the rich. As in all things, there are trade-offs.

One person's freedom is another's unfreedom

I've already introduced this central theme, and chapter 3 is devoted to explaining its multiple implications. For instance, this undeniable proposition leads directly to the related theme of regulation. Regulation is not the antithesis of freedom; restraints are necessary in a free society. Even in earlier, simpler societies, there was a need for regulations. Most of the Ten Commandments can be viewed as the minimal set of laws (regulations) required for a society to function.

One of the critical implications that I've also already introduced is that in discussing freedom there are often trade-offs. Sometimes, the balancing of rights is obvious. In all societies, killing someone is prohibited except in narrowly defined circumstances. The "right to kill" is subjugated to "the right not to be killed." There are many other instances in which the balancing of rights should be obvious if we would only clear away the cobwebs created by the false rhetoric of freedom and coercion. For instance, with the exception of someone for whom being vaccinated poses a health threat, the perils of an unvaccinated person spreading a dangerous and perhaps deadly disease far outweigh the "inconvenience" or the "loss of freedom" of an individual being compelled to get a vaccination. It should be obvious, too, that the magnitude of the imbalance grows as the contagiousness and seriousness of the disease increases.

There are, however, some instances in which the balance among trade-offs is not obvious; later chapters provide a framework for thinking about how we can approach such situations.

Free and unfettered markets are more about the right to exploit than the right to choose

A particular example of trade-offs in which I think the answer is easy entails exploitation. Exploitation can take many shapes: market power, including wartime price-gouging or drug companies keeping prices high during a pandemic; cigarette, food, and drug companies taking advantage of addiction; casinos and online gambling websites taking advantage of vulnerabilities. Recent advances in the digital economy have opened up whole new vistas for exploitation.

Standard competitive analyses in academic economics assume that no one has any power, and everyone has perfect information, and all are perfectly rational. They thereby assume away market power and other forms of exploitation. But in today's world, there are some individuals and corporations with considerable power.[13] It is as if people who take the stance that government should not interfere with the workings of the economy use a magic wand to wave away all the rent-seeking in a twenty-first-century economy. (A quick definition of rent-seeking: Rents are the returns to a service, labor, capital, or land over what would be needed to obtain their supply. Since there's a fixed supply of land, any money made from that land counts as rent; similarly, any extra returns earned from market power count as rents. When firms seek to increase their market power or exploit in other ways, we refer to it as rent-seeking.)[14]

   Exploitation enriches the exploiter at the expense of the exploited. Restraints on that exploitation may expand the opportunity set (freedom) of most, while constraining the opportunity set of the person doing the exploiting. There is a trade-off, and society must adjudicate between the winners and losers. In most cases, it's clear what should be done: the exploiter should be constrained. Here, the focus is not on the income or wealth of the exploiter versus the exploited but rather on the manner in which the well-being of one is enhanced at the expense of the other.[15] There is widespread support, for instance, for regulations that require certain disclosures—sugar in cereals, the risks of smoking cigarettes, the true interest rate on a mortgage, or the otherwise hidden risks in investment products. These disclosures reduce asymmetries of information, thereby reducing the scope for exploitation, and help markets work more efficiently. In a wide variety of situations, we can show that "coercion" that restrains exploitation increases economic efficiency even in the narrow sense that economists usually use that term,[16] expanding most, if not all, opportunity sets.

   This highlights another theme, perhaps even more puzzling than "one person's freedom is another's unfreedom": *Coercion can enhance everyone's freedom.* Stoplights are a simple regulation, easily enforced, that allow drivers to take turns going through an intersection. In their absence, there would be gridlock or accidents. Everyone would be worse off. It's clear that the little coercion of the stoplight—constraining what we can do—can increase the well-being, and in a sense the freedom to act, of everybody.

Property rights can restrain or free

We take property rights so much for granted that most in the West don't even think of them as "regulations" or "constraints." We simply accept the moral legitimacy of property and an economic system based on property rights.

The system of property rights is defended on grounds of economic efficiency. If there were no property rights, no one would have an incentive to work or save. That the preservation of some form of property is crucial to a functioning society is reflected in the eighth of the Ten Commandments: "Thou shalt not steal."

Property rights are a *restraint* on others (their freedom to trespass on my property is impinged, for example); but it is a restraint that, overall, is "freeing," that expands what people can do and consume. There is general agreement that property rights should be publicly enforced. Collective enforcement of property rights means we don't have to expend huge amounts of resources defending our property.

As ecologist Garrett Hardin, famous for his discussion of how to control excess grazing of common land (discussed below), wrote, "That we thereby infringe on the freedom of would-be robbers we neither deny nor regret." He went on to say, "When men mutually agreed to pass laws against robbing, mankind became more free, not less so . . . once they see the necessity of mutual coercion, they become free to pursue other goals."[17]

But this view gets us only so far. Property rights must be defined and assigned. The heated debates over defining new forms of property—intellectual property—clearly show that property is a social construction with trade-offs in freedoms. The freedom of potential users of the knowledge is constrained, while the freedom of the purported inventor or discoverer of the knowledge is enhanced. Chapter 6 shows the various ways that property rights can be, and in different countries are, defined, and the trade-offs involved.

Contracts: Private and social—
restraints voluntarily agreed to

Underlying the discussion so far is the simple notion that the public imposition of certain restraints may expand the opportunity sets of many, most, or even all people. People, of course, impose constraints on themselves in their dealing with others. That's what contracts are. I agree to do something or not do something (that is, I constrain what I do) in return for your committing to do or not do something. Voluntarily entered contracts make both parties better off. When we enter a contract, we believe that restraining our freedom in some way expands our opportunity set—our freedoms—in other ways that we assess to be more important than the losses imposed by the constraints. Indeed, one of the few roles for government accepted by the Right is the enforcement of contracts. Contracts are viewed as inviolable.

As we shall see, this view of contracts is unnuanced. Public policy dictates which contracts should be enforceable and enforced, when contracts can be broken, and what compensation needs to be paid when that happens. It is simply not true that allowing any contract voluntarily entered into by two freely consenting parties necessarily increases societal welfare. Restraining the set of "admissible" contracts can increase societal welfare—indeed, it can even increase the welfare of *every* person within society.

Similar reasoning can be and has been applied to thinking about a social contract that defines citizens' relationships with each other and the government. Or with the sovereign, as Thomas Hobbes (1588–1679) and John Locke (1632–1704), two of the earliest philosophers writing about social contracts, considered. It is not that individuals actually sign (or ever signed) a contract that entails a set of obligations, such as paying taxes in return for a set of benefits that might include protection. Rather, the idea of a social contract is meant to help us think about the moral legitimacy of collective action and the obligations and restraints it entails, a free exchange that might be voluntarily agreed on among the citizens of society.

Key Principles: More Modern Perspectives

Mill, Friedman, and Hayek wrote before the development of modern behavioral economics, which recognizes that individuals differ markedly from the way they are depicted in the standard economic theory. They are less rational, but also less selfish.

Traditional economics, especially neoliberal economics, has assumed away the power to shape beliefs and even preferences by assuming they are fixed and given; fundamentally, from the perspective of traditional economics, people are born knowing fully what they like and don't like and knowing how they trade off more of one good for less of another. In the standard theory, individuals change beliefs or actions (holding incomes and prices constant), only because of better information. But in reality, preferences and beliefs[18] can often be shaped, something that every parent, everyone working in marketing or advertising, and everyone waging campaigns of or against mis- and disinformation knows very well. Shaping beliefs and preferences entails more than just providing more and better information; it involves changing mindsets, a subject of study both by psychologists and marketers but typically beyond the reach of economists wedded to their model of full rationality with preferences set at birth.[19] Of particular concern is that our very economic system shapes preferences and beliefs—and this shaping is of first-order importance when we come to making judgments about the merits of one system as opposed to another.

When this kind of shaping of people makes them more "other-regarding," it may be all to the good of society because it provides a seemingly noncoercive way to "internalize" the consequences of a person's actions on others. Individuals think about the consequences of what they do on others. Recently, development economists have shown that changing beliefs may be far more effective (and less costly) in inducing behaviors that promote development or societal well-being, such as reducing fertility, gender discrimination, or domestic violence, than traditional approaches based on providing incentives or better information.[20]

But as the example of anti-vaxxers should make clear, beliefs and preferences can also be cultivated in ways that are antisocial and have harmful societal effects. Likewise, the line between pro-social behavior (that is, behavior that considers how one's actions affect others) induced by *social cohesion* and that induced by the more questionable *social coercion* is at best blurry. Because behavior and choices, including in politics, are so affected by beliefs, the power to shape them is critical. And unfortunately, in the twenty-first century, that power is concentrated in the hands of the relatively few who control the media in most countries.

When countries we don't like take efforts to shape beliefs, we label it pejoratively as "brainwashing" or "propaganda." But we don't recognize that the same thing occurs in market economies, often with "just" a profit motive but sometimes with the intent of affecting politics. As concerned as we may be with attempts to induce people to buy goods and services that they don't need, the effects of disinformation in politics, for instance, are of even greater concern. Citizens use their voting power to write the rules of the game, which enhance the scope for inducing or coercing others to behave in particular ways.

So, market power in the media matters, and we need to take a systemic view in thinking about freedom and such power. For instance, individuals can be induced to believe—contrary to theory and evidence—that markets are always efficient and government is always corrupt, leading to electoral outcomes that entrench the power and wealth of the elites. This, in turn, enhances elites' freedom at the expense of the rest of society.

Education can be freeing

Economists have traditionally viewed education simply as enhancing skills—creating human capital. But education does more than that; it shapes individuals.

Education is a two-, or perhaps I should say three-, edged sword. On the one hand, it can be used as a mechanism of social coercion, indoctrinating individuals into social conformity. On the other, it can teach students to be other-regarding and not impose unnecessary costs on society. But most importantly, a liberal education is freeing. It enables people to see matters more broadly, beyond the viewpoint they may have been given by their parents or their community. It enhances individual agency and autonomy, which is why the enemies of freedom and of an open society work so hard to restrict what is taught and are so skeptical of institutions of higher learning.

Tolerance and Enlightenment values under attack: Freedom to think

This intolerance of citizens who think or act differently pervades certain right-wing movements today and is increasingly evident on the Left as well. Yet tolerance is the central notion of the Enlightenment, the intellectual movement that dominated seventeenth- and eighteenth-century Europe and gave rise to modern science. Modern science, in turn, gave rise to enormous increases in standards of living during the two-and-a-half centuries that followed.[21] Certainly, one person's actions can affect others, but there are no such consequences associated with thoughts. This is why the liberty to think as one pleases and act in ways that one pleases—so long as the actions do not affect others—is central to the concept of freedom. These ideas also sit at the root of tolerance.

Applications: The Good Society and How to Achieve It

In the last part of the book, I ask what kind of an economy and what kind of global architecture is most likely to deliver on what I—and I hope many others—believe is the good society.

Understanding neoliberalism's failures, including why it didn't work, provides the basis for understanding what has to be done to create a healthier economy and society. One thing that is required, for instance, is a better balance between the market, the state, and civil society and a richer ecology of institutions, including cooperatives and not-for-profits.

From individual freedom to state sovereignty

The failures of neoliberal economic systems within countries have been replicated in the international order. There is a parallel between sovereignty of countries and freedom of individuals. The neoliberal system of international rules and institutions—including trade agreements, investment agreements, intellectual property rights, and the global financial system—has expanded the economic opportunities of the rich countries at the expense, especially, of poor countries.

There is an alternative: Progressive capitalism or a rejuvenated social democracy

One of the hallmarks of neoliberalism and neoliberal policies was the claim that there is no alternative. This was the chant recited by policymakers and others as Europe, under the influence of Wolfgang Schäuble, Germany's finance minister during the euro crisis of 2010, imposed punishing austerity—massive cutbacks in expenditures—on Greece and the other countries labeled the PIGS.[22] There were alternatives then for responding to the euro crisis, and there are alternatives now for creating a better economy and society. There are other ways to organize society and expand the opportunities of individuals. The system that I believe is most likely to do so I call *progressive capitalism*. (In Europe, I describe it as a rejuvenated social democracy.)

I use the term "capitalism" only to signify that large parts of the economy will be in the hands of profit-oriented enterprises; but what I have called progressive capitalism entails not only an array of institutions but also an important role for collective action. It is not premised on the canard that markets are the solution and government is the problem (as President Reagan famously claimed) but on a better balance between the market and the state, one that regulates to ensure competition and prevent exploitation of each other and of the environment. A central role of collective action is to expand the freedoms of all (by well-designed regulation and public investments, financed by taxes), but another key component is to balance expansions of the freedoms of some against the reductions in the freedom of others.

This only succeeds with a robust system of checks and balances, not just within government but more broadly within society, and these checks and balances can work in practice only if there aren't concentrations of power. But these power concentrations are inevitable if there are concentrations of wealth, and wealth concentrations will naturally occur in unfettered capitalism unless the state takes an active role in promoting competition, writing "fair rules" to guide the economy, and redistribution.

Political and economic freedom: Progressive capitalism promotes both

Finally, we turn to the relationship between economic and political freedom. Economists and others on the Right like Friedman and Hayek claim that free and unfettered markets are necessary for political freedom. They claim that it is essentially inevitable that any set of economic constraints will lead to still more economic constraints and that to sustain them, political constraints will follow, setting us on the road to serfdom. Selfish and self-aggrandizing bureaucrats and politicians ensure that this will happen. Give them more power to enforce one set of regulations and they will use it to further expand their power.

These predictions are wrong, partly because they are founded on an incorrect view of human nature and partly because they are founded on an incorrect view of democratic political systems. Fascist and authoritarian rulers have largely risen from a failure of government to do enough, not from government doing too much. In recent years, we have seen populism and extremist antidemocratic governments rising in Brazil, the US, Russia, and Hungary, countries that have done little to alleviate their inequalities. We don't see them, at least to the same extent, in Sweden, Norway, or Iceland, countries with a large state that protects citizens.[23] And, again contrary to Hayek and Friedman, the constraints imposed in the latter set of countries lead to *higher* standards of living—an increase in meaningful freedoms for the vast majority of their citizens.

Friedman and Hayek, like many other conservatives, have an unfailingly dismal view of human nature. It may have been because of deep introspection that they arrived at their extreme views about individual selfishness, which they then generalized to everyone. They fail to recognize that many, many people enter public service because they want to do good, not because they want to aggrandize themselves. Public servants could have done far better financially if they had gone into the private sector, especially in the era of neoliberalism. True, some people are utterly selfish and power hungry, and any political system must recognize this. Democracy, with its systems of checks and balances, is designed to limit the consequences.

Neoliberalism is not self-sustaining. It's self-negating. It has misshaped our society and the people in it. The materialistic, extreme selfishness that it has cultivated has undermined democracy, societal cohesion, and trust, resulting in weakening even the functioning of the economy. No economy can run well without a certain amount of trust; a world where everything is up to litigation is a dys-functional one. Well-functioning markets that serve society require competition—but without competition laws, firms on their own will subvert competition in one way or another and power becomes more and more concentrated. Without strong regulation, neoliberalism will destroy our planet. The extreme economic inequality it has created has given rise to political inequalities, and our democracy has shifted away from the idea of "one person, one vote" to the cynical reality that can more accurately be described as "one dollar, one vote," a political inequality that undermines the very notion of democracy. Internationally, neoliberalism's effect may have been even worse, as it foisted policies on countries that constrained their democratic space and condemned most of the poor countries—and the people within them—to remain poor.

These outcomes are the precise opposite of Hayek's and Friedman's claims that unfettered capitalism is *necessary* to preserve political free-dom. Unfettered capitalism—the kind of capitalism advocated by the Right, including by its intellectual leaders Friedman and Hayek—undermines meaningful economic and political freedoms and puts us on the road to twenty-first-century fascism. Progressive capitalism sets us on the road to freedom.

CHAPTER 2

How Economists Think About Freedom

Economists have long discussed the idea of freedom and the relationship between freedom and a society's economic system. Friedrich Hayek and Milton Friedman were the leaders of a pack of conservative economists who have tried to preempt meaningful discussions by the very vocabulary they use. They talked of "free markets," as if imposing rules and regulations results in "unfree markets." They relabeled private enterprises—companies owned by private individuals—as "free enterprises," as if giving them that appellation would bestow a reverence and suggest that they should not be touched and their freedom should not be curtailed even if they exploit people and the planet.

For Hayek and Friedman, unfettered capitalism was desirable not only because of its efficiency but also because it promoted freedom. A reexamination of whether it leads to more or less freedom, however, requires a reexamination of how the market economy actually works.

A Thumbnail History of Thought in Economics—from Adam Smith to the Middle of the Twentieth Century

Adam Smith, the founder of modern economics, provided a critique of the excessive statist (mercantilist) approach to economics. He believed in markets. He had conjectured in his 1776 book, *The Wealth of Nations*, that a competitive economy would be efficient. In the pursuit of self-interest, entrepreneurs would be led *as if by an invisible hand* to the well-being of society:

> By directing that industry in such a manner as its produce may be of the greatest value, he intends only his own gain, and he is in this, as in many other cases, led by an invisible hand to promote an end which was no part of his intention.[1]

Smith was, however, far less sanguine about unfettered markets than his latter-day followers. He would, I am sure, have been horrified at the extent to which he was taken out of context, and how other sage remarks of his were ignored because they were not consistent with the free-enterprise mental model—the way those on the Right understood market economies. Consider these examples. In the first, Smith emphasizes the proclivity of entrepreneurs to engage in anticompetitive behavior:

> People of the same trade seldom meet together, even for merriment and diversion, but the conversation ends in a conspiracy against the public, or in some contrivance to raise prices.[2]

In the presence of market power (collusion), markets are in general not efficient but distorted; and as Smith emphasized, firms can exploit both consumers and workers, effectively constraining their choice sets (their freedom), while expanding the freedom of the firms' owners.

Smith was not the first to question what an underregulated economy might look like. Even before the advent of the industrial revolution, philosophers had considered what society would be like without
adequate government. Thomas Hobbes, in *Leviathan* (1651), described
life in such a world as "solitary, poor, nasty, brutish, and short."[3]

Smith's less sanguine views of capitalism seemed to have played out
in the early decades of the industrial revolution. England's poor laws
of 1834 had made workers cheap fodder for the local public works
and factories. There was economic growth, but it was obviously not
being equally shared. The squalor in which the working classes lived
in England was documented by Friedrich Engels in his famous 1845
treatise, *The Condition of the Working Class in England*, and vividly
depicted in the novels of the time.[4]

Amid the industrial revolution, two schools of economics emerged.
It was remarkable that such markedly different views of the world
could develop, since each seemingly looked at the same picture. One
focused on what its proponents saw as the harmony of the economic
system and its ability to produce goods. This school was led by classical economists who took Adam Smith's quotation out of context and
developed theories of laissez-faire, which said, in essence, simply leave
the market alone to perform its wonders.[5] This theory was often called
liberalism and emphasized free markets, especially the elimination of
barriers to the import of cheap agricultural goods into the UK, which
would enable wages to be lowered. The other school, most famously
associated with Karl Marx, emphasized the role of the exploitation of
workers and the need to combat it.

In the succeeding decades, growth and exploitation occurred on
both sides of the Atlantic. The growth was fostered not only by the
accumulation of capital and innovation but also by the exploitation
of enslaved people, colonies, and ordinary workers. Parsing the relative importance of these roles is virtually impossible. Today, in the
pantheon of the great donors who founded or donated to the major

institutions of learning in the eighteenth and nineteenth centuries, it is hard to find men not tainted either by the slave trade or the opium trade—or both.

The Great Depression and the mixed economy

But not even market advocates could ignore the Great Depression, when one out of four workers in the US had no job. The financial crash of 1929, in which millions lost their savings, was only the worst of the financial gyrations the economy had experienced. Just twenty-two years earlier, there had been the panic of 1907, which had led to the creation of the Federal Reserve, but even it could not save the banking system and the economy; broader government help was needed, which President Franklin Roosevelt delivered through the New Deal.[6]

Economist John Maynard Keynes provided not just an explanation of what had gone wrong in the Great Depression but also a prescription for what to do about it. His recommendation included a large role for government—not the overarching role advocated by the Socialists and Communists but a more constrained role limited to managing the macroeconomy. Nonetheless, it was anathema to the capitalists.

The mixed economy that evolved in the years after World War II was distinctly antisocialist. Private enterprises were dominant, but government played a vital role in ensuring competition, preventing exploitation, and stabilizing the macroeconomy. Socialism was a regime in which the means of production were held by the state. By contrast, in the prevailing system in Western Europe and the United States, markets and the private production of goods and services remained at the center, with government contributing, too, through education, research, infrastructure, helping the poor, providing retirement insurance, and regulating financial and other markets.

This economic model was enormously successful. In the US, growth had never been higher,[7] and the fruits of that growth never better shared. The US and the world experienced the longest period of stability without a financial crisis or a deep downturn. The model had bipartisan support, with tax rates reaching new heights under Republican president Dwight Eisenhower, who simultaneously introduced major education, infrastructure, and research programs nationwide.

A variant of the model in East Asia, where the government took on a somewhat more active role in promoting development, turned out to be the most successful developmental model ever. Unprecedented growth narrowed the gap between these countries and advanced countries. Following this model, Japan became the fourth-largest economy in the world and China the second, at official exchange rates. But when measured in the more appropriate purchasing power parity (which adjusts for differences in costs of living in different countries), China by 2023 was the *largest* economy, exceeding the US by almost a quarter.[8]

The "theory" of why things worked so well during this era had, ironically, not been developed. It posed for economists the same problem that a giraffe posed for biologists. Giraffes exist, even if we can't fully figure out how a creature with such a long neck can survive. It was only during the second half of the twentieth century that we developed a deep understanding of the limits of markets and how well-designed government intervention could actually make the economic system perform better.

A New Economic Era

With the oil price shock of the 1970s, postwar economic arrangements faltered and inflation soared—not the type of hyperinflation that had prevailed in Germany in the 1920s but inflation the US and much of the rest of the world hadn't seen before. It was disturbing and worrisome.

The Right, joined by Democrats whose faith in the system seemed to have been shaken, seized the moment and argued for a new economic system.

Before long, regulations and restrictions were stripped away willy-nilly, in what was called *liberalization*, the freeing of the economy. This was supposed to free the spirit of human enterprise, enhance innovation, and improve the well-being of everybody. Even if there were an (enormous) increase in inequality, the thinking went, everyone would be better off as the gains of the richest trickled down to everyone else. Simultaneously, there was a wave of privatization, converting government-owned enterprises into private for-profit enterprises. In Europe, there were many such enterprises, from steel and coal to electricity and transport. In the US, where government ownership was more limited, privatization was accordingly more limited, from garbage collection and water companies in some cities to the company that made enriched uranium, the critical ingredient for atomic bombs and nuclear power plants.[9]

On both sides of the Atlantic and on all sides of the political spectrum there seemed to be support for the mantra of trade liberalization (eliminating trade barriers), deregulation, and privatization.[10] President Bill Clinton tried to put a more human face on it, but he pushed it nonetheless—notably with the passage of the North American Free Trade Agreement (NAFTA) in 1994 and the international agreement that led to the creation of the World Trade Organization (WTO) in 1995. Among the signal "achievements" of his administration was the deregulation of the financial sector, which led a decade later to the global financial crisis. These financial and trade policies also led to an acceleration of deindustrialization.

Clinton was not alone in promoting liberalization. Prime Minister Tony Blair in the UK and Chancellor Gerhard Schröder in Germany pursued similar agendas.

In the developing world, these ideas provided the foundation of what came to be called the Washington Consensus policy agenda, a set of rules foisted on countries coming to the World Bank and the International Monetary Fund (IMF) for assistance.[11]

The intellectual battles

Ronald Reagan and Margaret Thatcher were at the forefront of the political battle that reshaped economic policy and Western economies in the last third of the twentieth century. But long before the arrival of these political leaders, the intellectual groundwork had been laid by Friedman and Hayek. Both men were part of a circle of intellectual and business leaders called the Mont Pelerin Society, which worked to advance and refine the arguments for a very limited role for government and to push them politically. In its "Statement of Aims" on its founding in 1947, the Mont Pelerin Society provided a dire perspective on world affairs:

> Over large stretches of the Earth's surface the essential conditions of human dignity and freedom have already disappeared. In others they are under constant menace from the development of current tendencies of policy. The position of the individual and the voluntary group are progressively undermined by extensions of arbitrary power.[12]

The Mont Pelerin Society sought to advance an anti-state vision, one that was far more radical than even the Republican Party at that time.[13] Members saw free markets and private property intimately interlinked; without these, they suggested, it was "difficult to imagine a society in which freedom may be effectively preserved," as they put it in their "Statement of Aims."[14]

Of course, one may question the extent to which these Mont Pelerin Society members were really committed to an agenda of political freedom. Milton Friedman was only too willing to serve as a key adviser to the notorious Chilean military dictator Augusto Pinochet, and many other conservatives often seemed to be more focused on order than freedom. In pledging to restore an older regime, Pinochet, like other dictators, offered an end to the disorder and uncertainty conservatives fear will result from the kinds of change that freedom-seeking "leftists" want. The preference of order over freedom is reflected in another term often used in connection with markets—"market discipline." Markets "force" behavior in certain directions. If countries don't follow the rules set by Wall Street, they may be punished. Wall Street will withdraw its money, and the economy will collapse. In a sense, freedom is taken from people to act in any way other than what the market dictates. Of course, it is a mirage to think that change can be avoided—that old power structures can go on unaffected as our world, the structure of our economy, and our ideas change.

The post–Cold War détente

Political debates often don't take on quite the sophistication and complexity of the intellectual debates that lie behind them and, in part, motivate them. With the Iron Curtain coming down in 1991 and China declaring that it, too, was going to be a market economy, albeit "with Chinese characteristics" (whatever that meant), there was a broad consensus that the extremes of socialism/communism with government ownership (and implicitly, control) of everything, on the one hand, and a totally unfettered market (of the kind that the Mont Pelerin Society had been advocating), on the other, were things of the past. Political scientist and economist Francis Fukuyama[15] could even celebrate this as "the end of history," as our understanding of economic and political systems had converged into the "correct solution"— market economies and liberal democracies. There was a search for the best "third way" between the far left and far right, since there was a lot of space between the extremes of the Mont Pelerin Society and communism. It made a big difference exactly where between the two one situated oneself. Politically, this was reflected in battles within and between the center left and center right. The political debate shaped up most clearly during the presidency of Bill Clinton—for instance, between those in Clinton's administration focused on the environment, inequality, and making the economy more competitive, and those focused on debt, interest rates, deregulation, liberalization, and growth. For the most part, the latter group won out.[16]

The system that evolved in the last quarter of the twentieth century on both sides of the Atlantic came to be called *neoliberalism*.[17] "Liberal" refers to being "free," in this context, free of government intervention including regulations. The "neo" meant to suggest that there was something new in it; in reality, it was little different from the liberalism and laissez-faire doctrines of the nineteenth century that advised: "leave it to the market."[18] Indeed, those ideas held such sway even into the twentieth century that, decades earlier, the dominant economists had said "do nothing" in response to the Great Depression. They believed the market would restore itself relatively quickly as long as the government didn't fiddle around and mess things up.

What really was new was the trick of claiming neoliberalism stripped away rules when much of what it was doing was imposing new rules that favored banks and the wealthy. For instance, the so-called deregulation of the banks got government *temporarily* out of the way, which allowed bankers to reap rewards for themselves. But then, with the 2008 financial crisis, government took center stage as it funded the largest bailout in history, courtesy of taxpayers. Bankers profited at the expense of the rest of society. In dollar terms, the cost to the rest of us exceeded the banks' gains. Neoliberalism *in practice* was what can be described as "ersatz capitalism," in which losses are socialized and gains privatized.

Neoliberal economists constructed a theory to support their views, not surprisingly called neoclassical economics. The name evoked nineteenth-century classical economics, with the "neo" emphasizing it had been put on firmer foundations, which in practice meant putting it into mathematical scribbles. Some neoclassical economists were slightly schizophrenic, recognizing that markets often don't generate full employment on their own, so Keynesian policies are sometimes required; but once the economy is restored to full employment, classical economics prevails. This idea, pushed by my teacher Paul Samuelson, was called the neoclassical synthesis. It was a highly influential assertion, with no basis in either theory or empirics.[19]

The call for a return to liberalism with the new name neoliberalism, in the middle of the last century, flew in the face of what had happened during the Great Depression. It was akin to Hitler's Big Lie. In light of the Great Depression, the economic argument that markets on their own were efficient and stable seemed absurd. (It was a Big Lie in another sense: the reality was that the government *was* taking on a large role, no matter how one measured it—share of GDP or share of employment. Over time, democratic political systems had identified areas in which markets were not delivering what societies wanted and needed, like retirement benefits, and countries had figured out ways of doing so publicly.)

But memories are short, and a quarter century after that dramatic event, with the trauma of World War II and the beginning of the Cold War intervening, the Right was ready to move on and once again celebrate the alleged efficiency of free markets. When confronted with theory and evidence to the contrary, they closed their eyes and reasserted their faith, as I saw personally in my repeated interactions with Milton Friedman and his colleagues, both at the University of Chicago and at their West Coast citadel, the Hoover Institution, on the Stanford University campus. Belief in the market (and the materialism associated with it—the more GDP, the better) became, for many around the world, *the* late-twentieth-century religion, something to be held on to whatever the theory or the evidence to the contrary.

When the 2008 financial crisis happened, it seemed impossible that these conservatives would hold on to their market fundamentalist religion, that markets on their own were efficient and stable. But they did, which confirmed that it was, in a sense, a fundamentalist religion, the truth of which is virtually unshakable by reasoning or, as here, events.[20]

And they continued to believe in it even as the failures of neoliberalism described below became more and more evident.

They closed their eyes not only to the big failures but to the smaller ones that make life for so many so difficult—airlines with myriad delays and lost luggage, cell phone and internet services that are unreliable and expensive, and in the US, a health-care system that, while the most expensive by far in the world, is impossible to navigate and results in the lowest life expectancy of any of the advanced countries. In this new religion, markets are always efficient and government always inefficient and oppressive. We simply weren't appreciating fully the efficiency benefits of the two-hour holds on the telephone with our internet provider or our health insurance company.

There was another way in which this "economic religion" was similar to more conventional religions: proselytization. Conservatives' faith was assiduously spread through the media and, to a considerable extent, through higher education, effectively ushering out of the public and political zeitgeist any remnants of an alternative and more humane economic vision that had first emerged in the 1930s and then flowered again in the more turbulent period of the late 1960s and early 1970s.

There was still one more way in which neoliberalism was like a fundamentalist religion: There were pat answers to anything that seemed contrary to its tenets. If markets were unstable (as evidenced in the 2008 financial crisis), the problem was the government—central banks had unleashed too much money. If a country that liberalized didn't grow in the way the religion said it should, the answer was it hadn't liberalized enough.

The Failures of Neoliberalism

As we have seen, with a post-Depression generation in charge in the last part of the twentieth century, governments around the world adopted one version or another of neoliberalism. It pleased the capitalists, and the simplistic argument that free markets would deliver both economic success and freedom seduced large numbers of people. I've highlighted the role of the Right in pushing the neoliberal agenda; but the Right was enormously successful in creating the mindset of the time. I've described the embrace of neoliberalism by Clinton, Schröder, and Blair.

There were, let me emphasize, large differences over the details of neoliberalism between the center-left and center-right that dominated political and economic debates, especially in rhetoric. The former tried to put a human face on the reforms, asking for assistance for those who lost their jobs as a result of trade liberalization. The latter focused on incentives, worried that any adjustment assistance might weaken efforts of people to do their own part. The Right talked about trickle-down economics: if we made the economic pie larger, all would *eventually* be better off. Democrats and European social democrats weren't so sure that trickle-down would work, or work fast enough. But in the end, in spite of these differences and much rhetoric, the center-right and the center-left were both wedded to neoliberalism.

We've now had forty years of this neoliberal experiment that began under Reagan and Thatcher.[21] Its rosy promises of faster growth and higher living standards that would be widely shared have not been borne out. Growth has slowed, opportunity diminished, and the fruits of what growth has occurred have gone overwhelmingly to the people at the top. The results were perhaps the worst in the United States, with its greater reliance on markets and where financial liberalization was taken to the most extreme. The country experienced the largest economic recession in three-quarters of a century with the 2008 financial meltdown, a crisis that it exported to the rest of the world. By the early years of this century, America had become the country marked by the highest level of inequality and some of the lowest levels of opportunity of any of the advanced countries. Wages at the bottom, adjusted for inflation, hovered at the same level that they had been more than a half century earlier. The American Dream had become a myth, with the life prospects of a young American more dependent on the income and education of her parents than in other advanced countries. Only around half of Americans born after 1980 could hope to have earnings higher than their parents (down from 90 percent for the cohort born in 1940).[22, 23] This loss of hope also had political consequences, witnessed so clearly in the election of Donald Trump as president.[24]

Statistics do not tell the full story. That unfettered markets, or even inadequately regulated markets, lead to socially undesirable outcomes should be obvious to anyone living through the late twentieth or early twenty-first century. Think of the opioid crisis, created in no small measure by drug companies and pharmacies exploiting people in pain; think of the cigarette companies making addictive, lethal products; think of the multiple scams that prey on the elderly and others; think of the food and drink companies pushing their unhealthy products so aggressively and for so long that the country faces an epidemic of childhood diabetes; and think, too, of the oil and coal companies making billions of dollars as they endanger the planet. It is hard to think of a corner of our capitalist system in which some form of scam or exploitation is *not* going on.

It is not just the costs imposed on those directly experiencing the dark sides of capitalism; all of us are constantly on guard lest we be taken advantage of. The economic costs are large; the costs to our psyches far larger. They reflect systemic failures with major consequences—for example, the relatively poor health conditions (compared with other advanced countries) noted earlier.

The consequences of the neoliberal project elsewhere in the world are no better. In Africa, Washington Consensus policies led to a process of deindustrialization and a quarter century of near-zero growth in per capita income.[25] Latin America experienced what is widely called the Lost Decade in the 1980s. In many countries, the rapid influx and then outflow of capital under the policies of capital market and financial market liberalization led to crisis after crisis—more than a hundred around the world. The inequalities that marked the US were a shadow of what occurred elsewhere. Foisted on the countries of the former Soviet Union, Washington Consensus policies led to deindustrialization. A once-powerful Russia was reduced largely to a natural resource economy roughly the size of Spain's, controlled by a small group of oligarchs who resented how the West had guided the country's path away from communism.[26] It set the stage for the rise of Putin and everything that followed.

Economic theory and practice

But what about the theory that markets would lead to efficient outcomes? Conservative economists picked up on Adam Smith's "invisible hand" but left behind the qualifications he put on the idea. When economic theorists attempted to prove that competitive markets were efficient, they ran into a dead end. The conclusion was *only* true under very limited conditions, so limited as to be irrelevant to any economy. Indeed, these attempts to prove that the market was efficient *highlighted* the limitations of the market—what came to be called market failures. Such failures include limited competition (where most firms have some power to set their prices);[27] absent markets (one can't, for instance, buy insurance for most of the main risks we face); and imperfect information (consumers don't know the qualities and prices of all goods in the market, firms don't know the characteristics of all their potential employees, lenders don't know the likelihood that a potential borrower would repay, and so on). So committed were conservative economists like Friedman to their ideology that they were reluctant to accept these fundamental theoretical results. I recall a conversation with Friedman at a seminar I gave in the late 1960s at the University of Chicago showing the failure of markets to handle risk efficiently[28]—a result I established in a series of papers that have not been refuted in the half century since they were written. Our conversation began with his assertion that I was wrong, and that markets were efficient. I asked him to show me the flaws in my proofs. He reverted to his assertion and his faith in the market. Our conversation went nowhere.

Though writing earlier than Friedman, Hayek's reasoning in many ways was more subtle. Hayek seems to have been more influenced by evolutionary thinking, that somehow the struggle for survival resulted in the "fittest" firms (those that are most efficient and most successful at meeting consumers' needs) outlasting their competitors. His analysis was even less complete, based simply on the *hope* (or the belief) that evolutionary processes would yield desirable outcomes. Darwin himself had realized that this might not be the case, that the experiments on the isolated Galápagos Islands had led to quite different, and sometimes rather bizarre, evolutionary outcomes.[29] Today, we realize that there is no teleology in evolutionary processes. Put in economic terms, that there can be no presumption that they result in the overall long-run dynamic efficiency of the economy.[30] Quite the contrary. There are well-known shortcomings, of which the major failures described in earlier paragraphs are only the most obvious. Natural selection does not necessarily eliminate the least efficient. Firms that die in an economic downturn are often as efficient as those that survive; they simply had more debt.[31]

Friedman and Hayek were powerful rhetoricians who made seemingly persuasive arguments. The strength of modern mathematical economics is that it forces greater precision in both assumptions and analyses, which is also its weakness because such precision requires simplifications that may ignore essential complexities. Economic theorists, working in both the equilibrium tradition (to which Friedman belonged) and the evolutionary one (to which Hayek belonged) have shown that their analyses were incomplete and/or incorrect, as I've just explained. Economic theory predicted that unfettered markets would be inefficient, unstable, and exploitive, and, without adequate government intervention, would be dominated by firms with market power that would give rise to large inequalities. They would be shortsighted and not manage risks well. They would spoil the environment. And shareholder value maximization would not, as Friedman claimed, lead to the maximization of the well-being of society. These predictions by the critics of unfettered markets have been validated. Looking back on their economics from the perspective of three-quarters of a century of research, Hayek and Friedman simply didn't get it right and, unfortunately, didn't even set the right research agenda. They were great polemicists whose ideas have had, and still have, enormous influence.

How could such bright minds have gotten it so wrong? The answer is simple. Friedman and Hayek examined the economy from an ideological perspective, not a dispassionate one. They attempted to *defend* unfettered markets and existing power relations, including as reflected in the distribution of income and wealth. They were not really attempting to understand how capitalism actually worked. They assumed markets were essentially always highly competitive, with no firms having power to set prices, when it was obvious that critical markets were not competitive. They assumed in much of their work that there was perfect information, or at least that markets were informationally efficient—conveying costlessly and instantaneously all the relevant information from the informed to the uninformed and aggregating all the relevant information to be perfectly reflected in prices.[32] These were convenient assumptions, which helped to get the desired results on the efficiency of the market economy. And they were convenient in another way: they simply didn't have the mathematical tools necessary to analyze markets with imperfect information. But when shown analyses based on those more advanced tools, which showed that markets weren't and couldn't be informationally efficient, they and others in their camp looked the other way. They didn't want to engage with analyses that might lead to a conclusion that differed from their unfailing allegiance to the market.

Friedman and Hayek were the intellectual handmaidens of the capitalists. They wanted a smaller role for government and less collective action. They blamed the government for the Great Depression (poorly managed monetary policy) and for every other seeming failure in the economy. And they claimed that government intervention in free markets was itself the road to totalitarianism, ignoring the historical reality of the economic conditions that had led to fascism and communism. It is too little government—government not doing enough about the critical problems of the day—not too much government that has led to populism and has repeatedly set society on the road to authoritarianism.

Beyond Efficiency: The Moral Arguments for Neoliberalism

Hayek and Friedman wanted to go beyond the efficiency argument for capitalism. They argued that everyone would share in its success, the mysterious trickle-down that capitalism is supposed to generate. But most importantly, they wanted a moral argument for capitalism, an argument that could defend the inequalities of income, small by today's standards but still so large that for many people they were morally outrageous.

The "moral legitimacy" of inequalities

Under neoclassical economics, individuals were rewarded based on their contributions to society—a theory called just deserts. This "moral justification" of the income individuals receive also provides the moral basis against redistribution: the person has *justly* earned his income.[33] While many conservative economists thus thought there was a fundamental ethical justification for the grave inequalities that unfettered markets might generate, even these conservatives recognized that the levels of inequality produced by the market might not be socially acceptable. It was unconscionable, for example, to just let people starve to death. Children presented a special problem because their deprivations were not the result of anything they had done; they had simply lost the conception lottery. They had "chosen" the wrong parents.

Economists on the Right also argued that if it were desirable to ameliorate these inequities, it could and should be done within a market framework through the imposition of what are referred to as lump-sum taxes. These taxes would be paid no matter what the person does and no matter what his income is, so individuals' behavior would not be "distorted" as they attempt to avoid them.[34] This claim had at its root a more pernicious objective: to argue that one could and should separate questions of efficiency from distribution. It was argued that economists should focus on efficiency and ensure that the size of the economic pie is as large as possible, leaving the question of fair distribution to philosophers and politicians. Some, like Nobel Prize–winning University of Chicago economist Robert Lucas, went further, claiming in 2004 as the tide of inequality was rising: "Of the tendencies that are harmful to sound economics, the most seductive, and in my opinion the most poisonous, is to focus on questions of distribution."[35]

Such claims are morally wrong. I might almost say poisonous. But research over the past half century has shown that they are also analytically wrong. Efficiency and distribution cannot be separated. Even the IMF and the OECD (Organisation for Economic Co-operation and Development)—not left-leaning institutions—have emphasized that economies with greater equality perform better.[36]

Freedom as the critical virtue of a market economy

All this I've said by way of giving the lie to Hayek's and Friedman's (and like-minded conservatives') claims to having an account of and method for providing for equality within a market ideology. But returning to the topic of freedom, Friedman and Hayek each granted enormous import to the relationship between free markets and freedom. Hayek and especially Friedman worried that regulations and other government interventions, whatever their intent, would impair individual freedom:

> We shall always want to enter on the liability side of any proposed government intervention, its . . . effects in threatening freedom, and give this effect considerable weight.[37]

They argued not only that capitalism delivered more freedom than any alternative system but that freedom could only be sustained with a more purified version of capitalism. The market economy of the mid-twentieth century had, from Friedman's perspective, simply too much collective action and too much government.

These arguments, focused as they are on moral rights and freedom, have probably had as much or more persuasive force for those committed to free markets than the technical arguments on the efficiency of markets put forward by economists.

Questioning the moral legitimacy of markets and market incomes

Friedman's and Hayek's understanding of the nature of economics and the relationship between economics and society was badly flawed, as was their (often implicit) conclusion concerning the moral legitimacy of market-determined incomes. If, for instance, the economic efficiency of the market was an important basis of its legitimacy and the income distribution it generated, then the fact that free markets are *not* efficient undermines the claim of legitimacy.

Even within their own framework, though, Friedman and Hayek would have questioned the moral legitimacy of inequalities arising from market power and other forms of exploitation. They denigrated the importance of such deviations from the competitive paradigm because they believed that the economy was *naturally* competitive, and that exploitation couldn't exist. They argued that there were strong forces ensuring that markets would be competitive and exploitation would not occur. The fact that we see, every day, market power and exploitation should serve as a refutation of these theories. But theoretical work over the past half century has shown the fragility of the intellectual edifice on which they rest their case. Even small imperfections of information, small costs of search, or small sunk costs (costs that can't be recovered if one exits a business) completely change the standard results, giving scope for high levels of market power and exploitation.

Accordingly, any theory of liberty and freedom, Hayek's or Friedman's, for example, that rests on the contention that markets on their own are efficient and not exploitive rests on a weak reed. Later chapters will explain why the moral legitimacy of markets and the distribution of incomes and wealth that they generate is even weaker than this discussion suggests. And in the concluding chapter I will turn on its head the Hayek-Friedman contention that economic freedom somehow defined—and typically defined in a way associated with a minimalist state—is necessary for political freedom. It is neoliberalism that has led to the wave of authoritarianism that the world experiences today.

Beyond Neoliberalism

The financial crisis of 2008 may have marked the apex of neoliberalism. It showed that financial liberalization failed even in the citadel of capitalism. It required government to rescue the economy. Then came Trump, and even the conservative Republican Party seemed to abandon trade liberalization. Too many people had been left behind. The statistics kept rolling in: life expectancy in decline in the US, inequality growing in much of the world.[38]

Neoliberalism had given short shrift to externalities, but with climate change and then the Covid-19 pandemic, it became obvious that externalities are of first-order importance. Government is as necessary to helping society maintain the environment and public health as it is to helping sustain macroeconomic stability.

As I emphasize later in this book, when a system breaks down and fails to deliver on its promises, there will be change. That is the nature of evolution. But there is no guarantee about the direction of that change. The end of the post–Cold War détente on neoliberalism has given renewed energy to the extreme Right. It's as if they are saying that neoliberalism made too many compromises, and what's needed is the unfettered capitalism of the Mont Pelerin Society, of Friedman and Hayek. The beliefs of those on the Right, which I have described as essentially "religious," have the power to grab human imagination and enthusiasm. Their appeal to individuality is extraordinarily enticing. If only everybody works hard, is creative, and pursues their *own* interests, all will be well. But that claim is, regrettably, false. Holding on to that belief now implies ignoring both the intellectual developments and the global changes of the last half century. These ideas made no sense in the middle of the twentieth century when they were crystallized and even less in the first quarter of the twenty-first century when global externalities—climate change and pandemics—took center stage. As one would-be authoritarian figure after another appears in one country or another, they spout their words and ideas as if talking about free markets enhances *their* freedom to take freedom away from others.

John Maynard Keynes and FDR saw an alternative way forward from classical economics. Updated for the marked changes in the economy and our understanding of the past three-quarters of a century, their vision still stands as an alternative to the neoclassical and neoliberal economics that followed and to the new Right that is emerging. The Keynes and FDR approach was a tempered capitalism with government playing a key but limited role, ensuring stability, efficiency, and equity—or at least more than is provided by unfettered capitalism. They laid the groundwork for a twenty-first-century progressive capitalism that supports meaningful human freedom.

PART I
LIBERTY AND FREEDOM
BASIC PRINCIPLES

CHAPTER 3

One Person's Freedom Is Another Person's Unfreedom

E very day brings news of another mass killing in the US—almost two a day since the beginning of 2020.[1] These mass shootings, harrowing as they are, represent only a little over 1 percent of deaths by gun each year.[2] In some parts of the country, children have to pass through metal detectors to enter school, and training for what to do in the event of a school shooting begins as early as kindergarten. Even churchgoers and synagogue members have to worry about being gunned down. The US is not at war with a foreign enemy; the battle rages within the nation itself.

There is one reason that the US exceeds other advanced countries in gun deaths: It has more guns. Per capita, it has about thirty times the number of guns as the UK and about fifty times the number of gun deaths.[3] You can buy AR-15s and other automatic weapons far more easily in the US than elsewhere. The reason for that is a misreading by the Supreme Court of the Second Amendment, making ownership of virtually all handguns a constitutionally protected right.[4] Some states, like Texas, went further in allowing assault weapons. In the interpretation of the Court, and even more so in Texas, the right to carry a gun trumps the lives of the thousands who might be killed as a result. The rights of one group, gun owners, are placed above what most others would view as a more fundamental right, the right to live. To rephrase Isaiah Berlin's quote mentioned in the Preface, "Freedom for the gun owners has often meant death to schoolchildren and adults killed in mass shootings."

This is an example of an externality, an action taken by some people that negatively affects others. When there are such adverse externalities, enhancing the ability to take those actions—going so far as to enshrine it as a right—necessarily takes away other people's freedom. Externalities are pervasive in our economy and society. Today, they are far more important than they were when John Stuart Mill wrote *On Liberty* and far more important than Friedman and Hayek suggested. As we've seen, markets on their own won't adequately "solve" the economic distortions to which externalities give rise. Given the inevitable trade-offs in liberties, societies must come up with principles and practices that reflect which freedoms are more important.

The Ubiquity of Externalities

Externalities are everywhere. While they've always been present and important, ongoing changes in the structure of our economy and the world have put externalities front and center. Key questions of economic policy entail managing externalities—discouraging activities where there are harmful (negative) externalities and encouraging activities where there are positive externalities.

We live on a more crowded planet, whose population tripled between 1950 and 2020. In that short span of human history, global GDP increased some fifteenfold, pushing us against the planetary boundaries. The most important manifestation is climate change, an existential threat. But that is not the only environmental externality. We are all affected by air and water pollution and by toxic waste dumps.

It is remarkable that people still debate whether climate change is happening, or whether greenhouse gases in the atmosphere contribute to it in a significant way. In 1896, the Swedish scientist Svante Arrhenius predicted that increases in greenhouse gases in the atmosphere would lead to the warming of the planet. It was one of the great scientific insights, although it was confirmed only decades later. And now we see the effects of climate change all around us, and the world will almost surely feel its force even more in the coming years. Climate change is about more than the heating of the planet a few degrees; it is about the increase in extreme weather events. More droughts, more floods, more hurricanes, more extreme heat and more extreme cold spells, rising sea levels and increasing ocean acidity, and all the dire consequences that will ensue, from dying seas to forest fires to the loss of life and property.

It is striking that given the evident costs and risks associated with climate change, some economists argue that we should do nothing, or very little, about it.[5] Ultimately, what is at issue is a trade-off of freedoms (opportunity sets) across and within generations. We restrict this generation from polluting (thereby reducing coal company profits—their freedom), but in return we expand the freedom of people in later generations to exist on a livable planet without having to spend a huge amount of money to adapt to massive changes in climate and sea levels.

A moment's reflection shows the deep inconsistencies in how we view risk and lives in different contexts. The US went to war in response to the attacks on the World Trade Center and the Pentagon on September 11, 2001. Slightly fewer than 3,000 people died in that attack. In the subsequent war, some 7,000 Americans died, as well as more than 100,000 allied fighters[6] and millions of Afghans and Iraqis,[7] at a cost of trillions of dollars.[8]

By contrast, during the first two decades of this century, climate change and air pollution are estimated to have caused 5 million extra deaths every year, with risks of even greater mortality and huge property losses in coming decades.[9] Yet we cannot agree to make the relatively small investments required to moderate these enormous human and material losses, as well as the implicit losses to the freedoms of the multitude affected.

Similarly, we shrink in horror from an airplane crash, refusing to fly on a Boeing 737 MAX because of its safety record. But the risks of a problem with that aircraft pale in comparison to climate risk.

The Covid-19 pandemic made us aware of enormous public health externalities—and the debates about masking, social distancing, testing, and vaccination demonstrated a widespread lack of understanding of these externalities. The decision of some people not to wear masks or get vaccinated increased the probability of others getting the disease, being hospitalized, even dying.[10] And, as scientists keep pointing out, Covid-19 is not the last epidemic we will face.

We have become a more urbanized world. A hundred and fifty years ago in America, almost three-quarters of the population lived in rural areas.[11] By 2050, it is estimated that 89 percent will live in cities.[12] Externalities are at the core of cities, taking on multiple forms, including congestion, noise, and environmental pollution. That is why almost all cities rely on some form of zoning, city planning, and health regulations. The few that don't are a mess. Houston is an example. As one local newspaper described it:

> [There are] single-story homes next to skyscrapers. Car parks next to playgrounds. Or, even, primary schools next to sex shops. . . . Behold one of Houston's most famous no-zones nightmares. The Zone d'Erotica, a kink-friendly "adult" store, is located in the car park of The Galleria shopping centre which houses a private pre-school as well as many other slightly more wholesome facilities. And not just that: many Houston residents have complained that it is directly across the road from a heavily populated residential area that is also packed with children.[13]

Externalities can be positive as well as negative, and a well-functioning society needs to encourage activities with positive externalities even as it discourages activities with negative externalities. As we moved into a knowledge economy, information and knowledge externalities have also taken on a first-order importance. Advances in knowledge by one firm benefit that firm but may also benefit many others. Consumers may benefit from lower prices, and one innovation can inspire another.

At whatever level you look at the economy, externalities are ubiquitous and consequential. It used to be that when you traveled in an airplane or ate in a restaurant, there was a risk that someone near you would be smoking. If you were a nonsmoker, this could have been irritating. Your eyes may have started to water; you may have coughed; you couldn't enjoy your food. We now know that you confront serious health problems with secondhand smoke.

Your mood may lift when you look out the window at home and see flowers, or you might get depressed if you look out at a sea of garbage. You may be kept up at night by noisy neighbors, or you might be woken up early in the morning by noisy trash collectors.

The externalities may be there, but you may not be aware of them. There are now well-documented adverse effects on pregnant women who live near tollbooths because of the pollution cars and trucks emit. The extra pollution exerts its own toll, whether you understand the environmental science or not.[14]

Our economy has become more financialized, and that has increased the potential for enormous negative externalities. The 2008 economic crisis illustrates the central role of macroeconomic externalities and how increased financialization has, in turn,, increased the magnitude of these externalities. The collapse of America's banking system was a result of excessive risk-taking, poor risk management, and underregulation. The aftermath threatened the global economy to such a great extent that the US government bailed out the banking system to the tune of some $700 billion (with further hidden subsidies provided through the Federal Reserve). Derivatives and the host of associated complex instruments increased systemic risk—the likelihood that financial problems in one part of the financial system would cascade into the failure of all or a significant part of the entire financial system. The Lehman Brothers collapse had cataclysmic effects.[15] No one buying or selling these financial instruments had a glimmer of a notion about their systemic consequences—that is, how they affected those not directly involved in the transaction. They thought only of the economic benefits that they themselves got. They had little understanding that when they and others bought similar instruments, the financial system became so brittle that they, and everyone else in our society, were more at risk, or at least would have been, had the government not come to the rescue.

There was a further externality. The actions of the banking system not only affected the American economy but the entire world. There are many other instances of cross-border externalities, and these have been especially strong as globalization has progressed, making everyone everywhere even more intertwined.

We talk about "contagion," the spread of a disease from one person to another, which is a clear externality. Economists similarly talk about economic contagion, a downturn in one country spilling over to another country, which provides the rationale for massive global bailouts.

We also worry about the contagion of regional conflicts. Not only may conflicts spread, but they can have enormous impacts well beyond the borders in which they occur, as Russia's invasion of Ukraine reminded us. Food and energy prices increased enormously around the world, which led to knock-on effects of inflation and economic instability. The conflict also created insecurity in wide swaths of Europe and Asia. Conflict-induced migration has had big effects, especially in Europe.

While these externalities are obvious and have spectacular consequences, there are also more chronic, more pervasive, but somewhat less obvious externalities. My Columbia colleague Bruce Greenwald and I showed that whenever there is incomplete and asymmetric information (situations in which some individuals know some things that others don't) and imperfect risk markets (the ever-present situations in which I cannot buy insurance against risks I confront), there are externalities[16] that affect the efficiency of markets. Markets are essentially never efficient. As I have often put it, the reason Adam Smith's invisible hand is invisible (the pursuit of self-interest leads *as if by invisible hand* to the well-being of society) is that it just isn't there. To take but one example: If people smoke more, the risk of hospitalization and death increases, and that means the premiums charged for health and life insurance go up.[17] Insurance companies can't tell who is smoking and how much, so even those who don't smoke are made worse off by higher insurance premiums. The smokers impose an externality on the nonsmokers, and the heavy smokers impose an externality on lighter smokers.

The multiple dimensions of externalities

There's a standard list of externalities, both positive and especially negative, to which I have repeatedly referred. But at various points in this book we'll discuss still others. For example, mis- and disinformation can be thought of as polluting our information ecosystem because both make it more difficult to sift out the information garbage. This imposes large costs on those who want to know the truth, and there can be additional externalities when individuals take actions based on mis- or disinformation.

Also consider the many dimensions of our society in which trust plays a role. The economy would function far better if everyone could trust each other. We wouldn't need costly lawyers writing contracts that try to cover every contingency, every form of bad behavior. But untrustworthy people pollute society, forcing us to assess the trustworthiness of everyone we meet. Untrustworthy and dishonest firms force customers to spend more time and energy assessing the products they buy and investors to spend more time and resources assessing the financial products they purchase.

Managing Externalities Is at the Foundation of Civilization

When one person's actions affect others, we have to find ways to shape those interactions. We try to teach our children to be thoughtful. We tell them, "Do unto others as you would have them do unto you" and "Don't do unto others as you would not have them do unto you." Religions and philosophies have gone beyond these broad precepts to issue more narrowly defined injunctions against killing, stealing, and so on. Highlighting why this is so important, modern economics has postulated that people are deeply selfish, pursuing *only* their own narrow self-interest. A world populated by such selfish people without these rules would be a true dystopia.

A slight digression on the development of economics: Selfishness and human nature

While recent advances in economics and long-standing work in other social sciences have rejected the hypothesis of extreme selfishness, it remains strong within the economics profession. Economics long aspired to be a science, like physics, free from normative judgments about what is good or bad, right or wrong. Economists were inspired by Adam Smith's invisible hand. But Smith himself was explicit (especially in his 1759 book, *The Theory of Moral Sentiments*, published twenty-seven years before his better known *The Wealth of Nations*) that individuals are not *perfectly* selfish. He begins that book with the lines

How selfish soever man may be supposed, there are evidently
some principles in his nature, which interest him in the fortune
of others, and render their happiness necessary to him, though he
derives nothing from it except the pleasure of seeing it.[18]

Indeed, historians of economic thought looking at the totality of
Adam Smith's writing, including his *Theory of Moral Sentiments*, suggest that when Smith referred to the individual pursuit of self-interest
leading to societal well-being, he wasn't referring to a totally selfish pursuit, as modern economists think. Rather, he was focused on
people's well-being, *broadly construed*, including their instincts toward
the well-being of others.

In some cases, "other-regarding" behavior may really be a reflection
of direct self-interest. A person may realize that she might be worse
off *in the narrow self-interested sense* were she (and others) not to have
acted in the seemingly other-regarding way. The spread of Covid-19
may, in the end, increase her own probability of death so that it is in
her narrow self-interest to pay attention to the social consequences of
her actions. Or that her sense of security is enhanced if no one carries
guns, far outweighing the pleasure that she might get from having a
gun with her wherever she goes. She may realize that climate change
will have a devastating effect on her life and so willingly embraces
limits on behavior that curb climate change.

But alternatively, other-regarding behavior arises out of a true
empathy for others, including future generations.[19] I think it could
be well argued that in a good society individuals feel this kind of
empathy, at least to some extent. Economics has narrowed our vision
of what kind of economy and society is desirable by denying the relevance of empathy and not recognizing that the extent of it can itself
be affected by the economic system.

The two perspectives—pursuing social justice because it is narrowly in one's self-interest and, more broadly, because it is deeply ingrained in our identity—are, of course, normally intermingled and cannot be easily separated.

Where economics is right, however, is that individuals sometimes— and with some people, often—fail to take sufficient regard of others even after the best education and the deepest religious or philosophical training and the best sermons. So, societies have laws, rules, and regulations that reduce the magnitude of these externalities and their adverse consequences, with punishments for those who do not obey them. This is coercion. We reduce the freedom of some because it is necessary if we want a civilized society to function well, for others to have some of the freedoms they want, and for any society that thinks of itself as a free society.

Evaluating Trade-offs and the Absurdity of the Absolutist Position

Once one recognizes the interdependence of freedoms, one must begin to evaluate trade-offs. An absolutist position that says "any infringement on my liberty is unacceptable" would lead to chaos. We all accept *some* circumscribing, like prohibitions against stealing and killing.

The absolutist position is absurd and indefensible—it is even incoherent. In our complex, interdependent society, where one person's freedom frequently clashes with another's, not all freedoms can be "absolute." Someone's freedom will have to be impinged on. And if that is the case, then we must decide: Whose freedom is to be restricted so that someone else's freedom is enhanced? There are philosophical frameworks that might guide us as individuals and as a society to answer that question. I will discuss one more extensively below.

Simple and hard cases

Sometimes it is easy to come to a reasoned judgment of the balance of costs to the various parties. Requiring me to get tested for a deadly virus or wear a mask is an inconvenience (a loss of freedom). Is that loss more or less important than the risk of you losing your life or the inconvenience of staying at home if you want to avoid the risk of getting the disease? All, or at least almost all, reasonable people will agree that wearing a mask is a small thing when compared with asking people to stay home or risk their lives.

Many of the most politically contentious issues arise, however, when groups within society differ in their judgments about balancing trade-offs. Beneath the surface the disagreements are often based on *empirical* judgments about the nature of the world that, with twenty-first-century science, should be able to be resolved.

Consider the case above about the loss of freedom from having to wear masks versus the loss of freedom from dying from a virulent disease. Assessments of trade-offs are obviously affected by beliefs—in this case, beliefs about the effectiveness of masks. If someone wrongly believes that masks make no difference, then not wearing a mask wouldn't harm anyone else. Both values and cognitive elements are involved, then. The latter should be resolvable, but at this point many anti-maskers abandon science. They resort to stories about a place that has done well without masking. Obviously, the spread of a disease is a complicated process that's affected by a host of variables, and the scientific method attempts to hold all other things constant. That is how one attempts to assess whether masking works or not. And scientists found that, holding all else constant, masking and social distancing make a difference.[20] So the source of the dispute over masking must revolve around values. Are there responsible people who really believe that the right to not be inconvenienced by wearing a mask is more important than the right to live?

I'd go further. Even in the absence of clear, strong, and unambiguous scientific work in support of the efficacy of mask-wearing, so long as there is any significant *probability* that mask-wearing matters, wearing a face covering because it might protect others is almost surely preferable given the low costs of wearing masks and the potentially huge costs of the disease.

Simple principles may be less simple than they seem

Even in the apparently simplest case of externalities, murder, society has evolved a nuanced approach. We qualify the proscription. We accept self-defense. But then we debate whether, in any particular situation, the assertion of self-defense is legitimate.[21]

In response to many externalities, we have adopted the principle that the person damaging others pays for the damage. In the case of environmental damages, we refer to the principle of "polluter pays." This makes sense because it incentivizes a potential polluter not to pollute.

But the externality doesn't happen in a vacuum. One person's actions wouldn't harm another if that other person weren't there. A chemical company that pollutes a lake wouldn't harm anyone if no one swam in the water or drank it—though it would still harm the environment and *constrain* people from swimming or drinking the water. Even a reckless driver might say that if the other vehicle hadn't been there, he wouldn't have hit it.

In most of these cases, there is an automatic (and I think correct) response. It's obvious that I should have the right to swim in a public lake and safely drive down the road. That's because, for the most part, our society has settled on which of these freedoms are more important, but sometimes arriving at that reasoned consensus has not come easily. In Germany, drivers still have the right to drive at an unlimited speed on certain sections of their autobahns, though those extreme speeds increase the probability of someone else getting killed and are bad for the environment.

My objective here is not to answer the question of how each of these thorny trade-offs among freedoms should be resolved. There are complexities and subtleties in each area. Societal views on these matters can and have changed, sometimes rapidly, and they differ across countries. Rather, my *first* objective is to see freedom through the economist's prism of trade-offs, requiring a reasoned public discourse on how freedoms should be balanced.

There are two additional objectives of this book, to which I will turn after offering a better grounding for understanding the freedom trade-off: One is to provide a *framework* to help address these harder questions where it may not be so obvious which of a set of conflicting freedoms should be given more weight (see chapter 5). And the other is to ask what kind of economic/political/social system is most likely to provide just outcomes and societal and individual well-being (covered in Part III).

Externalities and the Conservative Perspective

I spent considerable time in chapter 2 discussing free market economic perspectives. I view the failure of the Right to see that one person's freedom is another's unfreedom as the most fundamental philosophical flaw in the conservative and libertarian positions. Freedom rarely stands alone. In an integrated society, we simply can't look at an individual's liberty without looking at the consequences of that liberty for others.

Hayek and Friedman were, of course, aware of externalities, both negative and positive. And they even wrote about the need for government intervention when there are externalities. For instance, Hayek in *The Road to Serfdom* (1944) wrote:

Nor can certain harmful effects of deforestation, or of some methods of farming, or of the smoke and noise of factories, be confined to the owner of the property in question or to those who are willing to submit to the damage for an agreed compensation. In such instances we must find some substitute for the regulation by the price mechanism.

While aware of the *possibility* of externalities, those on the Right make four mistakes: (a) they relegate externalities to being exceptions; (b) they fail to recognize the really important externalities; (c) they believe that, in most of the rare instances in which externalities occur, voluntary actions would suffice and there is no need for government intervention; and (d) they believe if government has to take action, it should do so by using a single instrument—by imposing a tax on the externality-generating activity.

In the following sections, I explain each of these fundamental errors.

Externalities are the rule, not the exception

I've already explained how, in our twenty-first-century world, externalities are ubiquitous and pervasive. But in the world of Hayek, Friedman, and others on the Right, externalities are the exception, something to be discussed in an economics course at the end of the semester, if there's time. Their training as economists meant that they couldn't *totally* ignore externalities, but they certainly weren't front and center.

If externalities were really as unimportant as Friedman and those on the Right today claim, then maybe we could mostly just rely on the free market. But as I've explained, externalities are ubiquitous and pervasive, and they matter. In that sense, Friedman represented a big step backward in our understanding of the economy from the more nuanced analysis of Adam Smith more than a hundred and seventy-five years earlier. Ironically, neoliberalism increased cross-firm externalities, especially those associated with the financial sector. The excesses of deregulation led to highly interconnected financial institutions, where the failure of one or a few could bring down the entire financial sector and the economy.

Focusing on the wrong externalities: Burdens on our children

In modern politics, the Right (prominently, the Freedom Caucus in the Republican Party) claims that they are the ones who are thinking about the *critical* externality of excess spending and what burdens it imposes on future generations. (Of course, they suspend this reasoning when it comes to debts that arise from tax cuts to the rich and to powerful corporations. Those debts are somehow different.)

From an economics perspective, there are fundamental flaws in their reasoning. First, we can't look at debt in isolation; we have to look at what we got with that debt. If we spend the money on infrastructure, education, or technology, then we have a more productive economy; there are assets that offset the debt liability. Most companies grow by incurring debts. No one in the private sector would look just at the liability side of the balance sheet. When a firm invests well, the value of the assets increases more than the liabilities, and the firm's net worth is enhanced. The same for countries.

To put it another way, *not* to make essential public investments is to leave a country impoverished. There's a broad consensus that that is what has been happening in the US and some other advanced countries. There are very large rates of return on each of the categories of public investment, far higher than the cost of borrowing, yet the Right's fear of deficits and debt has held society back from making these critical expenditures. The mere presence of debt doesn't automatically mean there's been an unjust trade-off, with the current generation benefiting at the expense of future generations. Incurring debt to make high-return public investments is in the countries' best interest, with both this and future generations being better off.

Second, debt is a financial liability, not a real liability. By contrast, environmental degradation is a real liability for future generations; it imposes real burden, with *real* consequences, such as climate change, which will damage health, lives, and our physical infrastructure. The consequences can only be limited by *forcing* future generations to spend money to reverse the degradation. By allowing environmental degradation, we give more freedom to today's polluters and less freedom to future generations. This is the real cross-generational trade-off.[22]

To see the difference between this real trade-off and the financial burden of debt that the Right focuses on, consider the case of a country financing its debt by borrowing from its citizens, which is largely the case for Japan, for example. The country as a whole owes money to particular citizens within the country. If the country passed a law saying that the debt was being restructured so that someone with a $100 bond would get a new bond worth only $50, the bondholders would obviously be worse off; the taxpayers within the country who would otherwise have had to pay for servicing the higher amount of debt would be better off. But the debt would have been cut in half and the relevant *real* variables (like the capital stock) would be unchanged. While a country's financial debt can be lowered by a stroke of the pen, its debt to the environment can't.

The situation is somewhat different for a small open economy that borrows from abroad. In that case, increased debt means that more of what is produced in the country will have to be shipped abroad to pay the debt. The liabilities reduce what future generations can consume, but again, if the borrowing is for productive investments, future generations are better off than they would have been had the debt not been incurred. Also note that private debt reduces or increases future generations' consumption opportunities just as public debt does (depending on how the money associated with the debt is spent). Indeed, unfettered markets may lead to systematically excessive private borrowing, as individual private borrowers don't consider the effects of their indebtedness on the exchange rate and through that, on the rest of the economy.[23]

There are a range of other situations in which important cross-generational externalities arise—where the current generation's expanded freedom comes at least partially at the expense of future generations' freedom. But these are far different from what the Right envisions. Financial liberalization, for instance, exacerbated the problem of private-sector indebtedness I mentioned in the previous paragraph. Increasing the freedom of today's bankers has come at the expense of more frequent financial crises, which have imposed enormous costs on the dozens of countries experiencing them, thereby reducing the freedom of future citizens. It has also been associated with real estate booms, which make it more difficult for younger generations to rent or buy and divert scarce savings from areas like industry where it would be more socially productive.

Leave it to the market

Even Friedman and Hayek thought that we couldn't just leave the management of externalities, when they exist, to the market. However, some of Friedman's colleagues in the Chicago School (the name often given to the conservative school of thought of which Friedman was emblematic),[24] most notably Nobel Prize winner Ronald Coase,[25] thought markets on their own could "solve" the problem of externalities with, at most, limited government action. They were obviously wrong, at least in some really important instances.

The intuition behind their reasoning can be seen in a simple example traditionally used to illustrate externalities. Beekeepers benefit from more apple orchards, but apple orchards benefit from more bees. The bees are critical for pollination, which enhances the apple harvest. But at least in those instances in which there is an isolated apple orchard, the problem can easily be solved if the apple orchard simultaneously keeps bees. In that case, we say that the externality has been internalized. If a community has relatively few apple orchards and beekeepers, they could form an association and work out an efficient solution.[26]

In many cases, Coase argued that the problem of externalities could be "solved" if only the government assigned and enforced property rights. Different assignments might result in one group's expanded freedom at the expense of another's.

Consider the problem of overgrazing or overfishing when citizens in a community share a grazing ground (as in parts of Scotland and England) or a lake or another resource. The problem is that each citizen doesn't consider the externalities—or at least some of the citizens don't.[27] If one person takes more fish from the lake there may be fewer fish for others, and those others will have to work harder to catch the same number of fish as before. Even worse, each may take out so many fish that the total fish population declines. Everyone is then worse off. This is referred to as *the tragedy of the commons*.[28]

A privatized commons, in which the ownership of the commons was given to a single person, would, Coase argued, be efficiently managed. As an owner, this person would calculate the optimal number of sheep to graze or fish to fish to maximize the profits to be earned off the land or lake. The gains would be so large that the owners who took over, say, the common land (typically the local lord) could pay the villagers an income equal to what they had previously earned when their animals grazed the land, and the lord could appropriate the surplus for himself. Indeed, if he shared even a slight amount of the surplus with others, everyone could be better off.

In practice, in many places in Britain, grazing land commons were privatized by big landowners in what were called enclosures, which began in the fifteenth century in England[29] and similarly in Scotland.[30] Because the landowners shared none of the gains with those who had previously had access to the commons, many were unambiguously worse off.[31]

Moreover, Coase's privatization "solution" can't work in many of the most relevant cases. It's fanciful, to say the least, to think we could "privatize" the atmosphere to avoid climate change; that is, give to any one person or corporation the sole right to put pollution into the atmosphere, with that party then selling that right to others and imposing charges for pollution.[32] There are a wide variety of important externalities that can only be addressed by government intervention.

But the Coase solution doesn't even work for much simpler situations. Think of the externality that arises in a room in which there are smokers and nonsmokers. Coase would resolve the problem by giving the property rights to one or the other—let's say the smokers. Then the nonsmokers would pay the smokers not to smoke. If the value to the nonsmokers of clean air were greater than the value to the smokers of smoking, the nonsmokers would bribe the smokers not to smoke and the room would be smoke-free; if not, it would be filled with smoke. But in either case, the solution is efficient, even if the nonsmokers think it unfair since they either have to pay the smokers not to smoke or suffer from the smoke. But there's a further problem. Each nonsmoker might think: If enough other nonsmokers speak up and offer to pay the smokers not to smoke, smoking will stop, and I won't have to pay. Some nonsmokers free-ride on the contributions of others to stop the smoking. But, of course, if everyone does this, the nonsmokers won't raise enough money to bribe the smokers not to smoke and the "bad" equilibrium with smoking will persist.[33] This is called *the free-rider problem*, and it's endemic in all situations in which positive or negative externalities exist, affecting large numbers of people.[34]

For these and a variety of other reasons,[35] the privatization/Coase solution typically is not the solution to the tragedy of the commons or broader problems of externalities. Typically, there is no voluntary solution.

*Reliance on environmental taxes is typically not the
optimal response to environmental externalities*

Because Friedman and Hayek sought to minimize the role of the state,
and because they minimized the importance of externalities, they
didn't devote much energy to thinking about how externalities, when
they existed, might best be managed. Friedman relied on economists'
knee-jerk dependence on prices. He believed that prices were essential in guiding firms to decide what and how to produce and households to decide what to consume. But he went further. He argued
that *only* prices should be used, so if society thought there should be
less pollution than the free market generated, then the government
should tax pollution, increasing the "price" of pollution to the level
that generated the optimal amount of pollution.[36] This would balance
the (marginal) cost of pollution with the (marginal) cost of pollution
abatement. The "solution" to cars producing pollution, Friedman said,
is to "impose a tax on the amount of pollutants emitted by a car." That
would "make it in the self-interest of the car manufacturers and of the
consumers to keep down pollution."[37]

While Friedman was right that prices provide incentives, as a matter of economic theory Friedman's contention that it is best to rely
just on price interventions is wrong. When there are *multiple market
failures*—imperfections in competition together with imperfections in
information, capital markets working imperfectly, and inequalities
that a pollutant tax might exacerbate[38]—it is necessary to combine a
tax on the amount of pollutants with other government actions, such
as a regulation limiting the amount of pollution and public investments in public transportation, for instance.[39]

Climate change provides a telling example. The effects of regulations may be more certain than price interventions. We may not
know with much precision how firms and households will respond
to a carbon price (a fee charged on carbon emissions).[40] We can't be

sure whether a particular carbon price will induce a power company to switch to renewables or a household to switch to an electric car, so regulations may be preferable. This holds especially true in situations like climate change, where we really care about the level of atmospheric concentration of greenhouse gases, which is directly related to the level of emissions, and where we know that there is a real danger of exceeding certain threshold levels established by science. I'll expand on the reasons why "optimal interventions" in response to an externality like climate change entail a package of policies, including carbon taxes, regulations, and public investments, later in this chapter.

The Regulatory Solution

Nobel Prize–winning political scientist and economist Elinor Ostrom pointed out that there is another way to deal with the commons that is fairer and potentially just as efficient as Coase's privatization solution: regulation. Restricting the number of cattle, sheep, or goats that each person can graze (or limiting the number of fish that a person can take out), solves the problem.[41] Historical research in the UK shows that in fact much of the common land was actually well regulated, as communities themselves adopted restrictions to prevent overgrazing. There was no efficiency argument for the land enclosures, and privatization was not necessary, just as Ostrom showed to be the case in many developing countries today.[42]

Both privatization and regulation are coercive. Privatization completely constrained the ordinary Scottish or English person who had grazed animals on the commons from doing what she previously could have done freely. In a fundamental sense, privatization of the commons entailed taking away the property rights of those who had grazed their animals there before. In the absence of compensation, the commoners who had had grazing rights were unambiguously worse off than they were before the enclosures.

Neoliberalism taught us to see the issue through the eyes of the landowners, who obviously were less constrained. But if we see it through the eyes of ordinary people, regulation would have been far less coercive. Restricting the number of sheep a farmer could graze was far better than granting the farmer no rights to graze at all. Each ordinary citizen would have had more freedom, a larger opportunity set.

How best to regulate

We have seen that it's intellectually indefensible to claim there should be no public intervention when there are important externalities. Regulations may be more efficient and fairer than other forms of intervention, and some regulations more efficient and fairer than others. Privatizing the common grazing grounds was far more inequitable and no more efficient than instituting well-designed regulations.

Environmental externalities are a further case in point. There is, on the Right, widespread criticism of the use of regulations to control externalities such as pollution. They prefer (if pollution is to be discouraged at all) that producers receive subsidies to induce them not to pollute rather than that they be taxed as punishment for polluting or operate under regulations to stop them from polluting, with huge fines should they disobey. Such subsidies (as this book goes to press, now estimated to be in excess of a trillion dollars) are at the core of the Inflation Reduction Act of 2022.[43]

Subsidies, taxes, and regulations can all lead to power plants that pollute less by switching away from coal. In all cases, profits can be higher from making the transition, even taking the related costs into account. The power plants prefer subsidies over regulations or taxes. The reason is obvious. They prefer to receive money from the government rather than pay the costs themselves. But the "expansion" of their opportunity set through subsidies has to be matched by the contraction of the opportunity set of others. The electricity companies' "freedom" (and that of their owners) is increased at the expense of the ordinary individual, who must suffer from increased taxation to pay for the subsidy. Moreover, from the perspective of pure efficiency, the subsidy distorts the economy because the electricity company is not facing the full costs of what it does, even if it is successful in curbing emissions. Indeed, electricity prices may end up lower than they should be and electricity consumption higher, which will worsen global warming, even though the emissions per unit of electricity have been reduced.

Conventional economists have a proclivity for using prices because they give signals to all members of society, each of whom can creatively find ways to best reduce carbon emissions. Prices are then a critical instrument in a decentralized economy. But we've seen that some economists, like Friedman, argue we should rely *just* on price signals, like the ones a carbon tax would send. A carbon tax, some have argued, is simpler to design and enforce than regulations. Regulations are necessarily complex and expensive to administer, they claim. But in practice, that often isn't the case. It's far easier to see whether an electric power plant is using coal than to measure its carbon emissions, or to see whether a car has an internal combustion engine than to measure its pollutants.[44] In the vital area of climate change, it turns out that a relatively few regulations can achieve a large fraction of what needs to be done.

There's another advantage to regulations that I noted earlier: the effects may be more certain. And there's yet another advantage. Sometimes regulations can be designed in a more tailored way that limits adverse distributional consequences. Remember how the neoliberal solution to overgrazing—privatization—was inequitable? Similarly, relying only on the price system may be unfair to certain groups in ways that are hard to offset through the political system.

That's why it's often better to use a package of policies, including regulations, prices, and public investments, to address externalities, especially in a case of the scope and complexity of climate change.

The packages can be designed to be more efficient and fairer than relying on prices or regulations alone.[45]

What happened in France in November 2018 illustrates this. The well-intentioned French president, Emmanuel Macron, announced a gas and diesel tax designed to discourage carbon emissions. There was an uprising, spearheaded by the working classes in some of the country's poorer regions—protests that came to be called the yellow vests movement (named for the safety vests worn by many of the protestors). Years before, in acts of government frugality, public transportation services had been cut off, which forced people to rely on their cars to get to work, to church, and to food shops. In short, to live their lives. The prosperity reflected in French GDP statistics hadn't touched these workers either. Along with cutting some taxes on the rich, this gas tax seemed to be the last straw. A petition against the tax garnered a million signatures. Massive protests broke out throughout the country, some of which turned violent. All told, approximately 3 million people participated in the yellow vests protests. Two months later, the government canceled the tax and France continued to contribute to global warming unabated. On the other hand, a well-designed package that included public transport and perhaps even subsidies to the most-affected groups, especially those least able to bear the burden of the tax, such as pensioners, might have garnered enough support to avoid this kind of backlash.[46]

A comprehensive package that includes regulations, prices, and public investment will expand the opportunity set of most people in some ways (they can now enjoy a life with a lower risk of climate change) and contract it for others (they may have to pay higher prices for some goods). In practice, even if most are better off, some will be worse off. There are trade-offs. But it is wrong to say that the regulatory system is more coercive than the price or subsidy system. We must evaluate the full consequences for both winners and losers. I believe that a society that does this is not likely to rely on just prices or just regulations. A mix is almost surely the best approach.

The central message that some seeming coercion, here through the regulatory system, can be freeing and expand the opportunity set of most individuals is even more relevant to broad areas of public investment that may require increased taxation, as we will see in the next chapter.

CHAPTER 4

Freedom through Coercion: Public Goods and the Free-Rider Problem

Consider what would happen without rules delineating which side of the road to drive on. Some would drive on the left, others on the right. There would be chaos and gridlock, as can happen in a developing country where economic growth has outpaced the development of the necessary regulatory frameworks. The chaos can be resolved with a one-time intervention: a law requiring everyone to drive on the right-hand side. This neatly solves the coordination problem, and after its initial imposition, it isn't coercive. If everyone drives on the right-hand side, I want to as well.

In congested areas, an absence of stoplights can also give rise to chaos and gridlock. The use of stoplights is a simple regulation that specifies when cars can proceed through an intersection. This law entails minimal coercion and relatively little cost to either the government or to drivers, but it has the enormous benefit of avoiding, or at least reducing, gridlock and accidents. To be clear, stoplights are coercive. And yet everyone benefits.

These examples contrast with the situations discussed in the last chapter, instances in which seemingly coercive government action is directed at limiting the harms one person imposes on another. There, the collective action of the group decides on a set of rules that enhances the well-being of the society *as a whole*, even if particular individuals or groups of individuals are worse off. In this chapter, I consider another important case in which coercion is desirable, in which there are benefits from *collective action* through the provision of a public good or facilitating coordination (like stoplights). Coercion, in many cases, takes the form of taxes to make it possible to provide the public good. The Right often seems most militant against these taxes, except when the money is used for national defense. But then, even they recognize that the benefit of the public good provided by tax revenues is worth it. Everyone, including those who pay the highest taxes, may be better off as a result of this mild form of coercion. Bill Gates and Jeff Bezos might not be able to enjoy their fortunes under a regime headed by Vladimir Putin or in a world dominated by China. To be sure, there may be disagreements about what particular publicly provided good justifies the coercion of taxes. In general, the Left may be less convinced of the value of military spending and the Right of the benefits of public spending on health. In 2023, both parties came together to recognize the benefits of spending on infrastructure and technology, particularly advanced microchips.

Everyone should agree on this principle. There are some types of government spending in which mild coercion leads to improved societal welfare and enhances our freedom in the more broadened, positive sense of freedom that I've been arguing for. Coercion is required, but the result of the coercion is to "loosen" the budget constraint of citizens, including those who have to be coerced into paying taxes. In that sense, people's economic freedom (the set of things they can do) is unambiguously enriched.

We see the fruits of these expenditures in every corner of our lives, and they enrich every aspect of our well-being.

Public Investments Enriching Our Lives

In our twenty-first-century economy, we have all benefited from public investments in basic research that result in advances in science and technology.

I constantly check facts and figures on the internet and keep in touch with friends and family through email. But the internet didn't just happen. It was the result of a deliberate research program by the US government through the Defense Department (DARPA, the Defense Advanced Research Projects Agency). Even the browser was a publicly funded invention. Though it was developed as a result of public spending, it was, in effect, handed over to the private sector, which has enjoyed enormous profits from it.[1]

Health

One important yardstick to measure advances in standards of living is increased longevity. As of 2021, life expectancy at birth was 76.4 years in the US, 80.3 years on average in OECD countries, and as high as 84.5 in Japan.[2] Much of that increased longevity is based on advances in medical science, which rest on publicly funded basic research.

The response to Covid-19 illustrates the value of public action as well. In record time, the world recognized the pathogen responsible for the terrible disease; in record time, a vaccine was developed, tested, and produced. None of this would have been possible without a long history of publicly funded research. The private sector was eventually involved, but only toward the end and, even then, with massive government support. Decades of research on DNA was followed by research on messenger RNA; that was followed by the development of the mRNA vaccine platform, which proved so fruitful in producing the highly effective mRNA vaccine against Covid-19.

Despite the mistaken general impression that the mRNA vaccine was the result of the skills and effort of private companies, the success was due to a partnership that worked. Pfizer's vaccine was actually codeveloped with BioNTech SE, a German biotechnology company that had received government subsidies. And every company's timely success was only possible because of previous government-funded and university-funded research on mRNA platforms.[3]

In the beginning, it wasn't clear how the virus spread but, again, largely publicly funded research came to the rescue. Understanding how it was transmitted enabled the development of social protocols that reduced the spread. Public campaigns disseminating these practices and encouraging and paying for vaccination went a long way toward bringing the disease under control.

Public goods and the free-rider problem

I've touched on only a few of the rich set of goods and services that are publicly provided; there are far more—policing, education, infrastructure, fire protection, national parks—the list is endless. To be sure, there has been some controversy around the edges, whether this or that service might be better provided privately than publicly.[4] But to a large extent, the controversy is about *how* public goods should be produced. This is distinct from the issue at hand, which is the necessity of using coercion—compulsory contributions through taxation—to finance these public goods.

Yet despite the enormous benefits of spending on public goods, there is a free-rider problem. Public goods make everyone better off,[5] regardless of whether any one person contributes to their provision. In a large economy, each person might reason that it doesn't matter whether he provides support because it won't affect the supply.

We can think of voluntarily contributing to the support of a public good as creating a *positive* externality. The person making the contribution benefits, and so does everyone else. I noted in the last chapter that just as market economies produce too much of those things where there is a negative externality (too much steel, for example, with its production causing pollution), they produce too little of those things where there is a positive externality. And this is especially true in the case of public goods. Each person has a strong incentive to become a free rider on others' contributions. But obviously, if everyone attempts to be a free rider, then there won't be any public good. Even if only some are free riders, there will be an under-provision, to the detriment of all.

In this key arena of public goods, so essential for our well-being, we get the seemingly contradictory result that forcing citizens to pay taxes to provide public goods can expand the options and the individual freedom of everyone, even though it seemingly restricts options.

I argued in the last chapter that not recognizing that one person's freedom is another's unfreedom was a grave intellectual failure of the Right. Another is to not recognize the enormous value of public expenditures, which can only be funded through taxes. And not recognizing the value of coercive coordination is a third. These failures together help to explain why the Right's discourse on freedom is so misguided and has such limited vision.

The Benefits of Coercion in Coordination

There are many other areas besides the provision of public goods in which government actions that appear coercive actually increase the set of options for all or most people. This is, for instance, the characteristic of a wide class of situations that economists have identified as "coordination problems," where, in one way or another, individuals interact, and the outcomes are better if they somehow coordinate. I began the chapter with an obvious example: We need to coordinate which side of the road to drive on. It doesn't matter whether it's on the left or right; it just has to be one or the other.

Much of what we do with others entails coordination, and failure to coordinate well has high costs. We miss seeing a friend because we failed to coordinate our trips. If the producers of baby formula don't produce enough formula, the costs can be enormous. This happened in the aftermath of the Covid-19 pandemic. These types of shortages were a pervasive part of life in the Soviet Union and were a mark of the failure of central planning to coordinate.

The theme of this section is that there can be enormous benefits to good coordination. Individuals and markets on their own may do an imperfect job in coordination, but government can improve matters. This may partly entail an element of coercion—indeed, some coercion may be essential—but imposing it is "freeing," because individuals' freedom to act, their opportunity set, is expanded.

Coordinating vacations

Consider the simple problem of a family vacation. When both parents work it requires coordination with their two employers as well as their children's school. Given that my spouse has a vacation at a particular time, my children and I want to have our vacations at the same time. France solves this coordination problem simply: Everyone gets August off. This coordinated equilibrium works better than the uncoordinated American equilibrium, where the value of vacation days is diminished because it's harder for both spouses to get vacation simultaneously. As a result, both take fewer vacation days. Not only are both individuals worse off, but productivity, and therefore profits, may be lower.[6]

Prisoner's dilemma

Perhaps the most famous coordination problem is referred to as the prisoner's dilemma, in which people would be better off if they could only cooperate, but each has an incentive to deviate from the welfare-maximizing cooperative agreement.[7]

Everyone wants to take Sunday off from work and enjoy a day of rest, consistent with the biblical injunction. But if all other stores are closed, it pays to open my store because I get all the customers who want to buy on Sunday, some of whom may stick with me for the rest of the week. However, if I open my store on Sunday, my competitors will feel forced to do the same; if they don't, they fear they will lose sales and profits. The equilibrium that emerges is one in which all stores are open on Sunday, and all store owners are miserable. In total, they may not sell more than if they were all closed on Sundays. Government interventions that force all stores to close on Sunday make store owners better off. Of course, those customers who really wanted to shop on Sunday are worse off.[8]

The regulation solves the prisoner's dilemma, making all the players better off. Each feels coerced and would like to deviate. But the coercion enhances the opportunity set of everyone—it is "freeing."

Welfare-reducing speculation

There are many other cases in which cooperation, while yielding a better outcome, can't be sustained because each person has a private incentive to deviate from cooperative behavior. Consider the weather report. We all benefit from knowing tomorrow's weather. If one more person knows, it doesn't detract from my knowledge (unlike an ordinary physical good, which you and I typically can't enjoy simultaneously). This is a quintessential public good, which, if the benefits of knowing the weather ahead of time exceed the costs, should be publicly provided.

Now consider the case in which the benefits don't justify the costs. Speculators might have a special interest in knowing tomorrow's weather just a little bit earlier than everyone else. It may enable them to buy up umbrellas and sell them at a high price the next day. The speculator can reap a large profit. But then most people will be induced to spend money to find out whether it will rain simply so they won't be ripped off by the speculator. A cascade of wasteful expenditure on information ensues, induced by the speculator trying to take advantage of the public and the countervailing spending by the rest of society.

A simple coercive rule—no price gouging when it rains—solves the problem. The speculator then has no incentive to gather the information. And this enables everyone else to avoid the counter-speculator expenditures. Everyone except the speculator is better off.[9]

Alternatively, if information about the weather *collectively* has sufficient value in enabling individuals to better plan their lives, government provision of the information would be welfare enhancing, even though that requires a coercive tax to finance the publicly provided good. Government provision of information preempts the speculator.[10, 11] It takes away the ability to price gouge.

Systemic coordination

I am concerned here, though, mostly about the role of government intervention and coercion in the coordination of the entire economic system. Some firms make cars, others steel. Some firms (called auto dealers) have an inventory of cars to sell, and some households are thinking about buying cars. How does this all match up? How is it that, by and large, the amount of steel produced is just about what is needed each year? And that the number of cars produced is just about what buyers need?

In the nineteenth century, a number of economists, most importantly Léon Walras (1834–1910), developed a mathematical version of what they thought Adam Smith had in mind when he talked about the invisible hand—the pursuit of self-interest leading in a competitive economy to the well-being of everyone, as it somehow produced what individuals wanted in the quantities they wanted. In the middle of the twentieth century, this model was further analyzed to show that if there is perfect information about the characteristics of all goods at all dates and times and perfect competition in markets for all goods and services at all dates in all contingencies (so there are, in effect, perfect risk markets) *and* there is no technological change, then all the coordination that is needed exists within the context of the economic interactions that occur in markets, guided by prices. And the equilibrium, where each person maximizes her well-being given the prices (themselves reflective of the actions of all others), is an efficient outcome. Prices are the coordinating mechanism, adjusting up and down depending on whether there is an excess demand or supply. Putting aside the unreality of the assumptions, the beauty of the proof of the result and its far-reaching implications are breathtaking. The two people who succeeded in providing the proofs, Kenneth Arrow and Gérard Debreu, deservedly received the Nobel Memorial Prize in Economic Sciences for their work.[12]

The result was interpreted in three different ways by different groups of economists. A small group, of which Debreu was the leader, took the result for what it was: a mathematical theorem to be analyzed and generalized, but that was it. It was up to others to decide about the relevance of the theorem to the real world.

Conservatives, on the other hand, thought of it as a vindication of what they had long believed. It reinforced their conviction in "market fundamentalism."[13] They ignored the limitations of the assumptions, just as they had ignored Smith's many caveats warning about the limitations of unfettered markets. They held to that view even when, in the decades after Arrow and Debreu's work, it became increasingly clear that the assumptions to prove market efficiency could not be weakened; Arrow and Debreu had found the singular set of assumptions in which the results were valid.[14]

The third group—to which Arrow largely belonged—held that what had been proven was that the market was not efficient. The fact that the assumptions under which the economy was efficient were so distant from the real world meant that Arrow and Debreu (together with later economists who investigated each of the assumptions in more detail) had proved that markets were, in fact, not efficient; that is, when those unrealistic conditions are not satisfied, in general the economy is *inefficient*. Indeed, matters that Debreu had totally ignored in his analysis turned out to be crucial. The results on the efficiency of the economy were destroyed even when there was just a little imperfection of information, just a small cost of search. In short, prices coordinate in competitive markets (say, between producers and consumers, so that what is produced is exactly what is consumed), but in ways that are not in general efficient.

A corollary of this analysis is that there are interventions in the market—sometimes coercive—that can make everyone better off.

Macroeconomic failures

In practice, things are better and worse than the market fundamentalists of the Right believed.[15] There are other coordination mechanisms; firms don't just rely on prices. They look at their inventories and the inventories of other firms. If inventories are building up, they know to cut back production. They consult with others—including economists—to understand where the economy and their sector are going. In contrast to standard market economics, which claims that prices convey all the relevant information, they make use of a host of sources of information.

But the dynamics of this more complex system are, in general, neither efficient nor stable. The macroeconomic fluctuations that have marked capitalism over the past two-and-a-half centuries—including the Great Depression and Great Recession—are the clearest manifestations of these massive coordination failures that have imposed enormous costs on society. Years after, growth is lower; the economy may never catch up to where it would have been had these crises not happened. But the costs to people are even greater—lives and fortunes ruined, educations interrupted, fear and insecurity abound.

Over the past eighty years, government interventions have done a lot to reduce both the magnitude and frequency of these fluctuations and their consequences. These improvements in macroeconomic performance have been a major contributor to societal and individual well-being. In enhancing the stability and efficiency of the economy, freedom is expanded not just in terms of the opportunity sets discussed earlier but in more general terms of well-being, including, importantly, freedom from hunger and fear.

But most of the interventions have entailed some degree of coercion: forced contributions to unemployment insurance funds so when workers face joblessness, the consequences are mitigated; taxes to ensure there are food and health safety nets, weak as they are; restrictions on banks to ensure they don't make excessively risky loans that plunge the economy into recessions or depressions.

The success of these interventions in the macroeconomy provides an answer to another objection the Right has to government intervention. Sometimes they begrudgingly grant that markets are not efficient and that, *in principle*, there are government interventions that might improve matters. But, they contend, government interventions rely on political processes and these *inevitably* muck things up. Even if welfare-improving interventions hypothetically exist, they argue, government interventions tend to do just the opposite.

But this simply isn't right. Though governments, like all other human institutions, are fallible, they can and have been successful in improving economic outcomes in this and multiple other arenas.

Pursuing Self-Interest, Broadly Construed

Economists, with their proclivity *against* government action, naturally wonder whether there is a way that people might solve these public goods and coordination problems on their own.

There are a host of voluntary associations, nongovernmental organizations, and other organizations partially addressing specific coordination and public goods problems. In some areas, things are not as bad as economists, who view people as *absolutely* selfish, might have expected. Humans aren't *that* selfish.[16] They give billions to charity. They care about others.[17] Around the world, voluntary associations and NGOs pushing some public purpose or another—better human rights, better treatment of the environment, better health care— have flourished, with contributors and volunteers donating money and time and employees accepting pay well below what they could get elsewhere.

In a wide swath of domains and situations many, perhaps most, people seem to act as if they are maximizing their well-being in a broader sense than their own *narrow* self-interest. They exhibit a greater sense of *enlightened self-interest*, taking into account the nature of the society that would emerge if everyone acted in similar ways. They explicitly eschew acting *totally* as free riders. This is especially true in politics, where many citizens ask themselves in the voting booth, "What kind of a society do I want?" Many rich people vote for high taxes on the rich in the belief that if everyone contributes (all are coerced), then public investment would reduce certain inequalities and increase societal productivity and welfare. Such coercion creates a better society. Given the tax system, they try to minimize their taxes in accordance with their narrow self-interest; but in voting on the rules of the game, they take a more enlightened view.

Most people feel it is part of their civic duty to serve on a jury; they do so voluntarily, knowing full well that they could present some valid excuse for not serving. Parents work hard to improve the quality of their local schools. While their children benefit, so do others.

In short, the right-wing perspective—and the standard economics perspective—on human nature is just wrong. Although, regrettably, some people are not so inclined to unselfishness. They behave just as economists theorize, and our society has to be constructed to take them into account. This is why we cannot solely rely on voluntary actions to resolve problems of public goods and coordination. There has to be coercion to solve the large-scale problems that require public (governmental) intervention.

But the Right has created a trap. They trumpet selfishness almost as a virtue and misleadingly claim that selfishness ruthlessly pursued advances social well-being. That means, as they have said, that governmental intervention cannot be trusted, because the selfishness they praise applies to public-sector employees, too; and public officials will advance their own interests at the expense of the rest of society. But they are wrong on all counts. People are not as selfish as the Right claims, as I have noted; many enter public service to advance the public interest. Most importantly, for my purposes here, we can create public institutions with checks and balances that prevent the abuses the Right so fears. Some countries have done a remarkably good job of this. And there is a virtuous circle. Countries that have done a better job at creating trustworthy governments have more trust in government and attract better people to public service. Indeed, so successful have some countries been that individuals *willingly* pay taxes, knowing that "taxes are what we pay for civilized society," as Supreme Court Justice Oliver Wendell Holmes famously said. In Finland, for instance, a survey commissioned by the tax administration reported that "95% of Finns consider paying taxes an important civic duty. . . . In addition, 79% of respondents were happy to pay taxes and felt that they get good value for the taxes they pay."[18]

In Part II, I will discuss how society can create more trust, more trust in government, and more trustworthy individuals, and I make note of the converse—that in societies without trust, not even the private sector can function well. Neoliberal capitalism has created untrustworthy people and has (understandably) eroded not just trust in government but trust in private institutions and trust in each other. It has created a system that devours itself. None of this, however, is inevitable.

Global Public Goods and Global Coordination

As we've seen, there is a parallel between what occurs *within* nations and what occurs *between* nations. What one person does can affect other people; what one country does can affect other countries. We need rules and regulations to prevent negative externalities exerted by one person onto another, and to prevent externalities exerted by one country onto another. The problem, which I discuss at greater length in chapter 12, is that the basic political unit in the world today is the nation-state, able to regulate only what occurs within its borders. There is no effective *global* body to regulate what occurs across borders. The same is true with international coordination and the provision of global public goods.[19] A little coercion could result in an increase in global societal well-being. The difficulties in taking cross-border welfare-enhancing cooperative actions mean there is less coordination, more negative externalities, and fewer global public goods than there would be otherwise.

The most important example of a global public good is protecting the world from climate change. Countries are voluntarily taking some actions, but far less than required if the world is to avoid the extreme dangers of temperatures rising more than 1.5 to 2 degrees Celsius.[20]

I have emphasized that there have to be rules and regulations—coercion—to avoid externalities and to generate coordination and cooperation, but I should also emphasize that enforcing these rules and regulations is equally important. Here the global system really falters. There is no global government to enforce even weak agreements. In some arenas the international community has succeeded and coercion (and the threat of coercion, including trade sanctions against countries that violate the agreement) has been effective. For example, before the 1987 international treaty referred to as the Montreal Protocol on Substances That Deplete the Ozone Layer,

use of chemicals like chlorofluorocarbons (CFCs) and halons was creating huge holes in the stratospheric ozone layer, which helps protect
us from skin cancer. The restorative forces of the Earth are amazingly
strong, and with these substances essentially eliminated the ozone
layer is expected to be restored by the middle of this century, with
enormous benefits. Those born between 1980 and 2100 will likely
dodge some 443 million cases of skin cancer, approximately 2.3 million skin cancer deaths, and more than 63 million cases of cataracts,
and the Earth will have avoided a temperature increase of 2.5 degrees
C from this source alone.[21]

The protocol can be viewed as a contract among countries in which
each gave up some of its "freedom" (to use CFCs) in return for others doing so, with obvious dividends. But the Montreal Protocol
included an element of coercion. Countries that didn't comply would
face a high penalty. Coercion expanded freedom—the freedom, for
instance, not to get skin cancer.

Similarly, in the private sector, there are voluntary contracts involving mutually agreed-on restrictions that include surrendering freedoms in some dimension in return for a more valuable expansion of
freedoms in another, with benefits exceeding costs. The next chapter
considers these situations in greater detail.

CHAPTER 5

Contracts, the Social Contract, and Freedom

W hen individuals sign a contract, they agree to do something; this contract constrains their freedom to act in the future in return for something from the other party. Individuals willingly agree to such constraints because the entire exchange benefits them, just like the "coercion" that the state may impose to regulate certain actions or to force people to pay taxes to finance public investments that make everyone better off.

In a fundamental sense, all contracts are constraints that expand opportunities for the parties agreeing to the contract in relevant ways. Without credit contracts, for example, people could not get access to the money they need to make high-return investments. In return, they accept constraints, including on how they can use this money, and possibly even constraints on other aspects of what they can do, such as not borrowing from another lender.

The fact that a contract is voluntarily entered into does not mean it is not exploitive—a subject I will return to later. Someone might sign an exploitive labor contract if it is the only way he can survive. In this situation, you could say the person is coerced—and even more if he has been deprived of alternatives, as in the case of South Africa, where Black Africans were deprived of the right to farm. There is, in this sense, a big difference between contracts among parties of roughly equal power and contracts between parties of unequal power.

The Concept of a Social Contract

Philosophers have long viewed the relationship between individuals and society[1] as governed by a similar *social contract*, which constrains citizens in ways that enhance their overall freedom and well-being. It is important to note that the social contract is a metaphor; there is no written or formalized contract.

A social contract defines the relationship between individuals and societies, much as an actual contract would, outlining the obligations of the parties to the contract and to each other.

There is one big difference between the social contract and ordinary contracts. When an actual contract is breached, there are consequences, both for the relationship and especially for the breaching party. The aggrieved party may attempt to impose a penalty on those who breach. When a person breaks a contract, there are clear rules about the processes for judging whether and the extent to which the terms of the contract (the rules and regulations) have been broken and the punishments to be meted out. But when the state violates what it is supposed to do there is no corresponding mechanism for enforcing the social contract. This is the fundamental difference between an ordinary contract and a social contract. Behind any ordinary contract, there is a government to enforce it. Social contracts are based on trust. With a social contract, there's the risk that if citizens believe their government has breached it, law and order can break down.

Writing the social contract
The notion of a social contract invites us to ask what kinds of rules and principles that form the basis of that contract might contribute

to societal well-being. Chapters 3 and 4 made clear that there are important societal trade-offs in writing the rules of the economy and society. Do we focus on the well-being of the wolves or the sheep? On gun owners or victims of gun violence? On the rich whose freedom is reduced by progressive taxation, or on the poor, whose freedom to live is greatly enhanced when the government helps to fund better education, health, and nutrition?

Once we see that freedoms entail trade-offs, we need to figure out a system for weighing the expansion of some people's freedoms with the curtailing of other people's beyond the law of the jungle, where the strongest expands her freedom at the expense of all others. John Rawls's *Theory of Justice* (1971) provides this kind of framework. We can think of how individuals would want to make these trade-offs if we imagine them behind what Rawls calls the "veil of ignorance," where they don't know where in society they will find themselves when the veil is lifted. Will they be rich, or will they be poor? Behind the veil, they don't know. In a pragmatic way, Rawls's framework is akin to Smith's "impartial spectator":

> Moral norms thus express the feelings of an impartial spectator. A feeling, whether on the part of a person motivated to take an action or on the part of a person who has been acted upon by others, is worthy of moral approval if and only if an impartial spectator would sympathize with that feeling.[2]

Both Rawls and Smith are simply suggesting that a person should distance herself from her self-interest when assessing what makes a good or just society. In fact, Rawls provides a method that *prevents* us from choosing principles biased in our favor when we select principles and policies to live by. This is what he calls *justice as fairness*. Smith's impartial observer is, in a sense, a personification of that method.

Rawls uses this framework to present a persuasive case for progressive redistribution as a desirable part of the social contract.[3] Here, I will use his framework to think about the wide range of institutional arrangements that govern society.

We can think of various provisions of the social contract as specifying society's rules and regulations. Markets don't exist in a vacuum. There is no such thing as a free market in the abstract. Markets are structured by rules and regulations. Behind the veil of ignorance, I think there would be broad consensus on the trade-offs involved in constructing the social contract. How do we weigh the freedom of the wolves versus the freedom of the sheep? Of the exploiter versus the exploited? We can ask: Behind the veil of ignorance, where we don't know where we will end up in society—the small chance of being a dominant monopolist or the large chance of being a potentially exploited worker or consumer—what set of rules and regulations would we desire? There is likely to be much less disagreement over these provisions, which we can think of as producing socially equitable outcomes. To put it loosely, we would choose provisions that promote as much equality as possible, consonant with overall economic performance.[4, 5]

This framework can be used to give guidance to the myriad laws, rules, and regulations required for a twenty-first-century economy, including those to protect workers, consumers, competition, and the environment. Interestingly, Adam Smith, whose name is so often invoked in support of laissez-faire economics that doesn't entail any government intervention, recognized how the design of regulations makes a difference:

> When the regulation, therefore, is in support of the workman, it is always just and equitable; but it is sometimes otherwise when in favour of the masters.[6]

Smith understood that laws concerning employees working together affect bargaining power, and he recognized, too, asymmetries in market power:

> What are the common wages of labour, depends everywhere upon the contract usually made between those two parties, whose interests are by no means the same. It is not, however, difficult to foresee which of the two parties must, upon all ordinary occasions, have the advantage in the dispute, and force the other into a compliance with their terms. The masters, being fewer in number, can combine much more easily. . . . In all such disputes the masters can hold out much longer.[7]

He went on to observe that:

> Masters are always and everywhere in a sort of tacit, but constant and uniform combination, not to raise the wages of labour above their actual rate. Masters, too, sometimes enter into particular combinations to sink the wages of labour even below this rate. These are always conducted with the utmost silence and secrecy.

Smith recognized that what we see differs markedly from what we might expect in a social contract written behind the veil of ignorance. The actual rules and regulations reflect power—in particular, political power, because they are set in political processes. Often the natural asymmetries of power that arise in an employment relationship are exacerbated by the regulatory framework, which in one way or another has restrained unionization (workers "combining" together) but sometimes looks the other way when firms combine to suppress wages. What is remarkable about these passages, written well before the dawn of the industrial economy let alone our knowledge-based economy, is that they still ring true. The technology giants, Apple, Google, and so forth, did conspire, *in secret*, not to poach workers from each other; the resulting lower level of competition lowered the wages of their engineers, whose intellectual prowess the companies' very successes depended on.[8]

The perspective of the Right

I have argued that people would want to accept regulations or taxes restricting their freedom because those restrictions ultimately expand their opportunity sets. The Right often has a peculiar and very limited view of the nature of this social contract. As they see it, there are a limited number of restrictions on actions that might be accepted as part of the social contract (killing, stealing). Property rights are critical; never mind how the property was acquired. The role of government is to enforce property rights and private contracts. This seems so obvious to them that there's hardly a need for justification.

Of course, without enforceability, contracts and property mean little. Without contract enforcement, many beneficial exchanges simply couldn't take place, particularly when they involve one party doing something today (like making a payment) and the other doing something later (like delivering a promised good). Likewise, without property rights, investment would be discouraged. Someone could simply take someone else's property. But as I will discuss in the next chapter, property rights have to be defined. Property rights and the rules governing contracts are social constructions, something that we design and specify to advance societal interests. They were not handed down from Mount Sinai, nor do they originate from some mysterious natural law. Society must also decide which contracts should be acceptable and enforced by government.

Many on the Right don't seem to understand this, or more accurately, they want rules that tilt the balance of power toward the powerful even more. Under the principle of *freedom to contract*, they argue that the government should enforce private contracts no matter how exploitive the agreement, so long as the contracts are entered into voluntarily. The Right insists on enforcement even if there are large asymmetries of information and even if one party has misled the other. They permit and even facilitate cooperative actions undertaken in certain forms through legal entities—corporations[9]—while they forbid as collusive other cooperative actions, such as workers unionizing to advance their interests. And they make cooperative actions to recover worker or consumer losses caused by corporations more difficult.[10]

These rules and regulations pushed by the Right (provisions that they implicitly[11] assert should be part of the social contract) have clear consequences for societal well-being and the distribution of power and wealth. People with low incomes, and even those in the middle, can only countervail wealthy interests by working together. When the Right impedes this route, they de facto encourage corporate exploitation, increase inequality, and decrease societal well-being.

I doubt whether the social contract desired by the Right, focusing only on protecting property rights and enforcing all contracts, would emerge from any reasoned discussion of what a socially just social contract would look like, or even a social contract that promoted economic efficiency. The changing nature of our society and economy requires more government intervention and investment today than in the past, and accordingly, higher taxes and more regulation. We can argue about the best way to deliver these investments,[12] but no reasonable person can deny the need for such investments, and the necessity of at least a large part of the costs being borne publicly.

What private contracts should be enforceable?

Contracts in and of themselves are, of course, ethically neutral; they can facilitate socially undesirable transactions as well as socially desirable ones. A good social contract would not encourage socially undesirable behavior, and accordingly, governments should not enforce private contracts that do. This is so obvious as to be banal—as obvious as the need for regulations against stealing and killing. A contract that obliges someone to do something illegal should itself be illegal, and clearly should not be enforced. Yet the Right, by emphasizing the "sanctity of contracts," does not acknowledge the distinction between socially good and bad contracts. Of course, there will inevitably be disagreement and debate in the margins about which contracts are socially good or bad. But once we recognize that contracts are social constructs, we recognize that they can be good or bad, and indeed that some contracts, far from being a sanctity, are actually abominations.

Admitting that there can be disagreement over what is a good and bad contract raises interesting questions. For instance, there is room for debate about what should be allowed to be sold. Even if there were universal agreement that people should not be allowed to sell their kidneys, should they be allowed to sell their blood? There is some evidence that outcomes are better both in terms of the quantity and quality (that is, free of diseases a blood transfusion might transmit) when blood is obtained only by voluntary donations, and doing so becomes a societal norm.[13] Similarly, whatever people think about prostitution, there is a legitimate question about whether a contract to provide the services should be enforceable under the law.

But while at the margins there may be controversy over which contracts should be acceptable and enforced through the rule of law, there is, today, broad agreement that the social contract should not allow, let alone enforce, contracts and contract provisions that countenance child labor, human trafficking, fraud and exploitation, slavery, indentured servitude, or the selling of organs and other vital parts of the body.

Another example of a questionable contract provision: nondisclosure agreements (NDAs) that corporations have increasingly inserted into contracts. There may be some circumstances in which secrecy (lack of transparency) is desirable, but often, secrecy is used to hide one bad thing or another. These provisions are frequently included in settlements when powerful men have sexually assaulted women, and they have proven to be an important impediment to holding these men accountable. The role of NDAs was highlighted in the infamous case of Harvey Weinstein, the movie mogul and sexual predator.[14] NDAs also make it difficult, if not impossible, to identify and correct other systemic problems such as racial bias[15] in banking, where there have been suits and settlements. There is, I hope and believe, a growing sense that such contract provisions should not be enforceable.

Chapter 7 will discuss other contract provisions designed to enhance market power and the ability of those with market power to exploit. In balancing the gains and losses of freedoms the answer should be clear: a just social contract would not allow exploitive contracts to be written, let alone call on or even require governments to enforce them.

Further Provisions of the Social Contract: Social Protection and Helping with Lifetime Management

There are several other aspects of the social contract that are important and that behind the veil of ignorance would be generally agreed to. Many relate to instances in which markets fail to work as they would in the idealized and fictional world of the Right. And many of these failures are inherent. Markets simply don't work in the way the Right envisions because information is inherently imperfect and asymmetric, and overcoming these information imperfections is expensive. It's also expensive to run markets.

When we talk about "perfect markets"—in which markets yield efficient outcomes—they *must* entail perfect insurance markets, in which every relevant risk can be insured against.[16] (This is not an obvious requirement, and establishing that insurance markets must be included was one of the signal achievements of economic theory of the last quarter of the twentieth century.) But some of the most important risks we face have, by their very nature, unknown dimensions and magnitudes. The Covid-19 pandemic and the war in Ukraine illustrate big risks the economy has faced—with enormous consequences for firms and households throughout the world—yet the market provided no insurance against these risks, and it is inconceivable that it would do so against similar risks in the future.[17]

Social protection in the social contract

One aspect of a good social contract incorporated into virtually all modern societies and representing one of the foremost social innovations of the past 150 years is social protection. This guards against the vagaries and vicissitudes of a person's life, especially the big ones like losing a job or having a major illness. Social protection aids in what I will refer to as lifetime management, the fact that individuals often don't have money and resources at the time they need them. Some of these big life risks are tied to the kinds of events described in the previous paragraph, against which private markets don't and can't provide insurance.

In addition, young people don't have the funds to invest in their own education and health. Struggling young parents don't have the money to provide for good childcare, and retirees may find they don't have enough resources to live a decent life. In the US, parents often don't have the money to send their kids to college, but they know that without a college degree their child's lifetime prospects are limited.

Given these obvious market limitations, it seems equally obvious that people *behind the veil of ignorance* would want a social contract that provides at least some social insurance and would make investments in young people to enable them to live up to their potential (rather than just relying on the resources of their parents). Virtually all modern societies do that.

Market failures and the conservative perspective

The standard economists' perspective—and the perspective of many a libertarian and others on the Right—*assumes* perfect capital markets, and it goes roughly like this: The young can borrow against future earnings. Young people (or their parents, acting on their behalf) make health and education investments rationally, balancing rates of return and the cost of funds, which, in a perfect market, would be low. Young parents can smooth their income over their lifetimes, so if they want childcare, they will purchase it on their own, and if not, one of the parents stays home. In the standard economist's mind, that's the efficient and desirable solution. Government mucks things up, according to standard economists, when it provides or subsidizes childcare because too many women end up working. It would be better if some of these women remained at home to take care of their kids. The income they earn doesn't justify the costs of having market-provided childcare. (The economist's sharp pencil in weighing costs and benefits doesn't, of course, take into account broader societal concerns about women living up to their potential or gender power relationships. Indeed, the standard model begins by ignoring the existence of any power relationships and assumes perfect markets.)

I illustrate the absurdity of this view about perfect markets with my economics students, virtually all of whom have low incomes now and will have much higher incomes in the future. Many of them would clearly like to have better apartments and enjoy more ski vacations now, when they are young. As they've learned in most of their other economics classes, the standard model says they should smooth their consumption over time, borrowing now against their future income. I suggest that they go down to the local bank and ask for a loan to enable them to do this. I know what would happen if they did: resounding rejections. They might be able to borrow *a little*, and even then typically only at high interest rates. In the real world, credit is rationed.[18]

On to risk markets. The Right, again following the standard economic model, assumes there are perfect risk markets. All of the "investments" described in the preceding two paragraphs are risky. People don't know the return on investments in health and education, or on pre-K education. They also don't know how long they will live. And in some of these cases, not even the experts agree about the magnitudes of the economic returns. We know that without adequate education and health care, no one can live up to their full potential. But in none of these cases can individuals buy private insurance even against the relevant future risks that affect the returns on investments in children's health and education. In general, risk discourages such investments,[19] and so in the absence of good risk markets, there will be lower levels of investment than would be socially productive.

There are many other risks that affect a person's well-being. Insecurity can have a devastating effect on people—which is why President Franklin D. Roosevelt's call for "freedom from fear" was so important.[20]

Health care, unemployment, and pensions

Over the past century, governments have increasingly recognized that there are key risks citizens face that are not being adequately addressed by private insurance markets. This has provided the impetus for social insurance.

Before President Lyndon B. Johnson passed Medicare in 1965, ensuring that the government would provide healthcare to older Americans, many couldn't buy health insurance and many who could were forced to pay extremely high prices. Before a number of laws and regulations were passed, most notably the Affordable Care Act in 2010, many people below age 65 couldn't buy health insurance either, especially if they had preexisting conditions like a weak heart or arthritis, conditions that made obtaining health insurance all the more important. And for many who could buy insurance, the cost amounted to a large percentage of their income.

The private market has never provided unemployment insurance, even though one of the most significant risks and sources of insecurity facing working families is the main breadwinner losing a job and not being able to find another quickly.[21]

Still another example of publicly organized social protections are public retirement programs like Social Security. Germany's chancellor Otto von Bismarck was the first to introduce an old-age social security program in 1889. At that time, relatively few people lived beyond a normal retirement age of 65. Today, the life expectancy in some countries is 80 years or more. In Japan, it's 82 for men and 88 for women, fifteen or more years beyond retirement. There remains enormous uncertainty about how long any particular person will live, though we have good statistics about life spans for various groups within the population. Annuities, insurance policies that pay a fixed amount no matter how long the insured person lives, mitigate that risk but at a very high price, well above the level that can be justified by data on life expectancies. Of course, this is not a surprise. Someone has to pay for the huge profits and advertising costs of the insurance companies, and that person is the customer.

Social Security can be viewed largely as a government-organized annuity, with transaction costs a fraction of the private sector's.[22] And there are provisions in Social Security critical to an individual's sense of security that are absent in private annuities, most importantly adjustments for inflation. Inflation may have been muted for decades following the burst of inflation in the 1970s, but the post-pandemic inflation reminded everyone that it can rise again. We need insurance against these kinds of events even though they occur infrequently. The market fails at this, but governments can provide it and have done so.

There is another provision in the US public retirement scheme that is important: Payments increase with the general increase in wages. Without this component, when wages rise rapidly—as they did in the decades after World War II—older people who depend solely on their savings would have living standards far below younger people's. There would be an unacceptable level of intergenerational income disparity. Public retirement programs provide for a modicum of intergenerational risk-sharing and income smoothing because one of the determinants of a retiree's benefits is current wage levels, even if the most critical determinant is his own contribution.

Surprisingly, some people on the Right still want to privatize various forms of social insurance, when the reason each was introduced was that there were risks the market wasn't adequately addressing; in many cases, it could not.

Much of the opposition to publicly provided social protection is driven by a simple ideology which claims that collective action impinges on our individual freedom and government is always inefficient.[23] (Much of it is also driven by naked self-interest. Some in the financial sector know they can make a bundle of money if, say, Social Security were privatized, never mind the costs to retirees.)

I've already addressed the claim about collective action. Social insurance has greatly expanded the freedom, or opportunity set, of most citizens.[24] For many, it has even succeeded in doing what President Roosevelt most wanted: it has given them freedom from fear, or at least it has diminished insecurity significantly.

The claim that government is necessarily inefficient is refuted by the evidence. As I've noted, transaction costs for private annuities are far higher than for Social Security. Repeatedly, in town halls and elsewhere, citizens have demanded that government keep its hands off Medicare and Social Security.[25] The two programs work so well that, for anyone captured by the Right's ideology, they *must* be privately run.

There's more that can be done: Enhancing education opportunities

Australia has a student loan program for people going to college in which the amount they repay depends on the income the graduate earns. Government (society) bears some of the risk associated with investments in education. It provides risk-sharing that the private sector doesn't. And it turns out that this public program is *much* more efficient than the private sector's loan program—even though the private sector's program might seem simpler. Bruce Chapman, emeritus professor of economics at Australia National University and the father of Australia's income-contingent loan program, jokes about a conversation he had with someone from another country who asked how many people the government employs to manage the country's loan program, which provides loans to almost the entire university population. When Chapman replied, "Seventeen," the person responded, impressed, "Seventeen thousand is really efficient." "No," Chapman replied, "just seventeen. Period." The point was that the loan program piggybacks on the income tax system; borrowers owing money on their student loans are automatically "invoiced" for the extra due by adding it to their tax payments. To administer the whole system, given modern technology, only seventeen additional employees are required.

Other Elements in the Design of the Social Contract

Many discussions about social justice and the design of the social contract have focused on distribution, implicitly asking, behind the veil of ignorance, what kind of tax program is socially just? John Rawls provided a convincing case for the desirability of progressive taxation.

I've argued here that one can and should look at *every* aspect of the social contract and societal organization through a similar lens, behind the veil of ignorance. In chapter 3, I analyzed the rules and regulations that help an intertwined society address externalities. In chapter 4, I addressed how a just society, behind the veil of ignorance, would think about public expenditures and resolve problems of coordination. In this chapter, I've discussed how we should think about what kinds of private contracts should *not* be enforced, and more broadly, what else to include in the social contract. I emphasized the need for social protection and lifetime management investments—in education and public provisions for childcare and retirement. Later chapters will discuss still other aspects of our economic, political, and social regime.[26]

Concluding Remarks: Seeking Guidance in the Design of the Social Contract

It's obvious by now that a socially just social contract is complex. It entails regulations and other provisions that curb freedoms narrowly defined, but in doing so broadens freedoms more generally. It is different from the Right's social contract, which is limited to the enforcement of private contracts and property rights, however broadly they attempt to define them. Indeed, I've argued that some contracts should not be enforceable—some are truly abominable—and later I'll explain how property rights are, and need to be, circumscribed. Behind the veil of ignorance, there never would be a social contract that enforces all contracts, nor one in which there were unfettered property rights.

In the US and other countries, governments often turn to financial and business leaders for advice on the laws and regulations for governing commerce. This is especially true in complex areas like financial regulation or international trade. But Adam Smith warned about asking the advice of these leaders:

> The interest of [businessmen] is always in some respects different from, and even opposite to, that of the public. . . . The proposal of any new law or regulation of commerce which comes from this order . . . ought never to be adopted, till after having been long and carefully examined . . . with the most suspicious attention. It comes from an order *of men . . . who have generally an interest to deceive and even oppress the public.*[27]

In this quote, Smith expresses a profound lack of trust in the advice of businessmen on public policy, recognizing that their interests do not coincide with the interests of society at large. (I only wish that the US government had paid more attention to Smith's sage words than to the recommendations of Wall Street financiers in the years preceding the 2008 financial crisis.)

Our discussion about Rawls helps to further explain why Smith was right: Society should be wary of the advice of businesspeople and financiers whose voices so often dominate, especially in economic matters. Most businesspeople don't think about what is good for society behind the veil of ignorance. They are used to simply asking, "How do I increase my profits and the profits of my corporation?" One answer is to convince government to make rules and regulations and spend money in ways that enrich their company.

Moreover, even if they have first-rate knowledge about dealmaking, or about their own sector, few are experts in understanding how the entire economic, political, and social system works. Academics who spend a lifetime on the subject grow humble when they recognize the magnitude of the task, but at least they are asking the right questions. They know that even voluntary contracts may not be desirable. Only by understanding how the system works can one assess this or that intervention and make judgments about what kind of social contract expands freedom, meaningfully defined, for most people.

And only then can one decide what kind of social contract would be adopted behind the veil of ignorance.

These considerations help us to think about key aspects of the economy, including property rights, distributive taxation, and regulations concerning competition and exploitation, which I will discuss in the next two chapters.

CHAPTER 6

Freedom, a Competitive Economy, and Social Justice

The fact that resources are limited—what economists call scarcity—constrains what we can do as individuals and as a society. We do not naturally call these constraints a loss of freedom. Yet when the government steps in and imposes taxes, taking away some of our hard-earned money, we often feel there is a loss of freedom. We can see how these public interventions may *seem* coercive, because they restrict our choices by reducing our income.

Libertarians especially make a big deal out of being forced to pay taxes. To them, it robs them of their liberty. They believe they have the fundamental right to spend their money as they please, for they claim that their high incomes are the result of honest, hard work, creative energy, and skills in investing (and one might add, for many, their skills in choosing the right parents).

A primary objective of this chapter and the next is to undermine these claims by arguing that for the most part there is no moral legitimacy to market incomes. This seems obvious when the incomes are derived from exploitation—whether it's seventeenth- and eighteenth-century slavery, nineteenth-century colonialism and the opium trade, or twentieth-century market power and seductive and misleading advertising. In the next chapter, I'll discuss how much of the wealth at the top comes, at least in part, from taking advantage of the people below.

This chapter, however, takes the hypothesis that markets today are competitive largely at face value but argues that, even then, the moral legitimacy of the incomes derived in seemingly well-functioning competitive markets is questionable. There are multiple reasons. It is partly because the wealth that people inherit is somewhat, or in many cases, largely derived from exploitation, and partly because there is no moral legitimacy to wages and prices even in a competitive market. This is because those wages and prices would be different if there were a different distribution of wealth. Morally illegitimate wealth gives rise to wages and prices that themselves lack moral legitimacy. Those wages and prices would be different, too, if there were different rules and regulations in the economy. But when they're written by the rich and powerful, the wages and prices generated have no moral legitimacy.

This is important. The libertarian claims that her income is hers, that she has, in some sense, a moral right to it. She further claims that, as a result, there shouldn't be redistributive taxation even in the face of huge societal inequalities and gaping public needs. But such claims rest on the premise that there is some moral legitimacy to whatever incomes markets give rise.

Just Deserts: The Moral Justification of Income and Wealth in a Competitive Economy

Historically, economists who attack direct redistribution—taxing the rich to provide public services and to help the less fortunate—claimed that incomes are the "just deserts" of people's efforts. Nassau William Senior, one of the great economists of the early nineteenth century, argued that the wealth of capitalists was the just reward for the "abstinence" of their saving, which generated the capital accumulation that was at the center of a capitalist system.[1] Neoclassical economics provided a more general justification. Each person was rewarded by the market according to his *marginal contribution*, what he added to the economic pie. But this argument ignored the presence of externalities and other market failures that were pervasive in their time, as they are today, allowing neoclassical economics to create a mythical universe in which the marginal *private* contribution—what the individual added to the profitability of the firm—was equal to the marginal social contribution—what the individual added to society.

Classical economics (and its twentieth- and twenty-first-century descendant, neoclassical economics) paid short shrift to why different individuals had different assets; why some had more education, others less; some more capital, and others less. Senior said it was simply a result of greater thrift. That was one factor, but there were others. During the period of their enslavement, African Americans in the South were denied the fruits of their labor. It was appropriated by the enslavers, who passed some of the illegitimately acquired (one could say "stolen") wealth on to their descendants. This is an obvious example of how wealth may lack moral legitimacy. When illegitimately begotten wealth is passed down the generations, it remains morally illegitimate even hundreds of years later (though societies can work hard to make memories short). Even when this kind of wealth is transferred many times over, the wealth inequality that eventually emerges still lacks any moral legitimacy.

The counterpoint to the claim that great wealth has some moral legitimacy is that we can draw a similar conclusion about people living in poverty. They "deserve" their misfortune because they failed to save, or for some other reason. But this contention is as fallacious as the other. There are many reasons for the poverty of so many descendants of the enslaved, including the fruits of enslaved labor were stolen; they were denied a decent education in the aftermath of abolition; the promise of "forty acres and a mule" never materialized; and there has been rampant discrimination.[2]

Bad schools, bad health care, food deserts, redlining, the inability to unionize or get mortgages, these are just some of the unequal and unfair challenges faced by many people living in poverty. It's not that they don't work hard or can't save; it's that they can't even get to the starting line.

Property Rights and Freedom

Any discussion of the moral legitimacy of wealth has to begin with an analysis of property rights. Consider a society without any fetters or restraints, where the strong are able to steal from the weak and do. The strong have their freedom and do as they please. But the weak have no freedom; they live oppressed by the strong. No one would call that a free society, because the weak cannot enjoy the fruits of their labor. It is not likely to be a productive society, either, because few would invest or even work, knowing that their savings or incomes could, and probably would, be taken from them. When we talk about a free market, we mean one in which such theft is prohibited, and the injunction enforced. And when we talk about the "moral legitimacy" of a person's wealth, we presume that her wealth was not stolen from others.

But defining theft requires defining property. What belongs to whom? And what can someone do with property that he "owns"? We take our system of property rights for granted, but different countries have markedly different views about property. As I have emphasized, property rights are something that we, as a society, delineate. Historically, property rights have been defined by the powerful to preserve their own power. If they are defined and assigned (or reassigned) in ways that have no moral legitimacy, then incomes derived from the ownership of property have no moral legitimacy. There is no reason *not* to take away income derived in this way. It is completely appropriate to retrieve the wealth stolen by a thief. And there's no moral justification to let the rich keep their income from ill-gotten gains rather than to give it to people with low incomes, especially if those incomes might have been higher had property rights been defined and assigned differently and perhaps more appropriately.

Property rights as social constructions: A variety of definitions

Property rights are social constructions—that is, they are what they are because we as a society define them to be—and so naturally our notions about which and what kinds of property rights have moral legitimacy are socially constructed. And whenever there are significant disagreements about boundaries, rules, and rights, you can expect powerful interests behind it, looking to secure more for themselves. The fact that they may give a legal panache to their wealth does little to solidify its moral legitimacy.

We have developed a framework for thinking about how to define property rights, from behind the veil of ignorance. They are simply a set of regulations that say what the "owner" is entitled to do and not entitled to do, and how (or whether) one can become the owner of a particular asset. There can, of course, be a disparity between how property rights are defined in practice and how they might be defined in a well-designed social contract, written behind the veil of ignorance. And whenever that disparity is large, questions can be raised about the moral legitimacy of wealth and property.

I wrote earlier about the change in property rights in the seventeenth and eighteenth centuries, when land that had been commonly owned—the commons—was privatized, enriching the landlords but impoverishing the vast majority of citizens. This was a simple property grab, subsequently defended by some economists as an efficient solution to the problem posed by the tragedy of the commons. But we saw that this approach looked at the matter through the eyes of the landlords, and that regulations were a fairer, more equitable, and equally efficient way to deal with it. The additional wealth the landlords acquired had no moral legitimacy, nor did the inheritances of their descendants. And this is true even if the land grab was backed by the political and legal system—it was a system in which these commoners had no voice.

Competing notions of property are at the root of many disagreements between the indigenous populations and colonialists around the world. In many instances, Europeans believed they had "bought" the land they settled and exploited. But, at least according to many accounts, the sellers didn't fully understand the nature of the transaction because they didn't understand land as something that could be bought or sold. It would be like someone coming up to me and asking if she could buy the Brooklyn Bridge. In general, people don't buy or sell bridges, so if that was the question I "heard," I must have misunderstood her, or she must have meant to ask the question in a different way. What she must have meant is, could she have the right to *use* that bridge, subject to certain regulations and norms, perhaps for a certain period?

To many indigenous peoples in Canada, Australia, the United States, and elsewhere, land was sufficiently plentiful that it could be shared, provided that it was treated properly (in ways that the settlers often didn't adhere to).[3] The notion that land could be "sold" was not part of the mindset of the indigenous people. Any modern interpretation of treaties and agreements made in the nineteenth century and earlier must take this perspective into account.

In a similar way, the idea of people as property is alien to most twenty-first-century Westerners. The thought that people could be bought and sold or rented out like ordinary property is intolerable. Yet, when it came time to end slavery in most countries, it was the enslavers who were compensated for their loss of property rights, not the formerly enslaved. That anyone would compensate people who had stolen the fruits of others' labor, not to mention their freedom, reinforces the conclusion that property is a social construction.

Another example: The US is one of the few countries in which the resources that lie beneath the land belong to the person who owns the land, and not the state. This provision contributes to random inequality without doing much to enhance economic efficiency, and in many cases gives rise to unnecessary complexities. If oil is discovered beneath my land, I will become a billionaire overnight—not because of my own efforts but by the luck of the draw. But the oil that I extract from my oil well may lie in a reservoir that spans the land outside my property, resulting in excess drilling as each landowner tries to get as much of the oil out as possible before anyone else does. This competition requires a host of regulations that would not be needed if the oil reservoir were declared (as it is in most countries) an asset owned collectively by all citizens, to be managed by the state. This example puts the lie to the claim that property rights systems are "naturally" defined to generate "economic efficiency," with efficiency in the production of goods and services being the presumed objective of a good system of social organization.

Economists also study a variety of implicit property rights that pervade the economic system. Tenure for professors is ultimately a property right, though non-economists don't usually frame it that way. I have the right to receive income from teaching a particular subject at the university provided I don't violate certain regulations, and typically provided the subject is still taught at the university. It is a circumscribed property right. I cannot sell the job to someone else, and I have to comply with the terms of the tenure contract.

Likewise, someone living in a rent-controlled apartment has, in effect, a property right—the right to remain there at a rent that may be substantially below market level. But it is circumscribed. I can't sell that right to another person and, typically, I cannot even give that right to my children.[4]

Property rights and freedom: Entitlements and constraints

This discussion of property rights makes clear the complexity of the concept.[5] It's not that I own something and thereby have the right to do anything I want with it, including transfer it to someone else at a price I decide. Property rights are always circumscribed. I've noted the right of the government to seize land through eminent domain, with appropriate compensation, when it is needed for a public purpose. A key characteristic of owning something, it is often said, is the right to sell or give that property right to others. In some countries, the government gives individuals the right to use a particular piece of land (called usage rights) but restricts their ability to sell it. And if they don't use it, they can lose it. That's also true of many natural resource licenses that governments issue.

There are sometimes good reasons for these limitations. Behind the veil of ignorance, a good social contract, while providing for *some* property rights, would circumscribe them. The question is, how?

Does or should owning a patent on a critical drug give me the right to charge as much as I want? The US and Europe differ in their answers. In the US, if my monopoly power is legitimately acquired, I can charge whatever price I want. In Europe, abuses of monopoly power are not allowed. This is another illustration that markets are defined by the regulations imposed. In this case, I think it is clear which system is better, but it is also clear why the US has adopted its system. It's not because America generates better outcomes. It's because the powerful, and particularly the powerful drug companies, hold greater sway in setting the rules. Looking at matters through the eyes of someone accustomed to European norms, the huge excess profits of American drug companies using their monopoly power have no moral legitimacy. Society has every right to take back those excess profits. This is not a hypothetical. American drug companies charge some ten times more for insulin than those in Europe do because of the exercise of this monopoly power, part of the US property rights system.[6]

Most importantly for our topic, property rights entail restrictions on the freedom of some while they expand the freedom of others in ways that we often take for granted; they seem natural and inevitable but are far from it. If I own a piece of land, I can stop you from trespassing on it. But that means that the property right restricts one person's freedom as it expands the other's (the right of the property owner to exclude others). "Free" markets with well-defined property rights do not maximize freedom, as some claim; they simply give freedoms to some and take them away from others. Sometimes there are efficiency defenses for certain assignments of property rights, but as I've explained, particular ways of assigning property rights may undermine efficiency. There are better alternatives, including collective ownership (as in the case of groundwater). And whatever the efficiency defenses, there are distributive consequences. Note that in the example I give in the previous paragraph—American drug companies' right to charge whatever price they want—there is an enormous social cost. Combined with inadequate public provision of medicines, people are almost surely dying unnecessarily as a result.

Concern for these distributional consequences motivates some of the important definitions of property rights. For instance, in the English countryside walkers have a defined right-of-way across land. Similarly, in many countries and states (including California), citizens have a right to walk on and access all beaches. Colorado, Montana, Wyoming, and New Mexico have recognized the "right to float" on streams, even through private property.

This discussion has highlighted the sometimes-arbitrary nature of property rights, with certain definitions and assignments leading to unjust outcomes—like the abusive pricing of insulin—and inefficient outcomes that would almost surely never arise behind the veil of igno-rance. But if property rights are defined in ways that are unjust and unfair, the wealth inequalities derived from those assignments and definitions of property rights are also likely to be unfair and unjust.

The intergenerational transmission of illegitimacy and advantage

If incomes and wealth at one time have a degree of moral illegitimacy associated with them, and there is some intergenerational transmis-sion of wealth (through financial bequests or simply access to bet-ter education), then incomes and wealth in subsequent generations will lack legitimacy. Consider the not-unrealistic case in which a few individuals inherit a large fraction of a country's wealth from parents who acquired it through land theft. The moral claim to wealth in this context is obviously weak.

Few would say that a policy of redistributing that ill-gotten wealth to citizens with lower incomes—particularly if the land was stolen from them or their forebearers—is a fundamental infringement on freedom, just as restitution of stolen property is not generally viewed as an infringement on the rights of the thief.[7] Many might say, in fact, that a policy of restituting stolen land would be morally justified. But that would raise questions about the moral claims to the land of those from whom the land was taken. Perhaps they also took the land from others.

Still other profound issues, which we do not address here, are the moral claims of restitution by descendants of those from whom the land was stolen, and who should bear the costs, when there is no clear link between today's wealth and past transgressions for particular peo-ple. Should the landowner who thought he had legitimately bought land with a clear title (and perhaps was told by the government at the time that he had clear title) be responsible? The economic and social costs of such a policy would obviously be enormous.

These are not just theoretical niceties. In the aftermath of the fall of the Berlin Wall and the Iron Curtain, many Eastern European countries where property had been nationalized adopted restitution policies. In some countries, certain groups came to view the property redistribution that occurred under a series of different governments as unjust. Property rights prior to Communist nationalizations had been, in many cases, affected by right-wing governments, and often entailed a redistribution from Jews and other minorities. Should today's restitution revert to the property rights held before the nationalization by Communists, or should it go back further?

The transfer of financial wealth down through generations is only one way the advantage gets transmitted. Even in the most progressive societies, there is a high level of intergenerational transmission of advantages and disadvantages.[8] There are many mechanisms by which this occurs, including education (human capital) and connections. Stolen or illegitimate wealth might give the descendants of one family an advantage even without financial inheritances, so undoing the effect entails more than just restitution. Though the US prides itself on being the land of opportunity, the life prospects of a young American are highly dependent on the income and education of her parents, more than in almost any other advanced country.[9] Ironically, the seeming move to a fairer system based on meritocracy—one doesn't "inherit" one's status but earns it by performance—entrenches inequalities, as students who are able to excel in school have well-educated parents who have the financial wherewithal and the knowledge of how the system works to provide them the best educational opportunities.[10]

Markets, Inequality, and the Rules of the Game

This discussion of property rights and how they are defined highlights the way rules determine both how the economy functions and the income distribution that emerges. As I've repeatedly noted, there are many possible sets of rules so there are many possible competitive market distributions of income. None is a matter of natural law or even the natural laws of economics, but rather of the laws created within our political system through a political process shaped by people with political power. And that's the point. We cannot divorce the current distributions of income and wealth from the current and historical distribution of power. Those in power typically, though not always, attempt to perpetuate their power. While they might appeal to notions of fairness and justice as they shape the economic and political rules, they might naturally, unwittingly, or actively tilt those rules to serve their own interests. Hence, there is no moral legitimacy to the income that is generated within even a competitive market.

There is an evolutionary process at play. Change is constant but initial conditions matter. One can try to untangle the long web of history but doing so fully is virtually impossible. Still, in most societies there are major breaks, well-defined points where history takes a big turn and as a practical matter, one can begin there. In the US, that point was the Revolution and the Constitution. But as is now widely recognized, the Constitution was not handed down by God. Rather, it was the product of its time (the Enlightenment) and of the people who wrote it (overwhelmingly, rich white men, many of them slaveowners), with their own interests and perspectives. It hardly reflected the interests and perspectives of the typical American at the time, particularly those who were disenfranchised.

The rest, as they say, is history. The electoral system entrenched in the Constitution—combined with the rules of the Constitution, which makes change very difficult—has contributed to the country's extremes in political inequalities, which, in turn, have contributed to its inequalities in market incomes. It's a vicious circle.[11]

As we've seen, even in the absence of the country's stilted politics, neoliberalism has had enormous influence around the world, leading to market economies afflicted by deep inequalities, even if not to the extreme found in the US. A major political thrust among progressive governments today focuses on changing these rules to generate a more equitable distribution of market income rather than redistributing the market incomes that emerge out of the current rules.[12]

Questioning the Primacy of Competitive Prices in the Absence of Market Failures

Even granting efficient markets and laws and regulations that reflect moral and economic considerations, and even granting that the market is perfectly competitive, the moral legitimacy of the incomes earned can be questioned on two grounds. The first we've already discussed: incomes depend on assets—how much wealth I have, including what I've inherited, and how much human capital I have, which typically depends on how the state allocates educational resources. And we've raised questions about the moral legitimacy of the distribution of those assets.

The second is that in a competitive market, wages and relative prices reflect the preferences of people with income and wealth. In competitive markets, prices and wages are determined by the law of supply and demand. But that abstract statement misses a key observation: What is demanded in a market economy depends on who has income and wealth. In a world without inequality, there might be little demand for Gucci handbags or expensive perfumes. Money would be spent on more important things. But that's not the world we live in. We live in a world marked by high inequality, with a very large proportion of total income and wealth going to the top 1 percent. Their desires influence demand. And accordingly, what they want determines prices, and what is scarce or not.

A simple thought experiment may be useful. Assume that tonight we redistribute the country's income and wealth so that everyone has the same amounts. That would have enormous consequences, including on wages and prices. Chauffeurs' wages would go down; childcare workers' wages might go up. Prices of beachfront properties in the Hamptons and on the Riviera would go down; prices of land elsewhere might go up.

Bernard Arnault and his family, owners of the luxury goods conglomerate LVMH (which owns a host of brands like Christian Dior and Moët Hennessy) and one of the richest families in the world, might not be so rich if there were not so much inequality. They have absolutely thrived on it. But if the distribution of dollars is the result of exploitation today or in the past—as is the case—then the prices and wages that emerge even in a competitive market lack moral legitimacy, even if the rules today were set in a morally legitimate way.

This should make clear that even in perfectly competitive markets the magnitude of the rewards may have no fundamental moral justification, even if there's a strong moral or economic argument that people who work or save more should be rewarded for their hard work and willingness to save.

The case is even stronger after we come to understand the multiple distortions in the economy. No market economy even approximates a competitive ideal of perfect competition, perfect information, and perfect risk and capital markets. Each "failure" can have significant effects on prices and, therefore, on the opportunity sets of different people. And even small deviations from the perfections required by the competitive ideal have big consequences. This is one of the important implications of the information revolution in economics over the past forty years.

Freedom, Moral Claims, and Redistribution

This brings us back to the central question of this chapter. Consider an economy with large disparities in income and wealth. Should the government impose progressive taxes to fund public goods, like investments in basic research and infrastructure? I have argued that behind the veil of ignorance there would likely be consensus that the government should. But libertarians retort that everyone has a certain moral legitimacy to his own income, well deserved because of his hard work, intelligence, and thrift. This chapter throws cold water on that argument.

The libertarian claims are even weaker once we think about what their incomes would have been had they been born in a poor country, without the rule of law or the institutions, infrastructure, and human capital that make the economies of advanced countries work so well. It is not enough to have assets such as entrepreneurial talents. If you are born into the wrong environment, those assets mean nothing. They yield the returns they do only because of the socioeconomic environment in which we live.[13] And if that's the case, we owe our income and the wealth that derives from it as much to that environment as to our own skills and effort. There is full justification, then, for imposing high taxes on high incomes even in a perfectly competitive economy in which wealth is garnered in ways that have full moral legitimacy.

Likewise, the moral claim against progressive taxes is slim if high incomes arise out of luck or inheritance—and even more so if they are made possible through exploitation or because the rules that generate or allow such incomes have been shaped by access to political power.[14] There is no presumption that the laws and regulations are themselves set in a fair way even in a competitive economy. Quite the contrary, with political power linked to economic power and economic power linked to the economic rules set in our political processes.

Trade-offs in freedoms

In a society with a fixed amount of resources, expanding one person's budget constraint—enhancing the freedom to spend—necessarily constrains others'. Redistributive taxation, of course, does this. Libertarians focus on the restraints that taxation imposes on the rich rather than on the loosening of the constraints on the people living in poverty who will have more to spend because of the income transfers or who will be better able to live up to their potential because of the education or health benefits they receive.

The world, of course, is more complicated; it is not "zero sum." Taxes, as actually imposed, may reduce work or savings, and therefore national output, because they reduce the return to work or savings.[15] The provision of better education and health can expand output enormously. How large the effects are in each case is a subject of debate; the magnitude clearly influences assessments of trade-offs.[16]

Assessing the economic trade-offs

Assessing the magnitude and nature of the trade-offs is hard, and it is the subject of inquiry of many an economist. I am of the view that conservatives typically exaggerate the adverse consequences of progressive taxation.

Some of the wealth of the very rich is the result of luck. To the extent that it's luck, redistribution and funding better social protection may increase economic output. The randomness of outcomes discourages work and investment. A good system of social protection may encourage people to undertake high-risk, high-return activities. Corporate-profits taxation with loss offsets[17] has long been seen as a form of risk-sharing, with the government as a silent partner, and long been shown to increase risk-taking and investment.[18]

Some of the high profits are a result of skill, but often skill in exploiting others and creating market power. To the extent that effort is directed at rent-seeking, we want to discourage it because it decreases GDP and increases inequality. Taxes on monopoly profits curb incentives to create market power and, together with rules curbing exploitation, redirect effort to more constructive activities.

But even when efforts at the *very* top are focused on socially desirable entrepreneurship, it's hard to believe that higher taxes, especially on exorbitant corporate profits, will matter much. Do we really believe that Jeff Bezos, Bill Gates, and Elon Musk would not have accomplished what they have if they could take home only $30 billion rather than the massive amounts they do? These entrepreneurs may have been driven by money, but also by much more than that.[19]

Beyond zero sum

We are not in a zero-sum world. The rules of the game affect the size of the pie in many ways. Today, there's a broad consensus on the desirability of at least some redistribution when inequality itself gives rise to an externality adversely affecting economic performance or having social and political consequences. I chose the title of my 2012 book, The Price of Inequality, to emphasize that we pay a high price for inequality even in terms of GDP, a narrowly defined measure of economic growth. Countries with more inequality perform more poorly. Since then, there has been a wealth of corroborating studies.[20]

There are multiple ways in which inequality has adverse economic, social, and political consequences. For instance, those not from rich families may not live up to their potential because of the inability to get a good education or decent health care. Moreover, some, perhaps many, of today's inequalities are the result of current or past exploitation, which undermines economic performance as it exacerbates societal inequities.

Making matters worse, the children of the rich may grow up feeling entitled, thinking the world owes them and that they have the right to break whatever rules society creates.[21] A prime example: Donald Trump. He was proud that he didn't pay taxes. Recent literature in behavioral economics confirms what many have long suspected,[22] that while Trump may be worse than most in flaunting his rule-breaking, he reflects a broader societal phenomenon. At the other economic extreme, people with low or no income feel a sense of despair, a conviction that the system is rigged. This hinders their aspiration and effort. Both entitlement and despair hurt overall economic performance.

Moral claims and redistribution

In the end, though, in assessing trade-offs we inevitably face the issue of societal values—whether, for instance, the enhancement of a poorer person's ability to live up to her potential and expand her freedom to act is more or less valuable than the associated restraint on the freedom of a rich person to buy another Rolex watch, a larger yacht, or a bigger mansion. I know how I and, I believe, most others would assess such trade-offs, were they to make those judgments behind the veil of ignorance. Redistribution, financing high-return public investments through progressive taxation,[23] and tilting the rules of the economic game toward ordinary workers through pre-distribution— that is, changing the market distribution of income to make it more equitable—are all desirable policies. They would emerge naturally as part of a social contract written behind the veil of ignorance.

Concluding Remarks

America's Founding Fathers did not take the extreme position of today's libertarians that all taxation is an infringement of liberty. Their rallying cry was "taxation without representation is tyranny." That is, our liberty is infringed if we have no voice in the political process of deciding taxation. Ironically, they did not then, and their followers do not now, appear to see the imposition of taxes on the many disenfranchised Americans as tyranny.[24]

Once we recognize there is no *inherent* reason *not* to impose taxes on the rich to benefit society more broadly or to help those less well off, we are back in the world of trade-offs. This chapter and earlier ones have shown that even in perfectly competitive economies without externalities, we need to look at liberties and freedom through the lens of trade-offs. The contraction of one person's liberty (from taxation) is set off against the expansion of another's (from increased government benefits allowed by that taxation). While I have expressed skepticism about any moral claim to the income a person receives in this type of economy, the grounds for redistributive taxation are even greater when substantial parts of the income and wealth of the richest citizens come from exploitation. I discuss this in the next chapter.

CHAPTER 7

The Freedom to Exploit

R ose and Milton Friedman titled their paean to free markets *Free to Choose*. They celebrated that a rich person could choose what he wants to consume, and they advocated policy reforms, such as student vouchers, that would expand freedom of choice in education. They argued that this freedom to choose was a central driver in the efficiency of the market economy and a necessary condition for a free society.

Twenty-first-century capitalism is a far cry from the kind of economy that the Friedmans glorified. It is defined by high levels of market power, with firms taking advantage of others' lack of information and other vulnerabilities. No real modern economy even approximates the idealized, pure, competitive market economy. Recent research has shown the extraordinary concentration of market power in the US in a wide swath of industries.[1] And it's growing, as seen in an increasing share of income going into profits, in stagnating real wages (wages adjusted for inflation) and incomes for ordinary Americans, and in increasing markups (the ratios of prices to costs). Matters were bad before the Covid-19 pandemic, but in the pandemic and its aftermath they got a lot worse, with sectors and firms that have more market power seeing greater increases in markups.[2] This meant that corporate profits increased significantly as firms exploited the increases in market power that resulted from the supply chain interruptions brought on by the pandemic.

This kind of exploitation eats away at economic efficiency and the health of the economy. Corporate profits went well beyond the level necessary for a normal (risk-adjusted) return on capital. When one party exploits another, her income may grow and her freedom expand, but the other person loses and his freedom to choose contracts.

Instinctively, we are repulsed by exploitation and most democracies enact policies to curb the freedom to exploit. They make it illegal, punishable with fines and/or prison. Defining precisely what exploitation is may not be easy. It may not even be the case that "you know it when you see it." This chapter is not concerned with fine-tuning policies to curb exploitation but rather in continuing our discussion of freedom, to understand why it is correct and appropriate for the government to curb such activities and to redistribute income from the exploiters to the rest of society.

For many perched at the top of the economic ladder, some or much of their income derives from one form of exploitation or another. One example is for-profit universities. Donald Trump, through Trump University, took advantage of individuals' aspirations to get ahead. While that operation was more brazen than most, it fits a wider pattern.[3] A large fraction of for-profit universities take advantage of the least well-informed, knowing that they may not be able to discern what constitutes a good education. Even worse, these universities have resisted government efforts to disclose their poor track records of graduation and job placement.

The 2008 financial crisis exposed how so many bankers got rich not only by excessive risk-taking—leaving it to the government to bail them out—but also by deception, fraud,[4] and abusive lending practices. Even many corporate leaders have gotten much of their wealth through the exploitation of market power. Bill Gates's Microsoft was found guilty of anticompetitive practices on three continents. Accusations of anticompetitive behavior have been leveled (rightly so, in my judgment) against Google, Facebook (Meta), and Amazon. Walmart's exploitive labor market practices have been well documented.[5] Behind these corporate façades lie some of the world's largest fortunes.

While we know today's stories, the making of many earlier fortunes seems even worse. In many cases, wealth was generated by the slave trade and the products the enslaved produced, namely cotton and sugar. The Lehman brothers are among that long list. The companies behind John D. Rockefeller, the richest person of his generation, and James Buchanan Duke, another of the plutocrats of the early twentieth century, were found guilty of anticompetitive behavior. Many men who made fortunes in the nineteenth and early twentieth centuries did so from the opium trade with China—a low point in Western history as the European powers, with American support, went to war to ensure that China remained open to opium. The right to free trade—even for a dangerous narcotic like opium—was seen as more important than the right to protect a population from addiction.[6] The language of war may have been about abstractly defined "rights"; the reality was much less noble. It was about the ability of Westerners to make money off the Chinese.[7] Money and power, plain and simple.

The fact that the incomes of so many wealthy people are the result, at least in part, of exploitation reinforces the earlier conclusion that we shouldn't give primacy to the distribution of incomes generated by the market economy. It is *not* a matter of "just deserts." There's no moral justification for such incomes, but there is a moral argument *for* redistribution, for taking away incomes derived from exploitation. We can even invoke the economists' central concern of efficiency and incentives: redistributive taxation, especially in ways that directly address exploitation and its ill-gotten gains, reduces incentives to exploit.

Exploitation can take many forms. In this chapter, we will consider two: exploitation through market power and through taking advantage of people's vulnerabilities and lack of knowledge. In a later chapter, we will consider abuses of corporate governance.

Market Power

Twenty-first-century economies are dominated by large corporations that enjoy significant market power—among other things, the power to raise prices, to treat customers shabbily, and to demand that any dispute be settled through arbitration, which is controlled by the corporation, rather than by a public court. Firms also have enormous power over their workers (this is referred to as *monopsony power*), giving companies the ability to depress wages. Unions have grown weaker and labor laws have further restrained workers' bargaining position. Globalization has meant that firms threaten to move their plants abroad unless workers accept low wages and poor working conditions. The results are stark: Hourly earnings of autoworkers declined by 17.1 percent between January 1990 and December 2018, a period in which prices doubled, implying real wages had gone down by two-thirds.[8] Well-paying jobs have been converted into badly paid jobs.

To the extent that wages are below what they would be in a competitive world, or food prices higher than they would be (as a result of the exercise of market power), there is a sense in which employees are coerced into working more. Is there much difference between the current situation and what happened in South Africa, where people were strong-armed into working in the mines because they were prohibited from working on the land?[9]

In many cases, one form of exploitation gets piled on another. In South Africa, miners' wages may have been lowered still further—coercion still greater—as a result of the monopsony power of the mines; or even worse, the mining companies may have colluded. And the legal framework made matters still worse. Before 1982, Black

South African miners were prevented from unionizing, which weakened their bargaining power.[10]

Many libertarians might accede to government interventions designed to limit deviations from the competitive equilibrium. For instance, a monopolist's "right" to exercise that power and raise his price to whatever level he wants obviously affects my budget constraints; it reduces my freedom to spend. If I want to buy a certain amount of his good, I am forced to consume less of other goods. Perhaps more telling is that if the monopolist has total control over a drug I need to live, he has real coercive power. He could force me to give up everything to survive. To what extent is this different from being held up at gunpoint?

Price gouging—extreme abuses of market power

There is common agreement, though a few economists dissent, that price gouging should be discouraged or simply not allowed, especially when it comes to essentials like lifesaving drugs, home heating, or fuels. One way to discourage it is to force the price gougers to give up their profits, effectively sharing them with the rest of society.

At different times, in different contexts, societies have held various opinions about charging prices markedly in excess of costs.

Earlier, I noted a critical difference between the United States and Europe in this respect. In the US, if a company acquires its monopoly power legitimately, it can do anything it wants with it—extorting as much as it can from the cancer patient who needs the drug or her insurance company. In Europe, this is not allowed. One might ask, why would different countries have different legal regimes governing the maximum prices a firm can charge? Isn't there an efficient answer? Economic theory provides an answer. Monopolies are distortionary, whether the monopoly power is legitimately acquired or not. The firm charges a price higher than its (marginal) costs (the costs it would incur to produce an additional unit), which results in production and consumption that is suppressed below the efficient level. (At the efficient level, price, reflecting the value of the good to the consumer, equals the marginal cost; this is also the level that would be realized in a competitive equilibrium). The US position that there should be no constraint on the exercise of legitimately acquired monopoly power implies that in these situations, prices will be too high and the quantities consumed too low. The high price leads to a transfer of income from ordinary people to the monopolist, creating more inequality.

The answer to the question of why the US and Europe have different legal frameworks is *not* that the laws of economics work differently across the ocean, or that there are different circumstances that would make the trade-offs different or cause them to be evaluated differently. In both Europe and the US, the unbridled exercise of monopoly power is bad on all reasonable economic grounds.[11] A difference in politics accounts for the differences in rules. The power of the drug companies is especially relevant here, and it is evidently far stronger in the US than in Europe.

One context in which price gouging is particularly reprehensible is wartime. The general sensibilities on these matters are reflected in wartime legislation that makes price gouging illegal, and when discovered, allows payments under contracts to be rewritten downward. For good reason: It undermines the kind of national solidarity needed for success in war. While young people are at least temporarily giving up their careers and even their lives, others are profiteering.

During the early days of the Russia–Ukraine war, while Ukrainians were giving their lives to resist Russia's aggression, multinational oil and gas companies and many energy traders made out like bandits, reaping tens of billions of dollars in extra profits for which they had done nothing. Indeed, remarkably, rather than taking that money and investing it to rapidly expand production to alleviate the pain that so many were feeling, they distributed the profits to their wealthy shareholders, either in dividends or share buybacks. While there is no evidence of explicit collusion, there seems to have been tacit collusion. The companies all apparently realized that prices would fall if they quickly expanded production, so the price signal (in market economies, higher prices are supposed to signal to firms to produce more) that was loudly saying to expand production was ignored; even the production of fracking gas, which could have been quickly brought to market, did not expand as one would have expected.[12]

Many economists argue against attempts to short-circuit the price system. High prices ensure that the oil gets to buyers who value it the most (or more accurately, have the most money to pay for it) and elicit desirable demand and supply responses. But what happened in the Ukrainian war largely contradicts this theory. There were some supply and demand responses, but they were limited. For instance, people who couldn't afford to pay high heating bills were forced to lower their thermostats. Why were the responses limited? The war was expected to be short, and hence there was no point in making the investments required. On the demand side, whether it makes sense for a household to redo the insulation or buy a more efficient furnace won't be affected much by a short-term increase in the price of energy. On the supply side, too, there's not much incentive to respond if the price spike is thought to be temporary; besides, the oil and gas companies were enjoying their profits.[13]

Stronger government actions should have been taken to increase energy production and to more equitably share the burden of the war and the post-pandemic adjustments.[14] A windfall profits tax—a tax on the excess profits arising from the increase in prices because of the war—would have been a redistribution from the corporations benefiting from the war to those who were sacrificing for it. This is true even if the companies were not engaged in price gouging but simply responding to competitive market forces. Because both employment and capital costs are deductible in calculating taxable profits, a well-designed windfall profits tax is nondistortionary. It neither encourages nor discourages investment or employment; it simply redistributes money from the war profiteers to everyone else.[15] Remarkably, the Right objected to a windfall profits tax. They supported the high prices charged by the oil and gas companies that simply wanted to enjoy the benefits of Putin's perfidy. In the United States, they prevailed, though not in many European countries.

Explaining the existence and persistence of market power

There are multiple reasons for the persistence of, and even increase in, market power. First, we've moved into a winner-take-all economy, where the market gravitates to one or two dominant firms—Google dominating the search engine, Facebook and TikTok dominating social media, and Microsoft dominating PC operating systems.[16] With the rise of the digital economy, where the marginal cost of production (the extra cost of producing an extra unit) is low, the "overhead" (fixed) costs have assumed an increasingly large role. Overhead includes things like R&D expenditures to design the product, build the factory, or write the computer code for a platform. When overhead dominates a firm's costs, markets are typically characterized by a limited number of firms.[17] Moreover, as we've moved toward a service-sector economy, local markets, in which one or a few firms dominate, have become more important.

There are other reasons for the increase in market power. Digital platforms glean and process information that gives them a competitive advantage over other firms, and the larger platforms may be able to glean more information than smaller platforms. Profits can be generated not by being more productive or selling more relevant products but by being better able to exploit consumers through sophisticated means of price discrimination. For instance, platforms figure out which consumers will pay more and charge them a higher price for the same product. This undermines the principles underlying the efficiency of the market economy, where all individuals and firms face the same prices.

Furthermore, firms have devised smart ways to exert market power, for instance, through cleverly designed contracts used to exclude competitors or at least make entry into a given market more difficult. That's, in part, how Microsoft became dominant. And it happens elsewhere in the economy, too, although we largely don't realize it. One of the reasons for high airfares is the exercise of market power by a handful of airline reservation companies that entrench themselves through contracts and bullying, intimidating entrants into the airline reservation business and airlines that might try their services.[18]

At one time, conservative, free-market economists hoped that even if there were large, fixed costs so that markets were dominated by one or a few firms, *potential* competition—the threat of entry—would discipline the market and drive down prices so profits would be zero. Even if there were a natural monopoly, with a single firm most efficiently serving all, advocates of unfettered markets claimed that competition *for* the market, competition to be that single firm, would replace competition *in* the market, and the resulting equilibrium would be efficient. From this perspective, any monopolies charging excessive prices would be temporary; they simply couldn't persist.[19] Simplistic economics said that such high profits would attract new competitors, which, in turn, would drive down prices and profits.

Modern economics has shown that these beliefs are not correct. Especially when there are sunk costs (expenditures on marketing and research, for example, which can't be recovered if one enters and then exits the market), high levels of profits can be and often are sustained.

The reason that potential competition can't replace actual competition is simple. Potential entrants know that their profitability will rely not on the *current* price but the price *after* they enter, because their very presence in the marketplace will cause prices to fall. They know that prices might fall by so much that they will incur losses. So potential entrants don't enter at all. Moreover, incumbent firms have learned how to *deter* entry, making potential competitors more convinced that if they were to enter, prices would fall even more, by, for instance, convincing them that should they enter there will be a price war.[20] And even if it were true that *eventually* there would be competition, the harm to consumers in terms of high prices and, at least in some cases, other forms of exploitation, can be enormous.

Perhaps most importantly, there has been less determination by government to ensure a competitive marketplace than there has been on the part of the private sector to create and maintain market power. And this is neither an accident nor a surprise. We've talked about how markets don't exist in a vacuum, that they must be structured by rules and regulations. An important area of those regulations relates to competition. But many people and corporations with power— including with market power—don't look favorably on competition regulations; they do what they can to limit the adoption and enforcement of the kinds of effective competition laws society needs for a twenty-first-century economy. Google, Facebook (Meta), and Amazon lobby against laws that would increase competition in the digital marketplace. As is often the case, Europe has gone further to ensure competition in this arena than the US through its Digital Markets Act that went into force in 2022. In the US, a conservative, business-friendly Supreme Court has interpreted existing laws in ways that have hampered keeping the economy competitive. More broadly, the courts have done what they can to expand the freedom of large corporations to exploit ordinary consumers, thereby curtailing the effective freedom (as I have defined it) of the rest of society, and so far, Congress has failed to constrain this market power.

There is still one more reason for today's disproportionate corporate power: the weakening of offsetting powers, in particular of workers. In his 1952 book, *American Capitalism*,[21] John Kenneth Galbraith described a system of *countervailing powers*, what might be thought of as a system of checks and balances within our economic system. He correctly saw that the American economy was not well described by perfect competition, unlike Friedman and other classical and neoclassical economists who thought it was. What kept a semblance of balance in the economy, Galbraith wrote, were countervailing powers. Perhaps the most important force countervailing corporations is unions, which represent workers not only at the bargaining table but in the political process, too, through supporting candidates and legislation that weigh in against corporate interests. But again, legislative changes, judicial rulings, and changes in the structure of the economy have led to the evisceration of unions, and that has weakened their ability to serve as a countervailing power. Fewer than 6 percent of private-sector workers were unionized in 2022, in contrast to almost 25 percent in 1973 and a peak of over 35 percent in the 1950s, when Galbraith wrote *American Capitalism.*

It is another instance of power begetting power—more akin to the law of the jungle than the harmonious relationship envisaged by classical economics. The power of corporations has increased as the power of workers has diminished.

Multiple ways to exploit power

Perhaps nowhere is that point clearer than in the dispute resolution process between corporations and people, whether they are consumers or employees. A just system, one that would be adopted behind the veil of ignorance, would entail impartial and unbiased judges adjudicating through fair, open, and transparent processes. But increasingly, corporations insist that their employees and customers sign arbitration clauses, which neatly move dispute adjudication out of the public courts and into the hands of private arbitrators, who are well-paid lawyers beholden to the corporations that hire them. No subject is of more concern to ordinary individuals than justice, and we turn to government to help us get it. But private corporations have used their power to cut government out of the loop, leaving anyone with a complaint at the mercy of a system that's stacked against them.

Corporations defend the practice as an exercise in freedom—it is part of the freedom to contract. They attack any attempt to restrict compulsory arbitration as an infringement on their freedom. But they know full well that forcing people to sign these contracts is an exercise of power and is part and parcel of corporations' power, and freedom, to exploit. A worker in the process of being hired by a firm is not going to have a lawyer negotiate the terms of his contract—indeed, he knows that if he brought along a lawyer, the firm would smell trouble and not give him the job. In most communities, there is one telephone company, at most two, with both insisting on arbitration clauses. If you want phone service, you have no choice but to accept the arbitration clause.

The US Supreme Court has made matters worse. When an employer exploits a worker, even by something as outrageous as wage theft (not paying a worker the wages owed), the worker is at a disadvantage because the costs of going to court or even going to arbitration are high. To wage a battle against a corporate giant with its large legal staff is a David-versus-Goliath proposition—but one in which Goliath almost always wins. If, however, all those who have been cheated and exploited could band together, it would be a more even battle, and in most areas, our legal system allows this (under fairly restrictive conditions), in class-action suits. But the Supreme Court has made such class actions difficult, if not impossible, in the context of arbitration.[22] It has weighed in on the side of Goliath.[23]

Exploiting vulnerabilities and limitations in information
There are multiple other areas in which companies may and do exploit their workers or their customers. Imperfect information and competition allow companies to take advantage of their customers by using vulnerabilities and information asymmetries (in which the company knows something that the worker doesn't and knows that it does).

Giving companies that freedom to exploit generates incomes for the exploiter at the expense of the exploited. The arguments for coercion, regulations that restrict the ability to exploit in these ways, are even more compelling.

Conservative economists have said not to worry about market power because markets are self-correcting. They make a similar case here. Firms that exploit their workers or consumers will lose customers or will be forced to pay higher wages, so the argument goes. The economists who say that we shouldn't worry about this exploitation go further by solemnly proclaiming that an economic system based on caveat emptor—buyer beware—is more efficient. This is just another instance of the sophistry that permeates these perspectives. (Famously, Lloyd Blankfein, former CEO of Goldman Sachs, when queried about his company selling securities that it had designed to fail—and which it actually bet on to fail without disclosing that information to investors—thought there was nothing wrong with what the firm had done: the buyers of these securities were all adults, he maintained, and should have been aware of the risks.)[24]

I explained earlier why it was desirable to restrict polluters from polluting. But companies that sell bad products are, in effect, polluting the marketplace. If firms stand behind their products, then a lower information burden is placed on consumers and markets work better. It makes sense to put the burden on the seller to ensure that the product is what it seems to be and as good as the seller claims.[25] That is why most countries have "truth in advertising" laws.

Curtailing Monopoly Power while Rewarding Innovation

One important source of monopoly power is patents, which give an individual or corporation exclusive rights to the use of a discovery for a temporary period (globally, twenty years). The Constitution gave the power to the US government to issue patents, and the reason, apparent even in those early days of science, was clear: to promote innovation, which has been the greatest source of advances in our living standards for the past 250 years.

The boundaries of knowledge are more ambiguous than the boundaries of a piece of property, and how expansive patents should be is a subject of serious debate. Should a patent cover all four-wheeled, propelled vehicles (as the original patent for cars did) or only a specific design, say, one involving an internal combustion engine? Another debate centers on what can be patented. The mathematical theorems that gave rise to computers, which are at the center of today's economy, could not be patented even though the ideas were of enormous value.

Both the US and Europe circumscribe monopoly power derived from intellectual property (IP). Consider, for example, a patent on a life-saving drug. Suppose the firm can't produce enough of it. In that case, the government can issue a compulsory license, which gives others the right to produce the good (with the company using the IP paying the owner of the patent a "fair" royalty, though a payment far short of the monopoly profits that the firm would otherwise have earned). Of course, the increased production will lower the price and, therefore, the profits of the patent owner.

This example illustrates another theme from earlier discussions: that property is a social construction, designed, we hope, to advance societal well-being. It is not a matter of nature or natural law, but of the laws *we* create. This is especially apparent with intellectual property, where we see the boundaries (of what is and is not included within a patent) constantly being contested, and for good reason. In a twenty-first-century economy, how intellectual property is defined has a big effect on the distribution of income and wealth, the well-being of citizens, and the pace and pattern of innovation. Changes in technology and the economy necessitate redefining the rules governing intellectual property from time to time—and this has occurred frequently in recent decades.

In chapter 3, I discussed the enclosing of the commons, allegedly done to increase economic efficiency and prevent its overuse. But a significant amount of intellectual property represents the enclosure of the intellectual commons, as intellectual property scholar James Boyle of Duke University has pointed out. Some of that knowledge may have even been previously held in the public domain.[26] This modern enclosure movement is worse than the older one because it diminishes economic efficiency by impeding the transmission, use, and even the production of knowledge. The most important input into the production of knowledge is knowledge itself. Walling it off with a patent impairs others' freedom to use it.

There is a growing body of evidence that shows that intellectual property, as currently constituted, leads to a slower pace of innovation and higher prices. A natural experiment was conducted when, in 2013, the US Supreme Court ruled unanimously that naturally occurring genes could not be patented. Myriad Genetics, a Salt Lake City company, had held the patent on two critical genes related to breast cancer and had used its market power to limit testing by others. Its tests were not as effective as those developed elsewhere, and the prices of its tests were exorbitantly high. The natural result: Women died unnecessarily. Again, a trade-off between Myriad's freedom to exclude—to deny the right of other companies to provide their own tests for the genes at affordable prices—and these women's right to live. With the patent removed, the market produced better tests at lower prices, and innovation proceeded apace.[27]

During the AIDS epidemic, the constraining effects of intellectual property were strongly in evidence. Drug companies charged prices multiple times the costs for life-saving therapies. The prices were so high many patients couldn't afford them. There were companies and countries able and willing to produce and sell drug therapies at affordable prices, but the patent holders said, in effect, our profits are more important than your lives. The inevitable result was that thousands died unnecessarily.

In this arena as in other aspects of property rights, there is no natural law. Individuals have no intrinsic rights to the income generated by a particular patent. Obviously, their incomes would have been different under different patent regimes. (A patent regime is defined by the length and breadth of the patent, the stringency of the conditions for the issuance of compulsory licenses, restrictions on charging abusive prices, the toughness of the disclosure requirements, and so on.) As in the case of other laws and regulations, we can evaluate the consequences of alternative regimes behind a veil of ignorance—each constraining the freedoms of some (innovators) as they expand the freedoms of others (those who might make use of the IP and benefit from the greater spread of knowledge). A longer patent life for a drug, for instance, would generate more profits for the drug company, but at the cost of forcing those who need the drug to pay the higher monopoly price for longer—with the possibility of patients who could not afford the drug dying. As we look at current IP regimes in the US and globally, we can ask: To what extent do they conform to what would likely emerge behind the veil of ignorance? And to what extent are they simply the outcome of power politics?

Overall, it's clear that power politics dominates. Nowhere was that clearer than during the Covid-19 pandemic. Early on, India and South Africa asked for an intellectual property waiver, which would allow others to use Covid-19-relevant IP, but the World Trade Organization (which oversees intellectual property rules) refused to grant it even as Covid ravaged the world. The result was vaccine apartheid, in which rich countries had access to vaccines, but poor countries were shut out. Many thousands of people in those countries got the disease, were hospitalized, and died unnecessarily. Almost surely, Covid-19 festered longer and mutated more because of the WTO's refusal to grant the waiver, with potential harms even to those in advanced countries. The WTO made a decision about the trade-offs in play. Drug company profits trumped the welfare of billions. The freedom to exploit beat the freedom to live.

Corporate interests have successfully affected the language we use. We refer to these ownership claims in patents and copyrights as intellectual property *rights*, thereby elevating this form of property to a right. It is as if these corporations are suggesting that reining in intellectual property is a deprivation of freedom akin to the abridgment of the other rights we cherish. But the boundaries of intellectual property have always been limited and ambiguous, and it is up to society to reason about and delineate what those boundaries should be. I was on the Council of Economic Advisers when the intellectual property provisions of what would become the WTO were being discussed (an agreement called TRIPS—Trade-Related Aspects of Intellectual Property Rights). It was clear to me that the provisions had not been chosen to maximize societal welfare behind a veil of ignorance, not even to maximize the pace of innovation in the US or the world, but simply to maximize the profits of a few companies, mainly in the pharmaceutical and entertainment industries (with perhaps a few constraints so as not to appear too unseemly). The copyright law included a provision derisively called the Mickey Mouse Protection Act, seemingly included to help Disney by extending protection for the Mickey Mouse brand for years after its creator's death, at great cost to scholars wanting to have access to the papers of critical literary figures. Disney enjoyed the extra benefits at the expense of the rest of society. Early versions of Mickey Mouse finally entered the public domain on January 1, 2024.[28]

Most economists would argue that extending the life of a patent or copyright beyond a certain point generates little benefit in induced incentives but may have large societal costs down the line, from the lengthened monopoly power. Most would agree that with the Mickey

Mouse provision, copyrights had gone well beyond the point where the additional monopoly costs could be justified.[29]

Concluding Remarks

A central theme of this book has been that in our interlinked society, any person's freedom can't be looked at in isolation. Expanding one person's freedom contracts the freedom of others. We typically have to make judgments about which freedoms are more important. Sometimes those judgments are easy, sometimes hard. This chapter has focused on what is normally an easy case: exploitation. The one area that requires some subtlety has to do with intellectual property, where there may be societal benefits from the innovation induced by the monopoly profits. Then, we have to ask two questions. The first concerns the balancing of freedoms, with more monopoly rights (more rights to exploit) being offset by societal benefits of innovation. Here, I've argued that in comparing current arrangements with what we might see behind the veil of ignorance, it's clear they are simply the outcome of the naked use of political power. The second goes further, asking whether there are better ways to organize our innovation system—to produce more knowledge and make the fruits of that knowledge more accessible. That is, are there other economic arrangements in which we might not have to face the balancing of freedoms so intensely? There are, especially in areas of health (but not universally). Government can finance the researchers themselves and/or it can provide a prize to the innovator. Of course, the "right to exploit"—the monopoly right granted to the innovator—can be thought of as a prize, but it's a very distorting and inefficient one. A cash prize would be more efficient and (per dollar spent) more effective.[30] The irony is that in current arrangements, we've managed to get the worst of all worlds. The government finances much of the research—the mRNA platform on which the Pfizer and Moderna

Covid-19 vaccines were based was largely publicly financed, as were many of the more immediate expenditures in developing the vaccine. But the drug companies are given full license to exploit. The public bore most of the expenses and risks, and the drug companies reaped the profits, with much of the costs of their high pricing coming out of the public purse. The government paid Pfizer and Moderna high prices for the vaccines, even though it had already paid for most of the research and development costs.

More generally, the societal benefits of curtailing corporations' freedom to exploit are obvious. Many on the Right live in a fantasy world in which no one has market or political power and everyone has perfect information. No one can take advantage of anyone else. Of course, when firms engaging in anticompetitive exploitation are charged with doing so under competition laws, well-paid economists come to the defense of these corporations. They look at behavior that seems on the face of it exploitive, doing little more, for instance, than extending and strengthening market power, and claim that it is not. They assert that for some arcane reason, an obviously anticompetitive action actually increases economic efficiency. Teams of lawyers and economists get paid hundreds of millions of dollars every year to convince courts that what is clearly the exploitation of market power is nothing more than a manifestation of the wonders of the market economy. They work hard to explain away the high and persistent profits of the firms with such obvious market power.

Over a hundred years ago, the US passed laws intended to curtail the ability of large behemoths to exploit ordinary Americans. But in the interim, business-friendly courts have reinterpreted the laws, expanding the right to exploit and making it harder and harder to prove that any particular action is exploitive.

It should be clear by now that current arrangements don't have the right balance of freedoms. Which poses a challenge: Are there alternatives that would do better? The answer, given in Part III, is an unambiguous yes. But first we must address questions that economists have largely ignored in the last century. How does our economic system shape people? How does it affect the extent to which regulations are even needed, or the sense of coercion we feel as governments impose the regulations needed for a well-functioning society?

PART II
FREEDOM, BELIEFS, AND PREFERENCES,
AND THE
CREATION OF THE GOOD SOCIETY

P art I of this book looked at freedom through the economists' standard toolkit—trade-offs, externalities, public goods, and coordination problems. It explained that every society must impose constraints and that, in some cases, limited coercion can make everyone better off, while in other cases, there may be trade-offs— one person gains, the other loses, with one person's freedom being another's unfreedom.

Designing the regulations, taxes, and expenditures that enhance freedom overall, even if that entails restricting it in one dimension or another, requires analysis and reasoning. It requires combining theory and evidence, not relying on a lazy ideological commitment to some unspecified, inchoate notion of freedom. We are concerned both about negative freedoms—freedom from want and freedom from fear—and positive freedoms—the freedom to live up to one's potential and the freedom to flourish. We are concerned about economic as well as political freedoms. Freedom is an important constituent of what we strive for in creating a good society.

But there is more to it than that. Much of our effort as parents is to bring up our children to be good people, honest, hardworking, empathetic, and so on. As children, it's hard for us not to have noticed those efforts on the part of our parents. Even when these efforts are not perfectly successful, they have consequential effect. So, the standard economic model that assumes we emerge into this world with fully defined preferences and beliefs is wrong, which, in turn, has important implications for society and how we think about it, including for the question at hand: How do we think about freedom? Different assignments of freedom to some and restraints on others, for instance, lead to the formation of different kinds of individuals, and over time, to a different society. As we think about these different regimes, we should think about the long-run societal consequences.

The recognition that individuals are malleable, with what economists refer to as *endogenous preferences and beliefs*,[1] is one of the important advances of twenty-first-century economics.[2] How people see the world—what might be called their cognitive lens—is shaped by their experiences, their peers, parents, leaders, and a host of others, including teachers and the media. To use the economists' jargon employed earlier, there are *social externalities*.

For two hundred years, mainstream economics proceeded as if individuals were not only "preformed" but infinitely rational and well informed (even rational about how informed to be). The standard model portrayed humans as cold-hearted calculators, weighing the costs and benefits (typically in material terms) of each act. Economists seemed to be a strange species themselves, somewhat schizophrenic, knowing as they did that those with whom they interacted and the subjects that they were supposed to be studying were far different from the humans portrayed in their models. The humans they *assumed* in their models were demonstrably more selfish than *most* people. But interestingly, some research suggested that, by and large, while even economists were not perfectly selfish (as their models assumed), they were indeed more like the individuals they assumed in their theories; in particular, they were more selfish than others. Moreover, the longer students studied economics the more like that idealized person they became. They took on more and more of the identity of the perfectly selfish individual that is the cornerstone of modern economics.[3]

Economists also assumed that all individuals are perfectly rational and perfectly consistent in the choices they make. In the latter half of the twentieth century, with the work of cognitive and mathematical psychologist Amos Tversky and psychologist and behaviorial economist Daniel Kahneman, economists began to explore systematic patterns of irrationality.[4] But in this literature, attention centered on cognitive limitations. As Kahneman explained in his bestselling book *Thinking, Fast and Slow*,[5] we often have to think fast and don't have time to reason things out fully. We use simple rules of thumb (what are called heuristics), and these may lead to consistent, measurable "biases" in our decisions and judgments. The research into the departures from infinitely rational individuals was called *behavioral economics*. But, of course, all economics is supposed to be about behavior; it's supposed to describe how people actually behave. It turned out that the economists' standard model, with infinitely rational and absolutely selfish individuals, often did not describe well how people acted.[6]

Twenty-first-century behavioral economics[7] argued that the key departures from the economists' standard hypotheses were not *just* that individuals had cognitive limitations and sometimes had to make decisions too rapidly but also that they knew imperfectly what they wanted, and what they wanted was changeable. The falsity of the assumption in standard economics that what individuals wanted was immutable, as I have already explained, is almost as obvious as the fact that people are not infinitely rational.

In this part of the book, I explore the insights of modern behavioral economics as it applies to our understanding of freedom and of how it can best be promoted in a meaningful way.

CHAPTER 8

Social Coercion and Social Cohesion

We are all social animals, sensitive to what others think of us. What we view as "acceptable" is shaped by our society. In some societies, it is acceptable to litter, go unmasked during a pandemic, spit in the street, or wear pants if you're a woman; in other societies, these behaviors are unacceptable. One might say in each instance the norms constraining what a person could do are no less constraining than a government fine and, in some cases, far more constraining. In that sense, norms could be viewed as coercive.

This chapter examines in closer detail how we form beliefs and the quandaries—and dangers—associated with social coercion. While I raise some hard-to-resolve questions, what emerges more clearly is that the current form of capitalism—neoliberal, unfettered capitalism—shapes people in ways that not only represent the antithesis of a good society but that actually undermine capitalism.

The Social Formation of Beliefs and Preferences

Twenty-first-century behavioral economics emphasizes that preferences are endogenous—they can change with our experiences—and that they are largely *socially* determined. We are who we are because of the people who surround us, influenced greatly (but not exclusively) by parents and teachers.

Parents and teachers not only transmit values down the generations, but socialize youngsters, making them more aware of how their actions affect others. Children are taught precepts like "Do unto others as you would have them do unto you," "Honesty pays," and "To do no evil is good, to intend none better." They are taught that a good person acts according to these precepts. When parents and teachers are successful, such other-regarding behavior becomes essentially part of the individual's identity. Of course, there are limits to the extent to which such socialization is successful.

The widespread support of public education in the nineteenth century was in no small measure directed at creating a workforce suitable for the emerging industrial economy, which required that people be sufficiently socialized so they behaved appropriately (and efficiently) in the workplace.[1] These behaviors included such everyday things as showing up regularly and on time to bigger things like accepting, even welcoming, directions from others and accepting hierarchical organizations and one's place in them. We sometimes refer to this process as "socializing" individuals.

Thus, schools do more than just impart skills and create human capital.[2] They try to inculcate norms, including those necessary for the economy to function, and values, including national and, in some cases, religious identities. History is taught in a way that glorifies the past, sliding over the atrocities that the country may have committed. All this is an attempt to shape individuals, to affect their future behavior, especially in particular situations and at particular times—for instance, when the country is under threat from an outside enemy. We economists shape our students to be as we assume they are in our models—not how *most* people are in life. But if economists were fully successful, say, in persuading all schools to have a required course every year in economics predicated on individuals being utterly selfish, we almost surely would wind up with a society with greater selfishness.[3]

Education plays another role. It creates "social commons," or common ways of looking at the world, including a common language with which to discuss it.[4] We are social beings, and want and need to communicate with each other. While all educational systems help to create these common understandings, good educational systems provide broader common understandings with greater nuance that enables differentiated meanings. It is not just about common understandings of what is said; it is, as I have noted, about the creation of norms, including norms about what goes unsaid.

Peer pressure and social norms play an important role in shaping behavior. If individuals act differently than dictated by the norms, they may be shunned and excluded from groups they belong to, which is painful. The role of peer pressure is perhaps most evident in teenagers struggling to find their identities; more subtly, it is part of our entire lives. Peer pressure can have enormous force, even resulting in bystanders being shunned if they don't participate in the group's exclusion of a particular person.

Internalizing Externalities and Inducing Social Cohesion

In some cases, society realizes clear and large benefits through the social formation of beliefs and preferences via the mechanisms I've described. Sometimes norms can help address an externality. Other-regarding behavior, whether a result of our own identity or of peer pressure and social norms, can lead to less littering, less drinking, and safer driving. Norms can also be important in creating and maintaining other elements of a good society, such as discouraging violence against women or encouraging tolerance. Today, emerging norms against unnecessarily emitting greenhouse gases—not eating meat, flying less, lowering the thermostat—are playing a pivotal role in saving the planet.

To the extent that these norms succeed in *internalizing* an externality, causing us to consider how our actions affect others, there is no need for public interventions that might be deemed coercive to deal with the externality.

Considering how one's actions affect others—whether because of peer pressure to behave well or because of empathy—can be viewed as part of social cohesion or social solidarity. Such pro-social behaviors define us. We think of ourselves as good citizens, as members of a community doing our part. It is not that we are coerced into behaving well; it's that part of our being requires us to show respect for others by helping our neighbors when a natural disaster strikes, for example, or by giving blood.

To the extent that there is social cohesion, a requirement to act for the good of society is not coercion—a regulation requiring us to offer the elderly or disabled a seat on a train is not coercive. It is also not coercive to be required to contribute to the support of people who are less well off—in other words, to pay taxes to support redistribution. We might do it on our own, but society as a whole is better off when we do it collectively so that no one can be a free rider in creating the kind of shared prosperity that is central to a good society.

Indeed, if individuals *fully* adopt norms as their own values, there is no constraint imposed by a regulation requiring these behaviors. They would not want to violate the norm by littering or refusing to give their bus seat to an older person; and a constraint that is not binding is not effectively a constraint. In well-functioning societies, much of the efforts at socialization (a key part of the social formation of preferences) entails inducing individuals to internalize externalities.

But the transmission of norms between individuals is imperfect. Some people will not have fully adopted the norm, and then the constraint posed by peer pressure and social coercion does seem like a restriction on the person's freedom to act. Ironically, from this perspective, the loss of freedom from a regulation not to litter is associated only with the imperfect transmission of societal preferences. Only people who have not adopted the norm of not littering feel a loss of freedom from a regulation against littering.

Donald Trump illustrates what happens when parents and teachers fail, and an individual does not become socialized. When norms, peer pressure, and tradition worked normally, we didn't need strong laws to define what a president could ethically do. Almost every president acted within the constraints. But Trump, with his brazenness, may force us to define the presidential limits more precisely by putting them within laws and regulations.

Social cohesion beyond internalizing externalities

Social cohesion enhances the functioning of society in ways that go beyond the internalization of externalities. In chapter 4, I talked about the benefits of public goods and social cooperation; social cohesion strengthens the support for public goods and facilitates cooperation. It enables even the rich to accept a certain level of redistribution for the public good and may encourage philanthropy. Social cohesion, and the lower levels of inequality that it may engender, in turn facilitate the inevitable political compromises that are hallmarks of a well-functioning society.

The other invisible hand

Norms, by internalizing externalities and developing a sense of social cohesion, help societies to function. The phenomenon of masses of individuals working together to produce the complex products that sustain and advance our standards of living is a subject that has long been of interest, especially to economists. As we've seen, Adam Smith provided one answer to the question of how this complex system works to produce the goods and services we need and want. Somehow, he said, the pursuit of self-interest leads to the well-being of society.[5] Modern economists have filled in the details. It is through the working of the price system that information is conveyed, so that the pursuit of the individual's self-interest is congruent with society's interests.

Norms and the shared lens through which people see the world provide another invisible hand, emphasized in a forthcoming book by Allison Demeritt, Karla Hoff, and me.[6] As I noted, if we all share the norm not to litter, we don't need regulations or even price incentives to induce us not to litter. We behave in ways that keep our cities clean. These norms and shared lenses are invisible in two senses: they are created invisibly and become part of who we are without our even being aware of it, and they function invisibly, so much a part of who we are that we typically obey them without even thinking.

Freedom and responsibility

The discussion in chapter 1 echoed the long-standing premise that with freedom comes responsibility. Parents tell their children, "I will give you more freedom *if you act responsibly*." What that means, of course, is that the children don't have unfettered freedom. There is an implicit set of rules and regulations understood between the parents and children. The same thing, in a way, is true in our broader family, our community. Just as parents attempt to shape their children to act according to the rules of the family, society—often through parents—works to shape all citizens to act responsibly, taking into account, for instance, the externalities that they exert on others.

There is widespread discussion within the disciplines of law and economics of the relative advantages of laws and regulations versus norms and other ways of inducing social (other-regarding) behavior. Of course, it is impossible to define what is appropriate under every contingency. Norms may have greater ambiguity than laws and regulations, and ambiguity itself may *normally* be helpful in constraining behavior. If there is a bright line, defined by a law or regulation, there will be a tendency to push against it.

Milton Friedman shows what happens when that perspective is taken to the extreme. He thought that as long as the government didn't regulate workers' treatment or environmental pollution, a firm should fully exercise whatever freedom it was given by the state to maximize profits. It had no moral obligation to treat its workers decently or care about the environment. Friedman flipped morality around, suggesting it was wrong for a corporate manager to do anything else. As he said, "There is one and only one social responsibility of business—to use its resources and engage in activities designed to increase its profits."[7]

In some contexts, it may be easier to induce cooperation through a social norm than through regulations or market incentives. A famous experiment at an Israeli day-care center discussed by economists Uri Gneezy and Aldo Rustichini[8] illustrates this. Because the staff obviously had to stay until all the children were picked up, it was important that parents arrive on time in the evening. To induce parents to be on time more regularly, the center imposed a charge for late pickup—but the response was seemingly perverse, as late pickups *increased*. The explanation was simple. Before there had been a norm. Now, a social obligation was converted into an economic relationship; parents judged whether the extra fees imposed as the cost of a late pickup were greater or less than the benefits to them, and in many cases decided they were less.

A related worry is that rules and regulations *crowd out* morality and other forms of pro-social behavior. We may feel better about ourselves if we don't litter because we care about others rather than because we know we'll face a fine.

Beliefs, preferences, and social externalities

The fact that our preferences and beliefs are shaped in relation to others gives rise to a fundamental social externality: If we are dishonest, there is not only the direct consequence of that behavior (itself an externality) but also an indirect effect. Trust in society is lowered, and others are more likely to behave dishonestly, undermining the overall functioning of society. Positive behavior, too, is likely to have a knock-on effect, as numerous experiments[9] have demonstrated. A gratuitous act of kindness is likely to lead others to engage in a gratuitous act of kindness. Honesty breeds honesty and nurtures trust in society.

As with other externalities, there is a compelling case for governments to encourage positive social externalities and discourage negative ones. They do this through market and nonmarket mechanisms. Governments punish egregious behavior (dishonesty in particular circumstances, like fraud and lying in advertising) and subsidize acts of charity through the tax system. And political leaders use the bully pulpit of their position to exhort what they view as pro-social behavior.

In Part III, I will discuss how the design of the economic and social system affects the extent of these externalities and suggest that neoliberal capitalism has encouraged negative externalities and led to a more selfish and less honest society.

Social Control, Social Credit, Advertising, and Individual Freedom

We may applaud the socialization of individuals when it makes them better citizens or better adapted to the workplace, but socialization can have problematic elements, too.

First, peer pressure is often not directed at curbing externality-generating activities or encouraging pro-social actions. Some of it may even generate social harms—for instance, when it enforces exclusionary behavior. It can encourage other troubling behaviors as well, such as disordered eating and bullying among young people. In the US, peer pressure undoubtedly aided the racist and exclusionary Jim Crow regime.

Neoliberal economists said this kind of discrimination couldn't persist. In his infamous book *The Economics of Discrimination*,[10] Nobel Prize–winning economist Gary Becker suggested it was hard, if not impossible, for discrimination to arise in a competitive economy. Those being discriminated against would have lower wages, so the goods they produced would accordingly be cheaper. As long as there were enough people who were not prejudiced, he maintained, they would shift their demands to these workers and the goods they produced. And— presto!—discrimination is eliminated. Teaching at the University of Chicago, an essentially white enclave in the midst of a low income African American neighborhood, it might have seemed hard to reconcile such reasoning with the massive discrimination that was going on right in front of him. But Becker had an answer: If it *seems* like there is discrimination because African American workers are getting paid less, it must be because they are not providing labor services of commensurate quality.

Put aside for the moment that there was discrimination in the provision of education. Becker lived in the mythical world of *perfect* competition and social fluidity. But even as he was writing, economists were studying how small deviations from that world had large consequences, and how economic punishments can enforce discriminatory arrangements. They reached conclusions contrary to Becker and more in line with what was in plain sight. Individuals who rejected Jim Crow and refused to discriminate could themselves be punished, possibly by being discriminated against. And anyone who, in turn, failed to punish nondiscriminators would themselves be punished. In this way, a discriminatory equilibrium can be sustained, even when many people were themselves not prejudiced; they simply were afraid of being punished for violating the discriminatory social norms. Social sanctions, reflected in peer pressure, can be as effective as economic punishments or even more so, especially when economic punishments are limited to boycotts (rather than kneecappings, lynchings, or arsons). Jim Crow, only slightly weakened, persisted after the Southern laws that had enforced it were abolished.

The argument here is the same as the argument about social capital, which is often thought to be an essential feature of a well-performing society. Social capital includes the trust people have in each other; it can also include social norms and the social commons that enable them to function well together. Some norms may be positive, but some may be exclusionary, with tightly knit groups excluding (discriminating against) those not in the group.[11]

Thus, norms can help create a better-functioning society, in which more people feel more free, but this isn't always the case. Norms and the peer pressure to which they give rise can be stifling and constraining,[12] and in some cases can lead to the antithesis of a good society.[13]

Is Orwell here?

There are well-grounded fears of Orwellian attempts to shape individuals toward social conformity, creating a dystopia. There has long been a concern that companies can use insights from modern behavioral economics and social psychology to make people behave in ways that are in the interest of corporations, going well beyond the socialization discussed earlier—for instance, getting people to regularly show up on time.[14]

Today, this is not a matter of speculation; it's a reality. Not of perfect control, exactly, but of moving at least parts of society in certain directions. China has a system of social credit, in which citizens have a "social" account. They are credited when they behave according to the wishes of the state and debited when they do not. This system, supported by mass surveillance, intends to incentivize people to act in the way China's leaders want. But the real intent is to create internalized social norms. China is attempting to develop a better system to motivate its citizens toward its state-directed goals than that of either Soviet Russia or Nazi Germany, with less reliance on explicit coercion and greater success in voluntary "cooperation," so there are fewer dissenters and resisters.

Westerners are revulsed by this twenty-first-century version of Orwell's *1984*, yet they allow private-sector firms to engineer similar results, only with greater subtlety. Corporations create advertising designed to induce consumers to take actions that, in their more rational moments, the consumers would not take, all in the interests of increased profits. Has the compulsive gambler who is enticed to gamble away her wealth lost, in some sense, her freedom to act by this seemingly noncoercive method? In one sense, she was "free" to ignore the enticement. But in another sense, the enticers knew she was unlikely to resist.

There are enormous social harms that arise from this kind of inducement. Think of food companies luring children and adults into eating processed foods, which has contributed to the epidemic of childhood and adult diabetes, or the Sackler-owned drug companies that contributed to the opioid crisis, or the cigarette companies that made their products more addictive without consumers even knowing it. Each of these examples can be thought of as a noncoercive threat to an individual's freedom.

Instagram promotes the alluring vision of a happy and successful teenage life. Kids, of course, want to be a part of that, so they post photos of themselves looking happy and successful. When enough do it, it creates a norm. Even though everyone knows that most of the pictures are posed, kids become anxious because they know that they themselves are not living this life. By now, the role of social media in inducing teenage anxiety and depression is well documented. The design of the social media platforms, with users sharing liked pictures with each other, reinforces these impacts.

I believe that public interventions in the free market are called for to limit antisocial activities, and while they restrict the freedom of, say, the Sackler companies, they expand the freedom of others in ways that enhance the well-being of society. Sometimes, judging among freedoms is easy. Few would defend the freedom of the Sacklers to create mass addiction. In others, it's more difficult. For example, with social media and advertising, we need to consider free speech implications. Later in the book, I will discuss how the Rawlsian framework of thinking about these issues behind a veil of ignorance, or Adam Smith's approach of the impartial spectator, can help us make practical judgments in these hard-to-assess cases.

Individual Autonomy and Peer Pressure: A Philosophical Debate

There's a debate about how to view peer pressure and conformist social norms. Do they represent a loss of freedom, no less than a government regulation imposes a loss of freedom? Are they a form of coercion, perhaps even worse than regulations, because they are harder to change and often operate invisibly?

There are some philosophers who argue that we should *not* view conformist social norms in the same way as regulations. We are sentient human beings, able, at least to some extent, to make judgments about whether and how much we will be influenced by others.[15] There have always been individuals who have stood against the herd, who have used "reason" to evaluate their own preferences, or behaviors, and the preferences of others to ascertain whether a particular set of preferences and beliefs is, in one way or another, undesirable. The capacity for reason is a critical part of a person's agency.[16] We have the ability to make judgments about whether we *ought* to follow the herd—either for our own long-term interest (especially important in the case of peer pressure on a teenager) or for societal well-being (which entails moral reasoning). As Columbia University philosopher Akeel Bilgrami has put it: "An embrace of prevailing social norms is something that one, with one's reason, allows oneself to be trained or acculturated into. That is why there is no intrinsic or essential link between individual autonomy and the self-regardingness that is so central to the standard economic outlook."[17]

But Bilgrami may be taking this argument too far: We do not freely choose the lens through which we see the world. It is largely, though not completely, determined by our environment, and especially in our most formative years, that environment is largely determined by our parents or whoever raises us. Much of the shaping of our perspectives and beliefs occurs subconsciously.[18] Even if one has consciously "allowed" oneself to be trained or acculturated into prevailing social norms, different people may feel differently constrained when it comes to bearing the potential costs of rejecting norms. One's background, social standing, and power deeply determine the "budget" one has for deviating from norms, especially when the stakes are substantial. Even if we all have equal ability to question the prevailing norms, our freedom to act on this accordingly is far from equally distributed.

Moreover, when our perspective is shaped by unseen forces, do individuals really have the *capacity* to choose a different lens? The fact that *some* individuals, possibly as a result of a liberal education, have been able to recognize the special lens through which they see the world and even understand how they came to see it that way doesn't mean that everyone has the capacity to understand that, particularly when they haven't been taught about "lens formation."[19] And even if people do come to understand it, many may not feel they are in a position to stand against the herd.[20] For them, social coercion does amount to a loss of freedom.

The Shaping of Beliefs and the Viability
of Neoliberal Capitalism

So far, I have provided many examples of how society shapes individuals. But there are many other ways that are more subtle but equally pervasive. Under capitalism, we tend to admire people who have made a lot of money without paying much attention to how they made it. Dig a little deeper, and you'll see that many of America's richest families acquired their wealth with more than a whiff of exploitation and bad behavior—abuse of market power (Rockefeller), pushing opioids (the Sacklers), or through the opium or slave trades. There are limits, to be sure. The Sackler family is now disgraced, its name removed from the art galleries that were the recipients of their ill-gotten fortune. The same for some people whose fortunes were made from the enslaved. But the names of many others who grew wealthy from the slave and opium trades continue to adorn prominent buildings at our leading universities as the origins of the wealth recede into the mists of history.

Markets shape us

Modern behavioral economics has detailed how our economic environment shapes us. Embed individuals in an environment defined by ruthless competition, and they become more competitive; embed them in an environment in which cooperation and collaboration are needed and rewarded, and they become more cooperative and collaborative. Behavior that is rewarded in one important context becomes, at least partially, ingrained, spilling over into others. It then gets reflected in organizational and institutional design and behavior, with broader consequences.

Many of the smaller banks in the US are cooperatives, officially owned by customers who deposit money in them or borrow from them. They're called credit unions. The credit unions take the deposited money and lend it to their members. The 2008 financial crisis provided a context to see how the cooperatives might behave differently from standard profit-oriented banks. As a whole, the credit unions did not engage in the abusive practices, fraud, or discrimination that pervaded many of the private, for-profit banks, even those with seemingly good reputations like Wells Fargo and Goldman Sachs.[21] As a consequence, the credit unions fared far better in the financial crisis and treated their customers far better after the crisis. They continued to lend, for instance, to small businesses even as the bigger banks drastically curtailed lending.[22]

The "shaving the truth" or outright lying to make an extra buck that has sometimes characterized the financial sector has become endemic in our society. It is at the center of the campaigns of mis- and disinformation that have played such a central role in our economy, and which I discuss in the next chapter. This morphing of dishonesty from one arena to another is to be expected.

Behavioral economists have also documented how monetization affects behavior. Think of the Israeli day-care center that charged for late pickups to no avail. But instance after instance of this kind of monetization begins to shape how a person lives and has shaped how we as a society think of societal problems.

It follows, then, that when students perform poorly in school, a well-trained neoliberal economist has an easy solution: Incentivize teachers to work harder by rewarding them with better pay when their students perform better. But that hasn't worked, which isn't surprising.[23] The extra pay may have simply reminded teachers of their already low pay. Many chose teaching because they were socially motivated and dedicated to working with children in poor communities. The miserly pay incentive converts this social relationship into a monetary one, possibly even discouraging work. More effective interventions might be to treat teachers with respect, recognizing them as professionals deserving of dignity, and to enhance their rights to act collectively through unions. As professionals, they have used those rights to demand better teaching conditions and better facilities. It's not a surprise that some of the states in the US with the highest teacher unionization are also home to some of the best-performing education systems.[24]

The importance of trust and honesty
for a well-functioning market

A market economy relies heavily on trust—that the product is as the seller claims, that the worker will work as he claims, that the working conditions in the firm are as advertised, that the borrower will repay the loan, that the company's management won't steal its funds.[25]

There are infinite ways one person could advantage himself at the expense of others. We have laws and regulations to prevent abuses of trust, but the reality is that if we had to go to court to get our due in every instance, society would be paralyzed. Fortunately, most individuals are inculcated to behave well, and to be basically honest, trustworthy, and hardworking.[26]

Will capitalism devour itself?

The question—and concern—is whether unfettered capitalism shapes individuals in ways that actually undermine the functioning of capitalism. Is capitalism as we know it viable in the long run? As hard as parents and schools are working to create honest, caring, and intellectually curious citizens, are there counterforces working within our capitalist system that undermine these efforts, shaping individuals in ways that jam up the functioning of the capitalist system itself?

Capitalism encourages selfishness and materialism; ruthless selfishness often leads to dishonesty; dishonesty undermines trust; and a failure of trust undermines the functioning of the economic system. We saw how it worked in the 2008 financial crisis. The sector imploded and would have brought down the whole economy if the government hadn't massively intervened, using methods at odds with unfettered capitalism.

It is not just that the economic system is not efficient in the way its advocates claim; it is neither sustainable nor stable. Again, the financial system illustrates that in the absence of strong government regulation (stronger probably than we currently have), privately profitable banks lead to an unstable financial system because their lending practices tend to be excessively risky and sometimes even fraudulent.[27]

Globally unrestrained materialism results in a world economy that is not living within the planetary resource boundaries, and yet we are not able to achieve the social and political cohesion that will restrain materialism sufficiently to put us back within those boundaries.

It gets worse. The current unstable neoliberal capitalist system naturally leads to excesses of inequality and pervasive exploitation. The latter undermines the moral legitimacy of our system, and the former leads to political divides and instabilities, which, in turn, undermine the system's economic performance.

There is still one more aspect of capitalism intimately related to the theme of this book: Capitalism and the way it shapes people may, it can be argued, deprive them of much of their freedom to act. What happens under capitalism is akin to what happens in some traditional societies, where everyone knows the role in society that they should and must play. If they deviate from that role, the social sanctions are enormous, so great that deviations rarely occur. Of course, within their well-defined role, there is some freedom. A woman might choose the menu for dinner, but she has no choice about whether to cook that dinner.

Similarly, under capitalism even the wealthy capitalist may have less freedom than is sometimes imagined. If she chose not to act like a capitalist, she would lose her identity and her sense of who she was. To survive in our system of Darwinian capitalism she must be ruthless, feeling she has no choice but to pay her workers the minimum she can get away with. Greater magnanimity would deprive her of the profits she needs to survive and expand. She may draw comfort by telling herself that without her, her employees would be even worse off because they wouldn't have jobs, and that they would not have accepted the work if they had received a better offer. Needless to say, there are systemic consequences to all capitalists acting that way. Wages are low all around, and so these capitalists are in a sense correct, that they have no choice but to pay wages below a level that is livable.

Of course, in reality, our wealthy capitalist has freedom—far more freedom to act than her poor workers do. She could take less money home and give more to her workers, leaving the same amount available for expansion. But to live in a smaller house in a less wealthy neighborhood would undermine her identity as a successful capitalist and might even undermine her credibility with other capitalists and, thus, her business success. She perceives herself, in this sense, as having limited choices, and in some sense, she is correct.[28]

Concluding Remarks

This chapter has centered around the *implicit* shaping of individuals that is an inevitable part of being a member of society, where views are shaped by our history and surroundings. The next chapter considers more explicit attempts to shape individuals, most notably through the media. I will also highlight that technological innovations—the development of AI and the platforms themselves—are undermining the very basis of the efficiency of the market economy, a system that conveys information about scarcity through prices, and in which all individuals face the same prices.

If this analysis has even a grain of truth it suggests even more strongly that capitalism, at least the neoliberal variety that has dominated over the past half century, is not a sustainable economic and political institution. There will be change. But whether the natural evolutionary process will be better or worse is an open question.

A key lesson of this chapter is that as we think about the design of economic and other institutional arrangements, we must carefully consider how they affect us as individuals and how we act with each other. We humans are malleable. Neoliberal capitalism has shaped us in ways that, in our better moments, we may not think well of. But we can be shaped into "better" individuals, too. And that will require a different kind of economic system.

CHAPTER 9

The Concerted Shaping of Individuals and Their Beliefs

The previous chapter explained how we are shaped by our society, often unconsciously and often without our being actively aware. We are shaped more overtly, too, by the private sector in its attempt to make money from us. In this chapter, I explore how these efforts to shape us can reduce our freedom in a meaningful sense, and more broadly, are often antithetical to creating a good society.

The discussion here touches on both economic and political freedoms. Who has the right, for instance, to control the dominant ways that information (using that term in its broadest sense, including mis- and disinformation) is distributed?

The Big Tech companies and social media platforms have presented democracies around the world with a challenge not yet fully resolved. Under current arrangements, these platforms have enormous power to set the metanarrative, our general understanding of how society and the economy function. In the narrative promoted by Fox News and other platforms and outlets on the Right, there should be no, or at least very limited, regulations, restrictions, or accountability.[1] And in the absence of these checks, their market power and their power to set the metanarrative only grows. Their business model and lack of accountability lead to a rash of societal harms and undermine the over-all efficiency of the market economy. A new freedom to exploit has been unleashed; this has reduced the freedoms of the rest of society.

America's devotion to the principle of free speech is embodied in the First Amendment to the Constitution, one of the country's core freedoms. But every government—including the United States', which typically takes the most extreme position on these issues—circumscribes freedom of speech. You cannot cry "fire!" in a crowded theater. You cannot disseminate child pornography. More narrowly, we have truth-in-advertising laws. Freedom of speech, like the other freedoms I have discussed in this book, is not absolute. It is a social construction with specified boundaries to enhance the well-being of society, and some of the thorniest problems are associated with draw-ing these boundaries. It is not, however, just a matter of what one can say and when one can say it. The advent of social media created a new issue not contemplated by the Founding Fathers—the question of virality. Governments can and have imposed conditions affecting the pace with which information (or disinformation) spreads. And there is no constitutional guarantee in any country, as far as I know, on restrictions on virality.

As the world evolves it may be necessary and desirable to change the rules concerning acceptable, or protected, speech and virality. This, I would suggest, is the case today. Current technologies, combined with a new understanding of how individuals and societies are shaped, have given rise to a dangerous prevalence of mis- and disinformation. The old rules are out of date. The balance of social benefits and social harms under past rules is now too often weighted to the harms.

This chapter begins by explaining what is wrong with the idea fashionable on the Right that a free marketplace of ideas is all that is needed to ensure a healthy democracy. I then examine the media's market power, especially social media's, and explain why the societal harms associated with this market power are far greater than with conventional goods and services. One reason is that democracy is being undermined. Along the way, we will look at how the big social media platforms can be regulated, both to curb their market power and to reduce the scope of their social harms.

Free Marketplace of Ideas

There is a popular idea that in a free marketplace of ideas, only the best win out. Accordingly, there are some people who say that just as in competitive markets in which the best, most efficient producers survive, in the marketplace of ideas only the best ideas survive. Simply release ideas into the world, they say, and the best, the most in line with the evidence and the most theoretically coherent, will dominate. Let a hundred flowers bloom, and the most beautiful flower will be chosen.[2]

This contention is built on misguided metaphors and misunderstood analytics. The metaphor is that the marketplace for ideas (beliefs, views about the world) is analogous to the marketplace for steel, chairs, food, and so forth. Adherents of this view also believe that the marketplace for chairs and other goods is efficient—a view I've dispelled. It is, to say the least, peculiar to appeal to the efficiency of markets to defend the efficiency of the marketplace of ideas when economics has already taught us that the private marketplace for goods is *always* inefficient.

This belief in the efficiency of the marketplace of ideas—ensuring that the best ideas prevail—assumes fully rational and well-informed individuals can distinguish between good (sound) ideas and hokum, just as they can distinguish between good and bad products in the marketplace of goods. "Caveat emptor" puts the burden on the consumer, and that opens up a wide avenue for exploitation through mis- and disinformation and taking advantage of individuals' vulnerabilities. In the case of goods, consumers want products that do as advertised. By contrast, in the case of beliefs, individuals may want to believe something false because it reinforces their own sense of self-worth or identity, at least temporarily. Or they may simply be misled.

Even if it were the case that the marketplace for goods was efficient, there are fundamental differences between goods and information and knowledge, differences that have been the basis of the development of the economics of information over the past century.[3] One of the key insights of that literature is that in the presence of imperfect information, markets are *especially* not likely to be efficient—even a little bit of information imperfection makes a very big difference. And, of necessity, the marketplace of ideas is one in which, a priori, there cannot be perfect information. If everyone knew everything there would be nothing to put out into the marketplace of ideas. Moreover, as I noted earlier, the firms that win out may not be the most efficient or the most popular, just better at exploiting their information advantage. The opportunity to exploit seems particularly vast in the marketplace of ideas.

The analogy to the *competitive* marketplace of goods is flawed in several other ways.

Transparency and disclosure laws: How freedom to deceive deprives others of their freedoms

The first principle of a competitive, free market is transparency.[4] For instance, firms that issue public securities are required to ensure equal access to information through the Securities and Exchange Commission's (SEC's) fair disclosure requirement and other disclosure requirements.[5] US regulations typically require firms to truthfully disclose all materially relevant information about the securities they are issuing. This goes beyond requiring "the truth, nothing but the truth, but not necessarily the *whole* truth." Implicitly, the regulators take the view that knowing that there is a serious downside risk to an investment and not disclosing it is effectively a lie. Their perspective rejects caveat emptor, which essentially puts all the burden of information on the buyer. If the seller knows something that he reasonably should know would be relevant for the buyer, he must disclose.

Banks, for instance, sometimes disclose information, but in ways that are misleading or unhelpful and not fully understood by many borrowers. Lenders have had a long history of presenting interest rates in ways that obfuscate what is really being charged to exploit vulnerable people. Laws today require lenders to disclose their true effective interest rate.[6]

There are several justifications for disclosure requirements and for why such requirements have been tightened again and again. Economic theory has explained why good information (transparency) is necessary for markets to work well—to deliver the socially efficient outcomes that its advocates claim. And it has also explained why firms may not voluntarily disclose critical information. The examples already given show that firms often try to obfuscate the truth, especially when there is a disparity between what the firm claims for its product and the reality. German automaker Volkswagen obviously didn't want to disclose what it had done to get a better fuel efficiency rating than it warranted, which ultimately resulted in the infamous Dieselgate scandal.[7] Firms have increasingly learned how to exploit individuals' irrationalities and vulnerabilities. It is even easier if firms are free to lie. They have learned how to deceive consumers better, to induce them to buy their goods and services, often at inflated prices, when the buyers wouldn't have if they had had all the information. Smart firms without scruples have used insights from modern psychology and behavioral economics that have exposed systematic irrationalities leading to what can best be described as "subpar" choices regarding health, borrowing, saving, and investing.[8] Providing standardized disclosure statements enables better and less-costly assessments of the relative merits of different products or investment opportunities.

Moreover, providing only partial information imposes costs on other market participants. In a real sense these firms are polluters—in this case, of the information ecosystem. Pollution of our information environment, like other forms of pollution, imposes costs on society that the polluter does not take into account. We expend time, effort, and sometimes money to undo the effects, to weed out the truth from the mis- and disinformation; and those providing truthful information have a harder time getting that across.[9] The fact that filtering out falsehoods is costly implies that the filtering occurs only to a limited extent; the market on its own won't take care of the problem. This failure is obvious. Just look at how flooded we are with inaccurate or false information. This is, then, a public "bad" because everyone is harmed by it. But detecting and discrediting misleading information is a public "good." It may not pay anyone *individually* to stop the production and dissemination of the lies and untruths, or to work to undermine them. Without public action, there will be an undersupply of efforts to counter misleading and false information.[10]

There is a strong argument for laws to regulate mis- and disinformation and fraud because they give rise to a loss of freedom as real as the harms associated with the other externalities I have talked about. This would include regulations to require firms to disclose relevant information, even if such laws might be viewed as an infringement on free speech interpreted in an absolutist way.

Freedom to contract, freedom to exploit, and the centrality of "truth" institutions

But if there are laws and regulations against mis- and disinformation, there have to be ways to ascertain what is true, at least with a high degree of reliability. There is no way around it. A functioning society *must* have socially agreed-on ways to assess the truth. People can't have different views of the truth in certain key areas, for instance, having to do with contracts, property, criminal behavior, and public health.[11]

I discussed in chapter 5 the importance of contracts and contract enforcement in the smooth functioning of a market economy—indeed, contract enforcement is one of the few things the Right believes government should do. But contracts would be meaningless if one party could simply assert that it had complied with the terms of the agreement, or that the other party had not. Contract disputes arise frequently, even between reasonably honest parties. There has to be some way to ascertain the truth, to know which of the parties' claims is correct, and this is what our legal system attempts to do.[12]

In the centuries since the Enlightenment, we've developed institutions that do a reasonable job of assessing the truth—independent courts, research and educational institutions, and professional associations. There was widespread consensus behind these institutions until the naysayers in the modern Republican Party and their counterparts around the world arrived on the scene.[13] Unless we restore trust in our truth-ascertaining and verification institutions, it will be hard to have a sustained, well-functioning society or a productive economy.

For the past 200 and some years, we have depended on public, independent courts to establish the truth when there is a legal dispute. It should be obvious that no one wants a dispute resolved by someone with a conflict of interest, whose own well-being depends on how she might rule. That's why we talk about an independent public judiciary. The adjudication of justice is a key public function. But some members of the corporate sector want to circumvent the courts and use *private* arbitration to resolve disputes.

Powerful corporations, for instance, insist that when consumers purchase their products and there is a dispute, they must turn to arbitration instead of a public court of law. Why? Because that's the arena in which businesses have disproportionate influence, so it neatly enhances firms' power to exploit consumers. Guarantees are an important way that firms ensure quality. If the good isn't of the quality claimed, consumers can get their money back. However, buyers typically don't have a lawyer with them to read the fine print and look for a hidden arbitration clause. But as more companies insert these clauses, the value of any firm's guarantee is reduced; consumers can't easily tell whether the guarantee is real. Guarantees then become an ineffective way to ensure quality. The fine print about arbitration represents a kind of pollution of the economic environment.[14]

The corporations claim that it's all part of a basic freedom, the freedom to contract. They say they have the right to insert whatever they want into the contract, and the other party has the right to sign or not to sign. I put it differently: It's all part of their freedom to exploit. A just and good society prohibits the freedom to exploit, and that means it must circumscribe the freedom to contract when companies abuse that "freedom" and exploit their customers, reducing their customers' freedom. This is just another example of a central point of chapter 5, that in every society the freedom to contract is restricted. A good society maintains a balance of freedoms, with a particular concern for how abuses of the freedom to contract may expand the freedom to exploit. But in this case, the contract provision undermines the credibility of society's "truth ascertaining" because transferring the functioning to corporate-driven arbitration leads to biased results that favor corporations.

This is not the only abuse of the "freedom to contract" practiced by the digital giants. Unless proscribed by government, the terms of service may give them unbridled rights to use, and sell, information they glean from our usage of their platform. We think they are providing their services for free, but they know they are the winners because they get *our* information for free. And, of course, if there is a dispute about whether there is a violation of the terms of service, it will go to a corporate arbitrator, not a public court.

Force and intimidation

There is at least one more ingredient necessary to make markets work well: no use of force and intimidation. Regrettably, intimidation and the use of force—unregulated trolling on social media, for example— have become a fact of life.

In "Facebook Does Not Understand the Marketplace of Ideas," which Anya Schiffrin and I wrote for the *Financial Times* in 2020, we concluded our discussion of the idea of a free marketplace of ideas with the following:

> In short, without full transparency, without a mechanism for holding participants to account, without equal ability to trans-mit and receive information, and with unrelenting intimidation, there is no free marketplace of ideas. One of the major insights of modern economics is that private and social incentives are often not well-aligned. If those who want to spread misinformation are willing to pay more than those who want to counter it, and if lack of transparency is more profitable than transparency, then [if we simply say] "so be it," we won't get a well-functioning marketplace of ideas.[15]

The Market Power of Social Media

The enormous profits enjoyed by social media companies are a strong sign of the lack of competition. Normally, such large profits would attract entry, which would lead to the dissipation of the profits. This has not happened.

Similarly, after Elon Musk purchased Twitter and threatened to abandon content moderation, advertisers fled because of the risk of their ads appearing next to an offensive or off-brand tweet. Users complained vociferously and discussed moving to another platform. But as this book goes to press, Twitter (renamed X), with all its flaws and faults, remains a dominant medium by which government and corporate officials and those in the public sphere communicate. And even Meta's well-funded attempt to replace Twitter with its Threads app has had only limited success, despite massive discontent with Twitter.

A central reason is simple: network externalities and a winner-take-all framework. The value of being on a platform like Facebook depends on others being on the platform. Initially, everyone may gravitate to the best platform, so only it survives. Even if, over time, it becomes relatively inefficient (in comparison to an innovator bringing new technology, for example) and doesn't serve users' interests, let alone society's, as well as an alternative might, it still can continue to dominate.

But there is another element to the growth of social media companies' enormous market power and profits. Their business model is based on gleaning, using, and hoarding the information garnered from interactions on their platforms. The platforms have monetized the value of user data. The efficient use of the vast quantity of information they have has allowed them to target messages (in particular, ads) in ways that engender more engagement, which generates still more information. With attention and time scarce commodities, "better" targeting could mean users receive messages that are more relevant, thereby leading to purchases that result in people enjoying a higher level of well-being. Unfortunately, that is not the objective of better targeting. The objective is higher profits, which are derived from advertising revenues, which, in turn, are derived from inducing more profitable purchases from the advertisers. Increased profits from sales can result from more effective price discrimination—from targeted pricing, in which different prices are assigned to different consumers. This allows the capture of more of individuals' consumer surplus, what they would have been willing to pay for the product in excess of what they actually have to pay. Profits can also arise from increased sales, including to people whose weaknesses the platforms exploit, such as gambling addicts. Higher profits for the advertisers are reflected in higher advertising revenues for the digital giants, making them still more profitable.

Platforms boost profits and increase their competitive advantage over rivals even more by hoarding information, enabling them to target consumers better than their rivals can. Digital giants like Google and Amazon have more information than others and can use that information advantage to gain a competitive edge either in direct sales or advertising. Hoarding the information, while privately profitable, is doubly inefficient. To the extent the information has social value, hoarding prevents its full use by anyone other than the platform gleaning it. But it also endows the platform with market power. With data a significant and largely unpriced resource, especially important in artificial intelligence, there is a vicious circle. Larger platforms sweep in more data, which gives them a competitive advantage over rivals, but one that does not necessarily reflect an ability or willingness to better serve others.[16] Their market power is then enhanced, as I've just described.

The special harms of imperfect competition in platforms: Undermining competition throughout the economy

There are tensions, of course, between the efficient use of information, the anticompetitive hoarding of information, and privacy concerns. One of the reasons that people are concerned with privacy is that the disclosure of information can allow exploitation, as I've noted. In the standard competitive market, there is no value to information about a particular person's consumer preferences.[17] But in the real world, with market power, it can be enormously valuable to a firm and significantly increase its profits.

While it is difficult to ascertain the extent, if any, of improvement in resource allocation resulting from the platforms' exploitation of the information they glean from users, one analytic result is clear: The use of this information to engage in price discrimination—charging different prices to different customers—undermines the standard argument for the efficiency of competitive markets that is premised on every household and firm being charged the same prices.[18] Such price discrimination is little more than a transfer of resources from ordinary consumers to rich companies, simultaneously decreasing efficiency and increasing inequality.

While the platforms have provided valuable services in the form of search engines and email, their business model is based on exploitation and advertising, not on increasing efficiency in the provision or production of goods and services nor on producing goods and services that better meet users' needs. The platforms are even willing to sacrifice the quality of the search function if it means enhancing their profits—exemplified by Google putting paid advertising at the top of the search results page.

There is something fundamentally strange about an economy in which the business model of the alleged engines of innovation is based on advertising and not on producing goods and services. And it's a dead end, because there is a limit to the amount of "rent extraction"—getting a larger share of consumer spending—that can be achieved through a better and more exploitive system of advertising. Of course, the larger the share of the consumer spending they extract, the smaller the share that goes into the actual cost of production of the goods and services that individuals need and desire.

The business model is directed less at enhancing well-being than at enhancing corporate exploitation. That cannot be the basis of a good economy or a good society.[19]

Why Market Power in Media Matters:
An Array of Social Harms

The market power described above has the usual effects of market power—higher prices and larger profits—distorting the economy and transferring resources from ordinary people to firm owners, which contributes to the growth of inequality. But market power in these sectors has several other important and adverse effects related to the fact that the private returns can be markedly different from social returns.

In this context, market power means a lack of equal and fair access to the channels by which information is transmitted to our society. Political interests with enough money can flood social media, using bots or other means. That's not a free market, and very different from how social media was initially championed as democratizing the information space. Corporations use their money to shape what citizens see and hear—and what they see and hear shapes society.

Market power also means the platforms control the algorithms, the rules that determine what gets amplified and what is targeted to whom. Mark Zuckerberg and Elon Musk have made no bones about the fact that they make the rules; they determine whether and when blatantly false statements are widely disseminated. In the middle of the Covid-19 pandemic, social media platforms were shamed into not transmitting false information about vaccines even if they could make money at it. They demonstrated that they have the power to not transmit false information. But in other arenas they have shown no such restraint. Zuckerberg and Musk decided, for instance, to disseminate false statements by politicians.

In our world of social media, with its multiple social harms and multiple aspects of what many might label noncoercive reductions in freedom (like cyberbullying), we again confront the dilemma that one person's freedom is another's unfreedom.

Social media platforms have been able to take advantage both of advances in AI, which enables better targeting of different information to different users, and of new understanding about human behavior and information processing. They have developed the ability to create separate online communities that reinforce disparate beliefs, fragmenting the information structure beyond anything that had been possible before and in ways that have increased polarization.

Online platforms have not only exacerbated societal fragmentation; they have also increased the problem of the rapid, viral spread of mis- and disinformation. Virality means that information can spread quickly, more quickly than "antidotes" to the misinformation can be designed. The lack of transparency in who gets what messages has meant that the antidotes cannot be effectively developed and delivered in the relevant time span, if at all.

Social media companies have enabled the incitement of violence and the spread of hate speech and induced antisocial behavior. Their claim that they are neutral is obviously false. Their algorithms make decisions about which messages to promote to whom, and, as I've noted, they do so in ways that enhance profits and further polarization.[20] There might be alternative algorithms that lead to less polarization or enhanced social harmony, but what is privately profitable does not coincide with what is socially desirable.

Explaining the success of mis- and disinformation

The success of mis- and disinformation and the persistence of wildly divergent views in many key areas seem hard to reconcile with any model of individual rationality. In the standard economists' model, nonscientific (for example, anti-vaccine) information would simply have no impact. The evidence is that in the real world, it does.

The magnitude of the divergences in beliefs even about scientific matters is partially explained by behavioral economics, which emphasizes the limited rationality of individuals.[21] Behavioral economics has, for instance, emphasized the importance of confirmation bias—the predilection to look for and give more weight to information consistent with our prior beliefs, and discount information inconsistent with those beliefs. The consequence is that if we start out polarized, we end up more polarized.

Twenty-first-century behavioral economics has, in addition, emphasized the formation of beliefs, as discussed in the last chapter. Of course, marketers have long sought to understand how to influence individuals' beliefs. Most advertising is not about providing information but about preying on people's aspirations and vulnerabilities. The Marlboro Man is emblematic. The hugely successful ad campaign, which ran for decades starting in the 1950s, did not say in so many words that smoking Marlboros would make you a rugged cowboy, information that, in any case, would be irrelevant for the majority of smokers living in urban areas. Instead, tobacco giant Philip Morris opted to create an image: Men who smoke Marlboro cigarettes are *real* men. And it opted to leave out, of course, the information that smoking can kill you.[22] Some ascribe the cigarette's success to that image of the cowboy. An advertiser's job is to induce people to buy a product, and advertisers are very good at what they do. So good, evidently, that companies justify spending hundreds of billions of dollars every year on advertising.

Why polarization is profitable

The platforms have devised a winning strategy—winning for them, but disastrous for the rest of society—based on polarization, or "engagement through enragement." Groups become enraged by different things, so the platforms' business model is to provide each user with whatever information will stoke anger. But splintering the information ecosystem naturally leads to societal polarization. Groups are fed information that reinforces their beliefs or their sense of injustice. Their feeds don't include articles or information that may counter them.

These effects are amplified because beliefs are interdependent. Our beliefs are affected by the beliefs of those with whom we interact. This is especially true if purveyors of information succeed in framing the information in ways that embed it into a cultural context.[23] If Republicans talk disproportionately to Republicans, their particular worldviews are reinforced. The evidence they see and their interpretation of that evidence reinforce their prior beliefs. The same goes for Democrats. And this amplifies polarization still further.[24] That's why a more important determinant of whether a person believes in the reality of climate change is not his educational level (as one might expect) but his party affiliation.[25]

This interdependence of beliefs gives rise to obvious social externalities that the social media companies, in their search for greater profits, pay no attention to—or, more accurately, pay attention to only so they can exploit it for their profits. (Even when these companies recognize the adverse effects of what is being transmitted and how the algorithms exacerbate polarization, they haven't been willing to do much, if anything, about it.)

Changes in technology and policy affect the extent of societal fragmentation. In the era after World War II, when television was a predominant vehicle for providing new information, there were only three major national TV networks in the US, and all aimed to provide broad, unbiased information. News programs were treated as a public service by networks (a practice that was changed, in part, by the program *60 Minutes* on CBS, which showed that news programs can also bring in revenue). Fairness doctrines ensured that major differences in views were given airtime.[26] Viewers across the political spectrum were at least exposed to similar information. While interpretations of the facts might differ, as well as the implications for policy, all viewers or listeners heard the same facts, providing enough commonality to reach compromise.

But the elimination of fairness obligations in 1987 by the US Federal Communications Commission, combined with the advent of cable TV and then the internet, meant that people of different beliefs tended to consume news that already fit their worldview.[27]

Market Power, Inequality, and the Creation of Society's Metanarratives

The greatest danger the platforms have, however, is the power to create society's metanarratives, the stories and understandings that shape how large portions of our population see the world.

As I have repeatedly noted, we respond to the information we get, and a major source of information in the modern world is the media, including social media. If we constantly watch videos of waves of refugees trying to cross the border—even when this occurs relatively rarely—rational individuals might conclude that immigration is a key issue. And this is exacerbated in a world in which preferences and beliefs are often shaped in ways that are not entirely rational. Rational viewers, for instance, might discount statements they hear on Fox News, knowing that the organization has an agenda and, at the very least, slants the news. But Fox has been caught propagating outright lies that reinforce some viewers' preconceptions. I've discussed the marked disparity between what is good for profits and what is good for society, even when individuals are reasonably rational. But when individuals are far from rational and media can shape beliefs, the disparity is even greater. The evidence is that what people see in the media matters. Viewers watching Fox News have a stilted view of the world.[28]

How people see the world is central to every issue—including freedom. As we observed in chapter 8, if people think it's wrong to litter, then they won't litter, and no coercion is necessary to stop littering. On the other hand, if people come to think they have a right to litter—that it's a basic human right—then we may have to pass laws that some feel are coercive to protect our environment.

The media has enormous power over creating the lenses through which the populace sees the world. It shapes beliefs about whether the government is the solution or the problem, whether material incentives matter, and whether raising taxes on corporations will destroy investment and lead to massive job losses.[29]

Fox actively promoted Donald Trump's false charges that the 2020 election was stolen, achieving remarkable success convincing a significant segment of the population, despite the enormous amount of evidence to the contrary. (In this case, Fox was held partially accountable in the $787 million settlement with Dominion Voting Systems.) By unwittingly becoming prey to how traditional media and social media are shaping us, we lose important elements of our freedom.[30]

Beliefs about collective action

If it were just individuals' privately held beliefs that were at stake, with no relevance to any action, this might not matter much. If people differed only in their judgments about whether red or green lettuce was healthier, it wouldn't be significant. The red lettuce proponents could eat more red lettuce. But there are a host of important decisions that we make collectively—what we as a society, especially through government, do together. A metanarrative, a lens, that sees governments as always inefficient, the private sector as always efficient, taxes as always harmful, and public spending as always wasteful, will lead to a small government and an underinvestment in public goods. It will lead to an underregulated, poorly performing economy, and almost surely a more divided society. But we've effectively been given this lens by some parts of the media.

Differences in worldviews are also associated with major differences in what decisions to take collectively. Extreme polarization in opinions about what the government should do, about what should be limited or permitted, has contributed to political dysfunction.

The lens through which we see the world defines the "moral legitimacy" of what all of us do, including what the government does about inequality.[31] In chapter 6, I explained that there was, in fact, little moral legitimacy to the incomes of large portions of the wealthiest citizens. They, of course, have always wanted everyone to accept the moral legitimacy of their wealth, because that would undermine the right of the state to take it away, whether for the purpose of redistributing it to the poor or providing for public goods. The owners of that wealth want us to believe that there is an inevitability, and perhaps even necessity, in their own wealth versus other people's poverty and deprivation. Before the Reformation and Enlightenment, it was a matter of "God's will," interpreted, of course, through the eyes of those whom God appeared to favor. In the era of capitalism, it was the "just deserts" for the wealthy's efforts and frugality—with neoliberalism throwing in the idea of trickle-down economics, so that all would benefit from the largesse to the top.[32]

But this begs the question: How did the wealthy get the rest of society to accept such ideas? A full answer would take us beyond the scope of this book, but part of the answer today is the central premise of this section: that at least some among the elites have a disproportionate hand in shaping the societal metanarrative through their control of the media. They've created a lens for viewing society through which our profuse, messy reality is rendered only as they see it. They decide what stories are told and what falsehoods are transmitted from user to user or to millions of users in an instant.[33]

This has been a long-standing complaint. But changes in technology and enhanced understanding of human behavior, combined with lax enforcement of existing competition laws and a slowness to adapt those laws to the rapid changes in technology, have provided a select few with unprecedented power to shape the metanarrative. The fact that the media is so concentrated and that social media can be so effective in targeting individuals with messages that shape their thinking has exacerbated the well-established problem of the power of the rich in the media.[34]

Take Argentina's mega-default on its debt in 2000. The *Financial Times* and much of the financial elite offered a simple story: Argentina was a serial defaulter; somehow, defaulting was in the country's genes. That begged the question that if this was so apparent to everyone in the financial community, why did they lend Argentina so much money?

There was another narrative, one that I think is closer to the mark. The financial sector is short-sighted and greedy. When right-wing president Mauricio Macri took office and promised market-friendly reforms, the financial elite's ideology held that these reforms would turn the country around. When Macri went further and offered them high-interest bonds—well beyond what the country could reasonably afford—they snapped them up without thinking through whether this was a reasonable financial decision. Macri snookered them, and they didn't want to admit it, so better to blame Argentina. Of course, in the end the Argentinians were the ones who paid the highest price for what happened.[35]

But we know which narrative prevailed. The first, that Argentina was a serial defaulter, because the financial elites linked with the creditors by and large controlled the relevant press. It resulted in cognitive capture, the capture of much of the citizenry in the advanced countries, and particularly of the relevant elites.

This, writ large, is what we are confronting. In many countries, control of both traditional and social media is highly concentrated and lies disproportionately in the hands of the very wealthy.[36] As a result, many throughout society come to believe a narrative that conveniently supports an economy that benefits the ultrarich.

When there is not sufficient media diversity, the ability to counter the prevailing narratives is limited. But even with some media diversity, the polarization effects described earlier mean that even if some outlets provide counternarratives and "true" facts, their impacts may be inadequate.

Media moguls have tried to shape our metanarratives on the question of how we should view freedom, including freedom from regulation and taxation. They've been so successful that their framing of the issue became well accepted, especially in the era in which neoliberalism triumphed.

A Growing Consensus on the Need for Regulation

There is now an increasing consensus that we need to regulate social media—perhaps surprising given its influence (and testimony to how badly wrong things have gone); that is, we must reduce the freedom of social media companies in a way that, in effect, increases the well-being of society and the freedom of others. The disparities between private and social costs and benefits are so wide in this arena that they make the differences in other sectors look minuscule—for example, those that arise from the market power of the automakers.

Interestingly, the profit-seeking ethos of a company like Meta is so strong that even where there are regulations concerning privacy, for example, that proscribe certain behaviors, and even when the company has agreed to mend its ways, it has gone ahead and acted as if it were above the law. This has resulted in Meta paying billions of dollars in fines—so imagine what it would do in the absence of regulations or if the market were regulated by the companies themselves.[37]

The losses of freedom imposed by social media companies are all the more grievous because they are often invisible. People are sometimes unknowingly preyed on by companies that understand how to prompt them to act or believe in ways they otherwise wouldn't. They've lost some freedom without even knowing it. It's a bit of a different loss than when our choices are explicitly limited. And it's also somewhat different from social coercion and peer pressure. But it's a loss, nonetheless, even if we do not see it at the moment it's happening.

While the arguments above suggest that social media and digital platforms should be more tightly regulated than traditional media, they are actually less regulated. In the US, the platforms are almost *encouraged* to behave badly. Section 230 of the Communications Decency Act (1996) exempts them from liability for what they transmit across their platforms in a way that standard media is not. Conventional media, for instance, can be sued under libel and fraud laws. Not their social media cousins. A legal provision originally designed to encourage a nascent industry has led to the viral dissemination of mis- and disinformation with no accountability. And even as this has become increasingly clear, it has proven impossible to stop.[38] Again, this should come as no surprise given the political power of the tech giants and the role of money in American politics.

Devising rules and regulations that serve society better is not easy, but it is possible. Even if all the social harms can't be prevented, more can be done to mitigate them. The EU, for instance, has adopted the Digital Services Act (DSA) in an attempt to regulate the social harms of social media. A central question in the design of these regulations is how to prevent harms within democratic frameworks that emphasize freedom of speech. Societies, including the US, have not taken absolutist positions on free speech. As I noted, there are prohibitions in America against fraud ("lying" in commercial contexts where the lie results in harm), false advertising, child pornography, and crying "fire!" in a crowded theater. Some countries ban hate speech. In each of these situations, there is a recognition that one person's freedom is another's unfreedom; that there is a high social cost to the absence of a constraint. Clearly, the greater harms emanating from mis- and disinformation on social media change the balancing entailed in the design of all regulations toward greater intervention.

Speaking and disseminating a thought is different from just thinking something, because it affects other people's behavior—indeed, that is often the intent. Of course, the preservation of the *right* to influence others is a central part of democracy. Governments need to be careful about restrictions because at the center of political repression is the deprivation of freedom of speech and the press. Absolutists effectively impose a lexicographic ordering on rights, with the right to free speech, regardless of its societal consequences, dominating all others. No society has taken such an extreme position because context matters. It is understandable to have bans on hate speech associated with race and ethnicity in countries like Germany, because of the Holocaust, or the US, with its history of slavery, lynching, and massive discrimination. To interpret the spreading of misinformation and disinformation about vaccines as "political speech" is a stretch. If nearly everyone ignored the dishonest statements, they could be tolerated as having, at most, limited societal harms. But in a world in which large numbers of people believe such nonsense, the spread of the information can impose enormous societal harm. Context determines what should be restricted.

There is, in particular, a strong argument for restricting the pace with which information (or disinformation) can spread, for restricting message targeting and for requiring transparency in algorithms. Obviously, no clause in the US Constitution discusses virality because it hadn't yet been created. This is just another illustration of the absurdity of trying to interpret that document in terms of original intent.

Regulating market power in the media and platforms

Regulating the multiple social harms of social media is hard, partly because of free speech and free press concerns. But regulating market power is somewhat easier. The EU has taken a comprehensive approach to regulating the evolving technological landscape, with the Digital Markets Act (DMA), adopted in 2022, attempting to limit market power. The DMA complements the EU's other actions on privacy and social harms.[39]

The difference between the EU's stance and the US's can largely be explained by the influence of digital giants in US politics. A central theme of modern economics is the link between economic power and political power. Concentrated economic power leads to concentrated political power, which results in policies that enhance concentrated economic power.[40] In this case, societal consequences go far beyond the harms usually associated with market power of the kind the antitrust laws attacked in the early twentieth century, such as oil and cigarettes.

There are some easy steps to take to limit the market power of the digital giants, especially social media, and to limit the increased market power that the information they glean gives to firms. In past decades, public policy recognized how price discrimination undermines efficiency (and equity). The Robinson-Patman Act of 1936 outlawed it, saying that firms couldn't discriminate in the prices they charged. Instead, price differences had to be justified by cost differences. But unfortunately, because of the influence of free-market economists who argued that markets were *naturally* competitive and therefore there was little scope for distortionary price discrimination, US courts have not enforced these provisions in decades. It's time they start, because it's another restriction on the freedom of firms to exploit that would enhance societal welfare.

Notably, the informational advantages enjoyed by large tech firms are qualitatively different from the monopoly or collusive advantages that the key antitrust laws, the Sherman Act and Clayton Act, enforced by the Federal Trade Commission and the Department of Justice, were designed to regulate. It is clear that there is a need for a new generation of antitrust legislation designed specifically for settings in which differential access to information confers an advantage.[41]

The Future of Neoliberal Capitalism

The discussion in this chapter has implications for the future of capitalism in its current form. Earlier in the century, there were concerns about so many of the most talented young people going into finance instead of producing goods and services or knowledge that enhanced societal well-being. After the primacy of the financial sector came tumbling down with the crash of 2008, many of the most talented young people went into tech. That seemed to entail doing something *real*, and the profits that these companies garnered seemed to suggest that it was big.[42] But at this point, we have to wonder about the long-term viability of an economic system in which many of these most talented young people are doing little more than making a better advertising machine.

There are also implications for the future of democracy. We are seeing the results of an insufficiently restrained market economy, leaving the media, including social media, open to the highest bidder. This creates societal polarization, where there is not even common ground on basic realities. A central message of modern economics is that information is a public good. We have long recognized the importance in a democracy of a well-informed citizenry, but many countries have not seriously taken on board what that entails. It means that government should support an independent and diverse media.

It may not be possible to fully counter the mis- and disinformation provided by a distorted private media with an extreme conservative agenda. Still, a more diverse and independent media can provide some checks. An array of countries, most notably the Nordics, have shown that democracies can create such diversity and independence in the media.

Ideas are always contested, so the game is not over. But we're not headed in a good direction, and we need to do something about it. There has long been a fear of an Orwellian world in which government shapes us to the point that we lose our human agency—in a deep sense, our freedom. We are now entering quite a different dystopia, in which certain private-sector firms have an almost Orwellian power to shape us, including the power to convince others to allow them to continue unchecked. But there is still time to put an end to this. We have the means to ensure that these powerful innovations serve society; we just need the collective will.

CHAPTER 10

Tolerance, Social Solidarity, and Freedom

In the examples so far, norms are related to individual actions that have externalities on others; they are ways by which society internalizes externalities and thereby increases social welfare. But in many societies, norms go well beyond that in an attempt to influence actions and even beliefs that have no direct impact on the well-being of others.[1]

Enlightenment values, themselves social norms shared by many and to which I subscribe, say that one should not allow others' beliefs to affect one's well-being and that, whether they do or not, others should be free to choose whatever beliefs they want for themselves. In particular, public policy should certainly not discriminate against people with different beliefs. Similar attitudes extend to actions that affect only those who have voluntarily agreed to the actions or its impacts. Sexual acts between consenting adults are a matter for those involved and only those involved, although consent is a complicated subject.[2]

This kind of tolerance was not only core to the Enlightenment; it was also central for John Stuart Mill and others who wrote about liberty in the nineteenth century. While these writers gave short shrift to the externalities that I have argued are central in a modern economy, they elaborated on the idea of tolerance at great length.

The absence of tolerance was manifest in the centuries before the Enlightenment when Europe was ravaged by wars, in part motivated by religious conflicts (though many think that deeper economic issues lay underneath). Intolerance to different religious beliefs led countries to expel certain groups and force conversions, sometimes to the detriment of their economic well-being. Some of the early immigrant groups that arrived in the US had fled intolerance or persecution in their home countries. This kind of liberty underpinned the notion of freedom for some of the Founders of the American republic. Some of the early colonists had seen the tendency when there was a state religion for the state to oppress citizens of other faiths. It was this history that informed demands for freedom of religion and the separation of church and state.

In the US, these seemed well-settled issues with a broad societal consensus. But today, around the world, including the US, some of the most heated controversies center on them. Growing up, I took the separation of church and state—with its concomitant prohibition on state support for religious education—as a pillar of America, part of the established institutional structure that ensured freedom of religion.[3] I never thought I would see the day when this would be questioned, as it has been by a series of court decisions. At the same time, I took freedom of speech to be another pillar, though of course I understood that there were reasonable exceptions. In the end, I'll argue that the Enlightenment perspective is still correct, that actions, not thoughts or beliefs, should be the subject of public intervention. But I've come to understand that speech itself in certain contexts is a form of action that can have momentous societal consequences.

Two Critical Distinctions

In thinking about tolerance, two critical distinctions are useful. The first is between ideas that can be verified and those that are metaphysical and cannot be verified; and the second is between thought and action.

Religion versus science

Today's divisions are quite different from those that prevailed 250 years ago. While a few might be rooted in religious convictions (for example, about when life begins), many are about the functioning of the economic and social system and, implicitly, about trade-offs on rights. Religious differences are metaphysical and not subject to verification; they are matters of faith that will never be resolved by evidence. This is not the case in science. Galileo may have been sentenced to life imprisonment (which he served under house arrest) because of his beliefs about the solar system, but his views had scientific validity—which we now recognize—unlike the Earth-centric views of those who condemned him. As uncomfortable as the scientific evidence about evolution or climate change may be for some, the evidence is overwhelming. One can believe what one will, but that won't change the nature of the universe. There are still people who belong to the flat-Earth society even as we've seen beautiful pictures of a spherical planet Earth taken from outer space. We can tolerate their beliefs so long as they don't lead to actions that cause harm to others.

Likewise with our economic and social system. We can ascertain with some confidence the consequences of balancing the budget or some other public policies. And it should be self-evident that it is absurd for Congress to pass legislation specifying taxes and expenditures and then pass separate legislation limiting the deficits and debt that arise from the differences between expenditures and taxes. The deficit is simply the difference between the expenditures it has authorized and the taxes it imposes. If it specifies expenditures of $6.1 trillion and taxes of $4.4 trillion, the deficit will be $1.7 trillion. It's simple arithmetic. Passing a law that the deficit should be not greater than $1 trillion can't change that arithmetic; it only poses the question: Which of the three numbers (expenditures, taxes, deficit) should be ignored? Likewise, the debt is nothing more than the result of adding up deficits. If last year's debt was $21 trillion, this year's deficit is $1.7 trillion, and next year's debt will be $22.7 trillion, again a matter of arithmetic. Passing a law that the debt shouldn't exceed $22 trillion can't change the arithmetic; it only poses the question: Which of the three numbers (today's expenditure, today's taxes, or the debt ceiling) will have to be ignored or changed? (It is akin to the US state legislature that considered passing a law in 1897 that pi—the ratio of the circumference of a circle to its radius—should be, variously, 3.2, 3.24, 3.236, or 3.232, rather than 3.1416. Simply writing a law stating something doesn't change the reality of the world.)[4]

Advances in economic science have enhanced our understanding, though to be sure there remain significant controversies. We can reason through the consequences of different rules and assignments of rights even if we may not agree on how the trade-offs that emerge can be evaluated. It should be clear that the right to carry a gun results in more innocent people dying. The right to live has been taken away from the victims. The Right seemingly asserts that those rights are less important than the right to bear arms and the pleasure the objects give to gun owners.

Thoughts versus actions

An even more fundamental distinction in understanding Enlightenment notions of tolerance relates to the difference between thought and action. Thoughts that are not acted on have no direct effect on others and therefore should not be circumscribed. Akeel Bilgrami has suggested that one of Christianity's greatest tyrannies was to go beyond saying, "Thou shall not commit adultery," to saying (in the Book of Matthew), "You have heard that it was said, 'Do not commit adultery.' But I tell you that anyone who looks at a woman to lust after her has already committed adultery with her in his heart." Even earlier, the Ten Commandments enjoined coveting thy neighbor's house, or wife, or male or female servant, ox or donkey, or anything else that belonged to "thy" neighbor (see Exodus 20:17). Coveting concerns one's inner thoughts.[5]

We obviously don't act on every thought—human agency is about our ability to decide what we do—and Enlightenment values provide freedom of thought, but not freedom of action when those actions adversely affect the freedoms of others.[6]

The Limits of Tolerance

Tolerance gets stretched in today's world when misguided beliefs—verifiably false based on the best science—get translated into action. I can tolerate people believing all kinds of foolishness; if it makes them feel better, so be it. But how are we to think about actions based on those beliefs that objectively affect *us* adversely? That, of course, is the standard case of an externality. The fact that people behave in a certain way because of mistaken beliefs doesn't in any way change the harm done, though it may influence the way we think about the trade-offs. We may (I believe we should) give less weight to their loss of freedom to inflict the harm if the reason for their action is a belief that contradicts scientific evidence.

Consider those who thought that drinking bleach would cure Covid-19. Even the president of the United States promoted false remedies. One could take a laissez-faire attitude—whoever drinks bleach bears the consequences of acting on those beliefs. But she is not alone in bearing the consequences. If, as a result, she is hospitalized, much of the medical costs will be borne by society. There are financial externalities that result from those misguided beliefs turned into action. There are also externalities on her family and friends, who suffer with her suffering out of empathy. And swallowing bleach rather than taking an effective drug means the disease lingers, which increases the likelihood that someone else gets it. Another externality. To be sure, there is an element of paternalism in preventing someone from drinking bleach to cure herself, but there are other arenas in which we show such paternalism, for instance, seatbelt and helmet laws and drug restrictions.[7] (Again, a full justification of this paternalism or analysis of its consequences is beyond the scope of this book, but it is clearly related to the bounds of liberty that we're focusing on.)[8] But so long as there are externalities, there is a social justification in preventing her from ingesting bleach.

There are still other limits to tolerance: To what extent should we tolerate the intolerant? Again, addressing this question would take us beyond the confines of this short book.

Tolerance and collective action

But there is one issue I want to say a few words about. I've emphasized that tolerance about beliefs is one thing; tolerance about beliefs that lead to actions that impose harms on others is something else. I've also explained the importance of collective action in a twenty-first-century society. Views about what actions society should take are, of course, affected by beliefs. If a person believes nonsensical things, he may vote for nonsensical actions and support political leaders who advance nonsensical ideas. This is a context in which externalities do arise from beliefs.

The ideological divides that mark society today unfortunately involve beliefs on one side that run counter to modern science. There is overwhelming evidence that, for example, climate change is real, that it is related to the increase in greenhouse gases in the atmosphere, and that it foments extreme weather events that impose enormous costs. If we believe in science, we have to believe that not all views on this should be given equal weight. We can't just declare, "Who's to say?" Science, in that sense, is fundamentally undemocratic, and that's part of its problem in today's world. In encounters with climate deniers, I often hear the refrain, "I think for myself." Many who say this resent the elitism of science, the seeming authoritarianism that says some views are right and others wrong, though to be sure the evidence is not always as clear as it is with the climate.[9]

In the last chapter, I talked about the need to restrict digital platforms from disseminating or facilitating the dissemination of mis- and disinformation when it gives rise to social harms. And they give rise to social harms when there are important collective decisions to be made that are affected by these verifiably false beliefs, often based on verifiably false information. When individuals believe wrong information—when there is a demonstrable inability of many to identify lies and false information—there may have to be restrictions on its dissemination. We did that during the pandemic; it would have been foolish—socially harmful—if we had not. We should have complete tolerance for what people themselves believe; but that tolerance should be limited when beliefs are converted into actions. Speech intended to influence others is, I've said, clearly an "action."

Though Americans champion free speech—it's the First Amendment, after all—there are still multiple restrictions. We constantly redefine those boundaries as the world changes. And as we become aware of new social harms and new ways of creating social harms, we need to reexamine the balance of the costs and benefits of restrictions, and on that basis impose new restrictions. Countries have done this balancing differently. In the US, almost anything can be said against a political leader, but in Singapore and many other countries, a statement considered slanderous may get you put in jail. In the UK, publishing a true statement that defames an individual may have serious consequences. Truth is no defense. In the US, truth may be a defense. Most countries have laws against fraud—one can't just say, "I have the right to say what I please." In the US and many other countries, there are laws governing truth in advertising. And incitement to riot, which usually means just speech, is a crime in most countries. Sometimes there is "forced speech," that is, firms are required to make certain disclosures. They can't just declare, "I have the right not to disclose that the product I sell causes cancer and other health problems." Conspiracies to commit a crime (such as overturning an election) are illegal, even if they fail; but typically, at the center of such conspiracies are discussions—speech.

It is clear, then, that all societies, even those committed to free speech, put restrictions on that freedom when it imposes harms. As I wrote earlier, there are a wide range of social harms arising from mis- and disinformation, and so it is understandable that governments would want to restrict their dissemination. But that requires institutional frameworks that can distinguish between dangerous falsity and the truth.

These were, in essence, the questions posed in the last chapter: How do we determine which statements are not truthful? And among those, which are harmful? How do we institutionalize these limits to tolerance? In the context of Covid-19 it was easy to ascertain false statements (drinking chlorine would cure you), and it was easy to ascertain the social harms of such statements. The social media platforms also showed that they had the power to filter out much of the false information. These successes stand at one end of what can be done. The platforms cooperated; there was scientific consensus on what was untrue and what was harmful.

Unfortunately, the platforms have often not been cooperative—indeed, they have generally resisted the idea that they have any responsibility toward policing and have demanded freedom from liability of any resulting harms. Most of their activity in content moderation has come about because of regulation or their user base demanding it. Some have taken the position that if a political figure says something that is false and harmful, it is not only beyond their responsibility to take it down but doing so would be a violation of some basic political set of rights, which include the right of politicians to spew venom and falsities. That would be political censorship, they maintain. So, if the president or a senator were to assert the false claim that microchips were implanted during Covid-19 vaccinations, the platforms would transmit that "information," and algorithms might even promote it, helping the false statements go viral. This, I think, is wrong. It strikes the wrong balance between freedom of speech of the politician and freedom from harms for the rest of society. *At the very least*, the politician's false claims should not be amplified, and attention should be drawn to the falsity of the claim and the harms to which it might give rise. The algorithms act as editorial mechanisms, deciding what gets brought to users' attention. In this case, the algorithms have a responsibility to do no amplification. Let the politician's statement appear on her website for anyone to read, but that's all.

In areas of science—and here I include climate change—there are well-established protocols to determine what is known with a reasonable degree of confidence and what is known not to be true. But that is not the case in many other areas, even in the social sciences. I see no way to limit the dissemination of false and confused ideas in these arenas. We will have to live in a world in which some may believe in dark forces, grand conspiracies, and an array of notions that can't be scientifically proved but that can induce clearly harmful effects.[10] Those of us who believe in science will have to do what we can to create a more informed and more reasoned populace. Knowing that the marketplace of ideas does not work perfectly, there is no assurance that the battlefield of ideas will be any better. The sad truth is that the world may become even more divided than it is today. We may end up with societies committed to science, reasoning, and Enlightenment values, where these perspectives, if not universally accepted, at least provide the basis of a social consensus, and societies that, in one way or another, are trapped in a pre-Enlightenment world. In the latter, science and technology may even continue (as it did, in a limited way, in the Soviet Union), but with compartmentalized societal influence—for instance, in developing better smartphones, electric cars, and rockets. It will be doubly sad if my own country winds up in the second category.

Thinking about tolerance behind the veil of ignorance

The approach to social decision-making that I've been advocating, thinking about matters from the perspective of Adam Smith's impartial spectator or behind John Rawls's veil of ignorance, may be helpful in thinking about the limits of tolerance. If, behind the veil of ignorance, I don't know whether I will be born rich or poor, or become a religious zealot or secular scientist, one question I might ask is how different perspectives on tolerance affect civic harmony. Civil wars are never good for anyone, and situations in which members of families are at each other, while not as deadly, are not pleasant for anyone. With too little tolerance of views that differ from one's own, it is almost inevitable that there will be conflict. But in that same vein, if there is too much tolerance, in particular of those who are intolerant, there will also be conflict. There needs to be social pressure to discourage intolerance. Only in a society where there is a norm of tolerance—particularly when directed at actions that do not directly affect others—can there be sufficient societal harmony for a democratic system to function well. It is clear that in some countries, including in some places within the US, that norm no longer exists.

In thinking about tolerance as *instrumental*, as something necessary for society to function well, I want to emphasize that I am not abandoning the Enlightenment perspective that takes tolerance almost as a fundamental value in itself. But I am suggesting that this approach helps us think through some of the inevitable conundrums that arise when we try to define the limits of tolerance.

Liberté, Égalité, Fraternité

"Liberté, égalité, fraternité" ("Liberty, equality, fraternity") was the rallying cry of the French Revolution. It connected equality and solidarity—social cohesion—closely with freedom and liberty, and rightly so. I have argued that equality, or more precisely, increasing the income of the poor at the expense of the rich, also increases the freedom of the former and decreases the freedom of the latter. I believe this move enhances societal welfare, possibly even the welfare of those at the top, partly because it increases social cohesion. The French revolutionaries realized that social solidarity is a virtue in its own right and is necessary for the well-functioning of society.

There is no solidarity when a few live in luxury while others starve, which was the situation in France that precipitated the revolution. When there is too much inequality in society, it is hard for people in different strata to see the world through the same lens, try as they might. Society will almost inevitably become polarized. I've attributed the polarization in so many countries today, including in the US, partly to the extremes of inequality; and I've argued that policies that lead to more equality will induce greater solidarity and greater freedom as I've defined it for more citizens. Greater solidarity—less polarization—will enable us to see the world more similarly, and this will allow us to reach greater consensus on the difficult issues facing society, including what kinds of statements and actions are untruthful and socially harmful, and in what ways can the dissemination of those statements be restricted consistent with other values.

Many communities in the US and UK have had to face the question of what to do with statues of slaveowners and (in the US) those who fought for the right to maintain slavery. In my Oxford college, All Souls, the beautiful 1751 library built by architect Nicholas Hawksmoor was formerly known as the Codrington Library, after the man who endowed it. Christopher Codrington made his fortune from owning plantations in the West Indies worked by enslaved people. In 2020, it became simply "the Library," as part of "steps to address the problematic nature of the Codrington legacy," as explained on the All Souls College website.[11] But rather than taking down the statue of Codrington, Oxford reached a compromise of displaying the names of those enslaved and retelling the story of the slavery of that era.

As it is, we face a series of troublesome conflicts that further undermine solidarity and polarize society. In the US, the Supreme Court, which might have taken on the role of making wise judicial decisions that represent intelligent compromises—Solomonic decisions—has become simply another instrument of partisan polarization.

Whence Enlightenment Tolerance?

This chapter has explored the many dimensions of Enlightenment tolerance. Whether the evolutionary view that better ideas will dominate is correct or not, whether Enlightenment values *eventually* predominate, is of no matter. As John Maynard Keynes put it, in the long run, we are all dead. The reality is that these values are not shared by a significant fraction of the population. Maintaining them is a constant struggle. As one of my colleagues in the Clinton administration put it, he felt like he had to relitigate the Enlightenment every day.

Deep and universal adoption of the Enlightenment value of tolerance is difficult, for it entails the commitment to a certain mindset, and there seems a natural human proclivity to shun those who do not share our values. Moreover, the monopolized media does not always promote notions of Enlightenment tolerance. It may not serve the interests of the media giants and their owners.

Still, of all the dimensions of freedom that we ought to be working hardest to expand, this is the most important.

Concluding Remarks

In this part of the book I have emphasized that our beliefs and preferences are shaped. A good and just society would not, I believe, give so much power to the wealthy and to large corporations to shape our beliefs and preferences. It is costly and harmful, and the advent of social media has only exacerbated the problems. In the same vein, market power in the media is far more invidious than in other areas of the economy.[12]

Tolerance—the freedom of people to believe whatever they want so long as the beliefs don't lead to actions that harm others—is at the center of Enlightenment views about freedom. And freedom of expression implies the right to communicate those views, no matter how much they go against the grain. But we've seen that matters are not that simple. Science, the pursuit of truth, and the creation of truth-assessing institutions are also core to the Enlightenment. And some decisions have to be made collectively. Should we allow greenhouse gas emissions to go on unfettered? How should we manage a public health crisis like a pandemic? In that case, the transmission of scientifically false information—especially targeted mis- and disinformation that goes viral—can have dangerous and destructive consequences. These are the treacherous shoals that twenty-first-century democracies must navigate, and absolutist positions on freedoms won't help us.

As we think about what a good society is and how to create it, a topic I turn to in Part III, we have to look at how our economic and social system shapes us and who gets the right—the freedom—to shape us and our beliefs.

There is a broad consensus that current economic arrangements are not working—and not balancing freedoms in the appropriate way. In the chapters that follow I try to better understand these failings and to define what kind of national and international system is more likely to produce the good society—or at least get us nearer to that aspiration than today's dysfunctional world.

PART III
WHAT KIND
OF ECONOMY
PROMOTES A GOOD,
JUST, AND FREE
SOCIETY?

The basic question of this book, which drove me to study economics in the first place, is, what kind of economic system is most conducive to a good society?

There is a long history of failed answers. Feudalism was marked by a high concentration of power and wealth, low economic growth, and slow social progress. Communism succeeded in generating greater security and more equality in material goods but failed on other counts, including low economic growth, an absence of freedom in all dimensions, a concentration of power, and a greater inequality in standards of living than Communist rulers would admit.

Neoliberalism, the dominant economic system in the West over the past forty years, is increasingly viewed as an economic failure because it brought slower growth and more inequality than in earlier decades. But I have also suggested that its failures run deeper. It increased societal polarization, created selfish, materialistic, and often dishonest citizens, and contributed to a growing lack of trust. In spite of embedding the concept of freedom in its name (neo*liberalism*), it didn't deliver *meaningful* freedoms to much of the population.

To find a better way forward, with shared prosperity and the broadest set of liberties for the most people, we need to think deeply and ask questions about what a good economy is and its relationship to a good society.

Ducking the hard questions: A pretense at science

For the past century or so economists have tried to avoid these hard questions. The standard theory *assumes* people enter the world fully formed. How we build our society has no influence on the kinds of people we are, they say. And even then, economists focused their analyses on those limited situations in which no one could be made better off without making someone else worse off, which they refer to as the Pareto criterion.

The *positivist* economics agenda, which holds that every assertion must be scientifically verified or capable of logical or mathematic proof,[1] tried to avoid judgments on the nature of preferences and on interpersonal comparisons.[2] Economists shied away from discussions of social justice. They didn't want to talk about who was more deserving, or the moral rights that people might have to keep their own income. They didn't even want to say that it was desirable from a moral or social standpoint to transfer money from an ultrarich man like Jeff Bezos, no matter how he had earned his income, to someone who is destitute, for whom those dollars mean survival itself. An economist might say, I know whether I think transferring that money is desirable, but those are my values; as a technician, I can't impose my values on others. There is no scientific or objective way to evaluate whether a dollar has greater social value to one person or another.

As long as the economy was efficient, producing goods at as low a cost as possible and delivering them to consumers who value them the most, the question was left to philosophers to decide whether an economy in which most of the income went to a few was better than one in which incomes were more equally shared. Income distribution was the responsibility of the political process, not economic technocrats.[3] As noted in chapter 2, scholars like Robert Lucas argued that economists shouldn't even discuss inequality. Obviously, I think Lucas was wrong. A society with a given amount of goods, more equally distributed, is a more just and better society than one in which those goods go to a few. I have presented a coherent way to explain why: from behind Rawls's veil of ignorance, it's the kind of society that most would opt for, but it is also a society in which more people have more freedom and greater opportunities to realize their potential.

The positivist economics agenda could only go so far. The Paretian criterion—accepting government intervention only when no one is made worse off—is simply insufficient for guiding moral judgments and public policy. It is impossible to say much without invoking judgments about whether firms should have the right to exploit or the right to pollute or the right to disseminate mis- or disinformation.

Policy entails facing trade-offs and moral judgments. Some people—even if it's only the exploiters and speculators—are worse off with a regulation that prohibits antisocial behavior.[4] Earlier, I argued in favor of government actions that limited cigarette advertising and the sale of opioids or restricting food that gives rise to childhood diabetes.[5] The broad consensus on the desirability of such interventions only reinforces the conclusion that economists' obsession with Pareto interventions (in which *some* people are made better off but no one is made worse off) is misguided. The technocratic approach of the last three-quarters of a century has led to a dead end.[6]

The arguments in Part II also exposed another limitation of the standard economic approach that assumes fixed preferences given at birth. Preferences can and do change. Who we are is affected by our economic system. Economic analysis can describe policies that might best achieve each possible outcome, but without knowing what we desire it cannot ascertain which of the alternative policies is ultimately preferable.[7, 8]

In a world with endogenous and changing preferences, we must ask the deeper question that economists have been trying to evade.

The economy is supposed to serve society, and a good economy helps create a good society. But what do we mean by a good society? Of course, economists shouldn't be the only ones to answer this question; society as a whole must address it. It should be at the forefront of our democratic discourse and dialogue. While this is not the place for a full articulation of the meaning of the "good society," I would like to comment on a few aspects of it.

It is intuitively clear to me that a society marked by greater equality (other things being equal) is better than one marked by huge disparities; that cooperation and tolerance is fundamentally better than greed, selfishness, and intolerance. The extreme versions of the latter that have appeared on the American scene in recent decades are truly loathsome.

Of course, it is important for economists to make clear when they are going beyond the positivist agenda, limited as it is by the Paretian criterion. As always, they need to state the assumptions underlying their analyses. Economists can be useful, too, in helping us understand why a good society embraces equality and tolerance. For instance, they can show how trust enhances social cooperation, economic performance, and general societal well-being and how equality and tolerance enhance trust.[9] But the arguments for a society based on trust, tolerance, and social justice go beyond instrumental in improving economic performance. Life is so much better and less stressful if we don't have to worry about being cheated by everyone we encounter.

The ideas presented here should be useful in thinking about what else we would like in a good society. For instance, I mentioned the positive freedoms that contribute to people being able to live up to their potential and lead fulfilling lives. A key attribute of a good society is that this is true for a large portion, if not all, of society.

We have to see this in the context of an ever-evolving world, not through the eyes of the nineteenth-century economists who viewed society in a harmonious but static equilibrium in which no one exerts power, either in economics or politics, and there are never any underlying changes. It's a tradition that continues too strongly within the economics profession even today. But it is obvious we do not live in such a world. A good society is structured so that we can learn about these changes and find just and equitable resolutions, adaptations, and responses.

As a matter of pragmatic philosophy, we don't have to answer the question of what every possible good society might look like. We begin where we are. We respect honesty, kindness, other-regardingness, cooperativeness, and empathy. We dislike suffering and deprivations, injustices, and so forth. It is noteworthy that throughout all the vagaries of time and space, across societies with different economic, political, and social structures, these are virtues in almost all.[10] We recognize prevalent traits, again which we see across societies, like an innate sense of fairness, a general aversion to risk, a desire for at least a certain level of security, and so forth. Are there social and economic arrangements that foster these virtues and satisfy these desires in a sustainable way? I believe there are.

CHAPTER 11

Neoliberal Capitalism: Why It Failed

Before we can answer the question of what kind of economy would deliver meaningful freedom to the most people, we should consider why neoliberal capitalism (neoliberalism, for short) failed, and failed so badly. Advocates of neoliberalism suggest that one reason is that we haven't really tried neoliberalism. Half of this claim is correct: We haven't tried pure neoliberalism. If we had, matters would have been much worse. Economic performance would have been weaker and inequality, polarization, and political and economic instability, greater.

Milton Friedman suggested that an unbridled form of capitalism is necessary to preserve capitalism, something more ruthless than the softer neoliberalism of the last forty years. Public education would be replaced by vouchers to finance private education. Public retirement programs would be replaced by private annuities. Public prisons would be made private. Taking the logic further, the federally funded military would be replaced by mercenary armies like the Wagner Group in Russia.

Advocates of free markets also argue that even when they are imperfect, the freedom itself allows a self-correcting mechanism to set in. I'll explain why this is not true. Far from being self-correcting, neoliberal capitalism is a system that devours itself.

There's more to neoliberalism's failure than just conventional economics. Neoliberal capitalism is not a sustainable political and economic system. While critics of capitalism have been saying this for 200 years, I think today we have a better understanding of why this is true. When a system isn't sustainable, it won't be sustained. There will be change. The question is: What can we do to ensure that the change heads in the right direction?

The Failures of Neoliberalism

The great irony of history is that neoliberalism became a global ideology just as economic theory was helping us to understand the limitations of markets. Any discussion of the failures of neoliberalism needs to begin with a discussion of these limitations, which I've dealt with at various points in this book but most importantly in chapter 3 in the discussion about externalities. But market failures go well beyond externalities.

In the table below, I summarize some of the critical market failures, the neoliberal view about what should be done about them, the consequences, and examples of what I believe to be more appropriate responses. Then I highlight three examples of the multiple interventions in the workings of the market economy that can and have successfully addressed key market failures beyond those already discussed.

Competition and exploitation

Twenty-first-century American neoliberalism is different from European neoliberalism in at least one critical and interesting way. European liberals recognize that markets work well *only* if there is effective competition, and they typically don't believe that markets on their own will necessarily be competitive. The dominant neoliberal strands in the US hold that markets are naturally competitive. This perspective has been incorporated into legal standards, so that in court, someone who claims that an action of a firm is anticompetitive has a high burden of proof.

The Chicago School economists and lawyers (most famously Robert Bork)[1] who pushed that view made unrealistic assumptions that are widely rejected today, even in the US. Nonetheless, while they were popular, they became embedded in Supreme Court decisions, implying that if there is to be change there will have to be legislation, something that is near to impossible in the current context.

To me, the evidence is overwhelming that government plays an important part in ensuring that markets remain competitive (through competition laws, also known as antitrust laws).[2] These issues have become of increasing concern with the growth of tech giants like Amazon and Google, which have enormous market power and have abused it.

Macroeconomics

One of the most obvious failures of unfettered markets is the episodic deep downturns, such as the Great Depression and the Great Recession, in which unemployment soars and output plummets. The Great Recession would have been even more catastrophic were it not for government intervention. Yet neoliberals and a major strand of modern macroeconomics argue that markets are efficient—that the observed fluctuations are nothing more than the efficient response to the shocks buffeting the economy. For those outside the closed fraternity of economists, it may be hard to believe that a major school of thought—one that is taken seriously, taught in graduate schools, and has several Nobel Prize winners—actually argues that there is no such thing as unemployment and that the variations in employment reflect changes in the number of individuals efficiently and voluntarily deciding to enjoy leisure.[3] Another major group of economists belongs to

Market failure	Neoliberal policy stance
Externalities Environmental Public health Knowledge Economic For example, excessive risk-taking by financial institutions, imposing high costs on the rest of society (Great Recession)	No intervention in the market (deregulation where there already are regulations) (Coase theorem says that if property rights are appropriately assigned, market will solve on its own)
Public goods and coordination failures	Leave it to the private sector When the government intervenes, rely on private production (Coase theorem says that market will efficiently solve public goods problems)

Consequences	Progressive capitalism policies
Too many negative externalities; too few positive externalities Excessive pollution Worse pandemics Too little innovation Financial and economic crises, at great cost	Regulation, "corrective taxation," government investment resulting in: • Better environment • Better control of epidemics Industrial policies to promote innovations with large spillovers—including possibly trade restrictions Financial regulations (both micro, which ensures bank solvency, and macro policies focused on economic stability and full employment)
Underinvestments in education, health, technology, and infrastructure Slower growth Less equality and less equality of opportunity Privatized firms pursue profits at the expense of social goals (private prisons) Privatization and public-private partnerships often mean socialization of losses and privatization of gains	Public investments Sometimes public funding, with private provision, and sometimes with public production

Market failure	Neoliberal policy stance
Imperfect information	Leave it to the private sector (no disclosure requirements, caveat emptor)
Imperfect risk markets **Absence of insurance against important risks**	Leave it to the market No attention to risk consequences of policies like financial and capital market liberalization—because markets perfectly manage risks

Consequences	Progressive capitalism policies
Insufficient disclosure, leading to suboptimal and distorted (rent-seeking) resource allocations and exploitation	Disclosure requirements Regulations (consumer, financial, labor) preventing taking advantage of information asymmetries and other forms of exploitation Liability laws making firms accountable, and class-action suits to enhance rights of injured Restrictions on compulsory arbitration

Loss of well-being (and productivity) as a result of insecurity
 	
   May even inhibit innovation
 	
Absence of health insurance leads to poorer health, reduced productivity
 	
Excessive economic volatility, high losses in well-being from volatility
	All policy (trade, finance, etc.) takes into account induced uncertainties and increased volatility
	
	Social insurance/protection
	   Safety net programs
	   Unemployment insurance
	   Retirement programs
	   Health insurance
	
	Income-contingent loans (where repayment depends on income), for instance, for education
	
	Public option

Market failure	Neoliberal policy stance
Imperfect capital markets (credit rationing, difficulties in borrowing or raising equity)	Denies relevance—leave it to the market
Macroeconomic fluctuations (macroeconomic externalities, e.g., firms undertake excessive debt, giving rise to excessive volatility)	Markets respond optimally to shocks and have no role in creating shocks If there is unemployment, it's because workers demand too high wages (blame the victim)—response: increase labor market flexibility
Macro-inflation	Central banks need to target inflation, raising interest rates when inflation increases above 2%

Consequences	Progressive capitalism policies
High-productivity investments aren't made, e.g., by small businesses	Small-business loans Development of green banks financing socially beneficial environmental investments
Episodic underemployment of societal resources/massive loss of well-being, especially with unemployment	Stabilizing fiscal and monetary policies Automatic stabilizers Social protection (unemployment insurance)
Large average output gap (disparity between economy's potential and actual output) High average unemployment Price stability comes at the expense of "real" instability (instability in actual output)	Response depends on source of inflation Supply-side shocks necessitate fiscal policies to address supply gaps

Market failure	Neoliberal policy stance
Lack of competition	Leave it to the market—markets are naturally competitive (potential competition, competition for the market, is a substitute for competition in the market)
Excessive inequality	Leave it to the market—or the political process

Consequences	Progressive capitalism policies
High concentrations of market power High prices Lower real wages Less resilient economy Less innovation	Antitrust/competition policies Restrict mergers Restrict abusive practices Restrict tacit collusion Public options providing an alternative
High concentrations of income and even greater concentrations of wealth and power Large numbers of people in poverty Lack of hope, opportunity—deaths of despair Undermining democracy and social cohesion Even harming overall economic performance	Pre-redistribution (policies like minimum wages and supportive labor legislation, increasing equality of market incomes) Redistribution through taxes Public expenditure programs (education, health care)

the blame-the-victim school: Unemployment occurs because workers demand wages that are too high. If only wages were perfectly flexible, the economy would be efficient and there would be no unemployment.

Neoliberalism has embraced these doctrines of abstruse economists in its efforts to defend the market and to limit government action. Consequently, it has failed to recognize that the source of the most important and severe fluctuations is the market itself. This is a lesson we should have learned from the Great Depression, the Great Recession, and the dozens of other crises caused by market excesses around the world.

In the aftermath of the Covid-19 pandemic and Russia's invasion of Ukraine, the global economy faced another problem: a large increase in the inflation rate. The underlying problem was not an excess of aggregate demand but supply constraints and demand shifts. The market lacked resilience. In the US, there were even shortages of baby formula. Automobile companies had failed to order the chips they needed and, as a result, production was curtailed and the shortage led to soaring auto prices. Germany and other European countries had become too dependent on Russian gas, and when the supply was reduced energy prices soared. European firms simply had not taken into account the risks of such dependence—something that I had warned about in my book *Making Globalization Work* more than fifteen years earlier. It seemed obvious to me at the time that Russia under Putin was not a reliable trading partner.

These episodes of inflation and unemployment reveal the fundamental weaknesses in unfettered markets, but they also expose the weaknesses in neoliberal policy prescriptions, which have centered on minimizing the role of government and its discretion. Neoliberals wanted government to obey simple—I would say simplistic—rules, such as governments should have no deficits, but if they do, deficits should not exceed 3 percent of GDP, as in Europe, or that macroeconomic stabilization should rely on monetary policy with interest rates hiked whenever inflation exceeds 2 percent. These magical numbers are plucked out of thin air. The prescriptions are based neither on theory nor evidence, nor have they resulted in stability, especially in *real* terms—in real GDP or employment. In many cases, neoliberal policies have resulted in disasters: the demand for austerity—massive cutbacks in government expenditures—in the euro crisis that followed closely on the heels of the 2008 financial crisis in the US induced deep recessions and, in some cases, downturns so deep they were rightly called depressions, with Greece yet (as this book goes to press) to return to its pre-crisis level of real GDP.

The pace and direction of innovation

Market advocates talk about markets' wonders in producing innovation. As we've seen, most of the innovation that increased living standards in recent decades rests on foundations of basic science, funded and often conducted by government.[4] But not only is it the case that markets on their own won't be insufficiently innovative, they push innovation in the wrong direction. We should focus innovation on saving the planet by reducing carbon emissions, but instead, enormous research efforts are directed at saving labor, especially unskilled labor, by reducing the need for it in production processes when we already have a global excess supply of such labor. These types of innovation may save private costs, but the induced unemployment and inequality impose large costs on the rest of society.[5]

Is Our Economic and Political System Self-Correcting?

Despite the failures of neoliberalism, there are many people—especially on the Right—who say, don't worry. Our political/social/economic system has built-in self-correction mechanisms, they insist. Once the excesses of neoliberalism have been exposed, we'll pass legislation to curb them. With a bigger dose of regulation here, a smaller dose of regulation there, a little more investment in education here, a little adjustment in other policies there, prosperity and social cohesion will be restored. The fundamental critique of neoliberalism, they say, is sheer hyperbole.

Historians naturally take the "long view" of history. One with whom I shared my glum perspective on the state of democracy around the world observed that it is also true that in the long run, dictatorships die. Think of the collapse of the Soviet Union, or of Francisco Franco in Spain, António de Oliveira Salazar in Portugal, Augusto Pinochet in Chile. True, the dictators in Latin America lasted less than a quarter of a century. But the Soviet dictatorship with its ruling elites lasted almost three-quarters of a century and was quickly replaced by another dictatorship and oligarchy. China's nondemocratic regime has lasted now for seventy-five years. There may be self-correcting forces in play, but they sometimes act slowly, too slowly for comfort.

There are several reasons for pessimism about self-correcting forces. Societies often respond slowly; there are marked societal rigidities even in the face of obvious dysfunctionality. For example, foot binding persisted in China for centuries in spite of its devastating effects on women. Slow responses occur in part because what each of us believes is affected by what others believe, in a self-reinforcing way.[6] If everyone believes (or if I believe that everyone believes) that foot binding is good, who am I to deviate? And almost all societies work to suppress deviants from norms. Too much questioning is too unsettling. It's almost as if societies have created antibodies to deviancy in the form of social and economic disapprobation (sometimes going further, with exclusionary behavior), whether the deviation from the norm might in the end lead to a better or worse society.

Probably a vast majority of people in advanced countries believe in some version of Adam Smith's invisible hand, in part because almost every pundit believes it; and the pundits believe it in part because almost every other person they know and respect believes it. Only a few academic economists and some radicals on the Left have argued otherwise. This is the lens through which the pundits see the world, a social coercion in thought, enforced not by party discipline but through a system of social approval and disapproval. As I described in chapter 9, confirmation bias allows most people to discount information that runs counter to their preconceptions and presumptions. When free market advocates saw the continued struggles of low-income Americans, they didn't see it as an indication of a fundamental flaw in the system. Instead, they rationalized according to the system's precepts: The victims were to blame because they hadn't worked hard enough, saved enough, or organized their lives in the right way. When that explanation seemed weak, since so many people did so poorly, the response of market-mentality adherents was to argue for minor policy changes without any fundamental change to economic structure.

Our institutions, rules, and regulations, of course, reflect these prevailing perspectives, and different parts of the system reinforce each other. It's hard to think through how each component of our complex system should change as our economy, our technology, our societies, and our knowledge of all these change. I've argued, for instance, that property law, particularly intellectual property law, needs to be rethought. That's a system that's been created over centuries. It has adapted, but typically only slowly—too slowly for the pace of today's changes.[7] It's hard to conceptualize alternative frameworks, but when we do, there is often resistance from vested interests and even from those without a vested interest, who see the world through older lenses.

Daniel Kahneman, whom I introduced earlier as one of the leading behavioral economists, describes in his famous book *Thinking, Fast and Slow* how individuals often need to make quick decisions or come to quick judgments. They think quickly, using rules of thumb that work well on average but are not fully reflective of what they really want or what their judgments would be if they had a chance to be more deliberative. It's the same for societies, except it's true even when we have time to think.[8] The pace of deliberative change, where deliberation can arrive at a reasonable consensus, either in formal laws or social norms, can be out of sync with the needs of our society. In the meanwhile, we use outmoded economic arrangements. This is perhaps particularly true in the US, where a majority of the Supreme Court justices attempt to interpret the Constitution from the perspective of the wealthy white male slave-owning drafters of the Constitution.[9] The drafters themselves designed the Constitution to make it difficult to change, in part as a way to protect entrenched interests.

Pessimism about the possibility of self-correction today

At the current conjuncture, any existing self-correcting forces may be particularly weak. First, in spite of its failures, neoliberal ideology runs deep in society. Too many have been brought up on it and believe in it.[10] Behavioral economics has helped us to understand these beliefs as a source of rigidity in society. We look for information that's consistent with our beliefs and we discount information that runs counter.

There are always differing views about a wide range of matters in society, including about the role of government. Opinions are affected by judgments about the importance of externalities, for example, as well as the efficacy of government interventions to address them. But at the beginning of these discussions there needs to be broad agreement about certain facts. Climate change is real. Covid-19 is a communicable disease with serious consequences. In the US, one of the two major parties has been taken over by politicians and voters willing to stare facts in the face and deny them. They deny even the credibility of science, the cornerstone of our society and the reason standards of living are so much higher today than 250 years ago. Large numbers of the Republican electorate are climate deniers, with many of the rest climate minimizers, even as their country is being ravaged by extreme weather events.

Much has been written dissecting this social pathology. It is part of a broader loss in the credibility of elites and trust in institutions, well documented in surveys around the world, including in the US. This, I believe, is directly related to the country's economic malaise—the income stagnation of the bottom 90 percent. It is natural for those at the bottom to reason, "The elites promised that the neoliberal market reforms would lead to faster growth, and we'd all share the benefits. If they were so wrong about that, how can they be trusted now?" The dominant paradigm focused on incentives, so it was natural for those whose incomes stagnated or fell as the incomes at the top soared to reason, "It wasn't just a matter of elites making a mistake about the economics. They were rigging the system to benefit themselves at the expense of the rest of us. They had an incentive to do so."

But economics alone can't provide a full explanation. Many other countries experienced similar economic trauma, and while they witnessed a growth in populism, few countries saw the same cultlike practice of truth denying. Perhaps it was because Americans expected more—there was widespread belief in the American Dream—so the disparity between what was expected and promised by neoliberalism and what was delivered was greater.

Moreover—and this is the second reason for my pessimism—the pathology itself creates conditions that are helpful for its self-perpetuation. The misunderstandings of economics combined with a willing blindness to facts means there is a good chance that the economic and social policies that are adopted will not be sustainable, and some will exacerbate adverse economic conditions. Trump's 2017 tax cut for powerful corporations and the wealthy didn't produce the investment he promised, but it did increase the fiscal hole and societal inequalities. His proposals for drastic cuts in basic research—fortunately never ratified by Congress—would have undermined the foundations of progress. The economic conditions of ordinary citizens may worsen, and this may strengthen populism.

In the same vein, while the neoliberal axioms on universal selfishness and greed are falsifiable—and falsified[11]—they have created large numbers of people who are well described by those axioms, and they constitute a particularly strong force perpetuating the system.

Probably most important are today's power dynamics. People in whose interest it is to perpetuate the status quo hold disproportionate sway in the political system.[12]

There are two distinct aspects to the situation in the US. The power dynamics are exacerbated by a political system in which money matters more than in most other democracies. American elections are very expensive, and donors who make more campaign contributions (more rightly thought of as "political investments") inevitably have more influence. Lobbying has also become a major business. Those who can afford more and better lobbyists are also more clearly heard. In some areas like finance, revolving doors are still a common practice, with companies and organizations offering good jobs to former government employees who've served their interests well. The distortions in incentives are obvious.

Moreover, the US Constitution, through its system of electing the president and two senators from every state, gave more power to less-populous states and, over time, the implicit disparities in the power of each vote have widened enormously. Even the value of democracy itself has come to be questioned by Republicans as they unabashedly work to suppress votes, gerrymander districts, and upset the peaceful transfer of power, a hallmark of any democracy.

The new technologies, moreover, have provided new instruments for entrenching power, and given additional powers to the few who control them to have undue weight in political outcomes.[13]

Where will change come from, and where will it take us?

Poor economic conditions, especially large economic disparities among different groups within society, give rise to demands for change in policies and systems.[14] But the direction of change is not always clear. There is an infinite supply of bad ideas. In times of despair, societies can seldom engage in the kind of deliberation that would allow a reasoned choice, the separation of good from bad ideas, the subtle restructuring of any nascent idea to make it work. As a result, the social change resulting from crises is not always positive. The Great Depression has often been blamed for the rise of Hitler, deindustrialization in the US for the rise of Trump. The worry among those who would like to see our democracy flourish is that the nation might elect a demagogue worse than Trump if the country's economic situation continues—its deep inequality accompanied by deaths of despair.[15] The rise of neoliberalism politically can be dated, at least in the US and UK, to times of stress, to the stagflation that preceded the election of Ronald Reagan and the early manifestations of deindustrialization, for example.

Of course, crises are sometimes moments to seize opportunities for positive social change. The Great Depression in the US led to the reforms of the New Deal, including labor legislation and Social Security.

In short, the economic stress that results from the failures of neoliberalism and its successors on the populist Right such as Trump and former Brazilian president Jair Bolsonaro may well induce movements for societal change. It is also possible that these movements will redirect our socioeconomic system in the right direction. But it is just as likely, perhaps more, that the economy will lurch the wrong way.

The US is perhaps distinctive in the influence it has on what is considered acceptable or desirable behavior by its leaders and government. To a large extent, it creates the intellectual environment in which other leaders and states function. Thus, Trump gave space for other demagogues like Prime Minister Narendra Modi in India and Bolsonaro in Brazil to advance their populist agendas. Trump almost surely changed the politics, at least in some of these countries, and made acceptable what would have previously been considered undemocratic ideas. After all, they didn't seem all that outrageous by the new global standards. Hungarian prime minister Viktor Orbán's notion of illiberal democracies might have been laughed at and dismissed out of hand were it not for Trump.

It is clear that intellectual waves travel around the world—the era of fascism in the 1930s, the era of military dictatorships in Latin America in the 1970s and '80s, and neoliberalism in the 1980s and '90s. In today's world, the US plays a large role in this trend setting.[16]

This leaves us with perhaps an even more pessimistic sense of the possibilities outside the US. If America is not on course to correct its growing dystopia, the likelihood is that more countries will have cult-like political leaders, which will make a return to a saner economics and politics slower and more problematic.

This democratic crisis could not have come at a worse time, since we are facing the climate crisis simultaneously. The unholy alliance among the demagogues, the populists, the fossil fuel sector, and the business interests that serve them is pushing us rapidly beyond our planetary boundaries.

The Time May Be Ripe: Notes of Optimism

As I noted in chapter 1, a hallmark of neoliberalism was the claim that there is no alternative. Proponents said there was no real alternative to their mantra of liberalization, deregulation, privatization, austerity, and central banks' ruthless and single-minded focus on keeping inflation at 2 percent. Of course, there were alternatives—but the neoliberals' claim was that any alternative policy would make everybody so much worse off they would regret it. This stance had a great advantage. We could leave not only the management of the economy but the writing of the basic rules to technocrats—indeed, to economists.

Their analyses were wrong, and most importantly, there were

realistic alternatives, both domestically and internationally. Earlier, I described neoliberalism as a mindset that begins with the *presumption* that markets are efficient, and that anything the government does is likely to ruin things. Economic realities are otherwise. Globally, government has played an important role in the countries with the highest growth rates. Everyone, everywhere, turned to government to save the economy and to contain Covid-19 in the pandemic. And it worked remarkably well. But that wasn't a one-time thing; it always happens. As the world faces the existential crisis of climate change, there is no alternative but government action.

The current neoliberal economic system is not environmentally, socially, politically, or economically sustainable.

Many within the establishment suggest that the slight tweaks to the system are all that is needed. In facing the climate crisis, they talk about "green finance" and unleashing the power of private financial markets. In facing the inequality crisis, they talk about improving the education system. Some may be so bold as to increase the minimum wage (in the US, it's at the same level that it was more than six decades ago, adjusted for inflation).

I and many others argue, however, that these slight tweaks won't suffice. Some say, accordingly, that we need a revolution. But the sad history of the last two-and-a-half centuries is that revolutions typically don't end well. To me, the only answer is to push for as large a change as our democratic system will permit. The US and other democracies have gone through periods of rapid change so large they can be described as radical, but at the same time they are short of a revolution. Examples of such rapid changes are the New Deal in the US and the creation of the welfare state post–World War II in the UK.

The fact that there is no alternative but radical change is one source of optimism. Our young people are another. One of the divides in our society is across generations. The young are struggling to buy houses and land decent jobs; they know that the likelihood is low that they will do better economically than their parents.[17] They also know that the reality of climate change may have devastating effects on the world they inherit. In many other ways, they are questioning their intellectual inheritance. And part of that questioning involves economic and social systems. Even in the US, I detect strong support for the ideas I am articulating here and an understanding of the principles I've enunciated. If we can keep the torch of a liberal democracy with Enlightenment values partially burning for long enough, and protect the kind of economy that comes with it, there's a good chance the next generation will come up with a consensus on how we might not only create a more stable, prosperous, sustainable, and equitable world but also begin the process of moving toward a good (or at least better) society.[18]

CHAPTER 12

Freedom, Sovereignty, and Coercion Among States

Many of the issues concerning freedom and coercion play out, often in related ways, at the level of nation-states much as they do at the level of individuals, though the language is sometimes slightly different. Countries worry about their loss of sovereignty in international agreements, such as the one that established the World Trade Organization. Countries that accept funds from the International Monetary Fund feel coerced into assenting to the conditions that come along with the money (termed "conditionalities")—demands that the country cut spending, raise taxes, or change some rule or regulation in order to get the money it needs so desperately.

It may be useful to distinguish two kinds of situations. The first is true coercion—the threat of violence with which colonial powers exerted their control. They were clearly intruding on the freedoms of the colonized even if the colonized signed an agreement that gave up their rights. That agreement was a mere façade.

The second is an agreement among two equals, made for mutual benefit, either to avoid exerting negative externalities on each other (as is the case with climate) or to make it easier to create positive externalities (as might be the case from a mutually beneficial expansion of trade). In both cases, each party agrees to do or not do something if and only if the other does similarly. Freedom to act in some dimension is constrained, but the expansion of the opportunity set of each as a result of the agreement, assuming the other side complies, increases freedoms to act in many other ways.

There is no coercion in truly voluntary agreements among equals even if they circumscribe sovereignty. These agreements can be viewed on the international scale like the contracts among individuals discussed in chapter 5. But, as I noted, seemingly voluntary contracts may still be exploitive and may seem coercive, especially when one party to the contract is more powerful than the other. Such imbalances of power, both economic and military, pervade the world today.

Over the past century, agreements between advanced countries and emerging markets and developing countries have had the appearance of being voluntary—there is typically no physical coercion—and have been supported by a rhetoric of mutual benefit. But that is not always how they are perceived by developing countries, who (rightly, in my judgment) often think what is truly going on is economic coercion.

Coercion can take many forms. Depriving a person of an opportunity he might otherwise have had may induce him to do something that he otherwise would not have done. While he is not "forced" to take the action he feels coerced into, it is the best *remaining* option. He may rightly say in such a situation that he was coerced. We saw an example earlier: Black South Africans "voluntarily" worked in the mines at low wages because the oppressive regime eliminated any outside opportunities like farming. There was no real choice.

A similar situation applies to nations. Colonialism left a legacy of deprivation in many countries. The best alternative for these countries was to accept economic relations, often called partnerships, which provided financial assistance and access to the large markets in the advanced world. But the terms were advantageous to the advanced country and would not have emerged in a world in which bargaining power was more equal. Much of my writing over the past two decades has been an effort to show the exploitive nature of international agreements and the exploitive workings of the international economic institutions and the disparity between the rhetoric of mutually advantageous fair agreements and the reality of unfair agreements written to promote the interests of advanced countries' multinationals, including large financial and mining corporations and, more recently, large tech companies.[1]

In many of the cases, the international agreements brought few direct benefits to the developing countries and yet limited what they could do. They entailed a clear loss of economic freedom for the poor country without sufficient commensurate gain.

In some cases, the international institutions talked about cross-border externalities as a justification of the constraints they imposed on poor countries (just as I've talked about regulations constraining individual behavior when there are externalities), but externalities from small developing countries or even emerging markets are typically minuscule, while externalities originating from the major advanced countries are large. Yet many agreements have sought to limit behavior of the developing countries and emerging markets in one way or another while doing next to nothing about the large externalities emanating from the advanced countries. This suggests that something else is at play. The large and rich countries use the agreements to advance their interests at the expense of the small and poor. Worse, the agreements typically aren't fully enforced against the large and rich but are enforced against the small and poor.

The agreements are little more than the latest manifestation of power politics, which constrain the freedom of the developing world as they expand the freedom of the developed world. It's not unlike the outcome of the Opium War discussed earlier, which constrained the ability of China to protect its citizens from a dangerous narcotic but expanded the free trade rights of the West to export it. I should be more precise: Those with power in advanced countries attempt to ensure that their government uses *its* power to secure the interests of power elites; the policies may be, and often are, contrary to the welfare of the vast majority of citizens in advanced countries.

The externalities from the large and rich countries to the small are evident not just in trade. Over the years, US monetary policies have created global externalities. Federal Reserve chair Paul Volcker's sudden increase of interest rates in 1981 to more than 20 percent precipitated the Latin American debt crisis. But the US has seldom taken these externalities into account when designing its policies. Yet the IMF, the World Bank, and others have put pressure on developing countries to run their monetary policies according to neoliberal dictates that focus on inflation, which means having to raise interest rates as soon as inflation rises above 2 percent regardless of the source, even though there are no significant global externalities arising from the monetary policy of a small country. More egregious, these organizations have used their muscle to make loans conditional on the borrowing country following such orthodoxy.[2]

There is one exception in which small countries have exerted an externality on the large. Some provide tax-avoidance options for corporations and the wealthy that undermine other countries' abilities to raise taxes. The Cayman Islands, Panama, and British Virgin Islands are notorious for this. It's not just poor countries—Luxembourg and Ireland have done the same within Europe. But large countries, and special places and sectors (like real estate) within those countries, have also become global centers for tax avoidance and evasion, helping rob other countries of the taxes they're owed. And, perhaps more to the point, if the rich and powerful countries wanted to shut down these tax havens they easily could, simply by restricting their citizens and corporations from taking advantage of their tax avoidance services.

They persist because it's in the interests of some of the rich and powerful in the rich and powerful countries to allow them to persist.

Intellectual Property

Nothing could better illustrate the imbalances in the international rules and regulations than intellectual property (IP) regulation. I noted in chapter 7 the disastrous effects when, during Covid-19, restrictions on the freedom of companies in the poor countries to produce Covid-19 vaccines, tests, and therapeutics led to thousands of additional hospitalizations and untold deaths. The irony was that there had already been a global agreement stating that during an epidemic, countries could have unfettered access to IP after paying a fair royalty. The poor countries believed this agreement meant that during pandemics lives would be considered more important than profits; without that understanding, they might not have signed on to the WTO agreement. But the drug companies had learned how to stall. Every day of delay meant millions more in profits—even if it resulted in thousands of more deaths. Regrettably, key governments, including Germany, Switzerland, and the UK, supported the drug companies during the Covid-19 pandemic.

The West's decision to put drug company profits over lives will have lingering effects. The waning support of so many developing countries for Ukraine against Russia's invasion was not a surprise, given the West's cruel response to the cries of help during the coronavirus pandemic. But in a world in which global cooperation is urgently needed to solve existential problems, like climate change, we must rewrite international agreements so that they are significantly more balanced than they have been in the past.

Global Governance and Taxing Multinationals

There is an imbalance of power within the international setting that is perhaps more obvious and greater than within most well-functioning democratic societies. And this imbalance is reflected in how decisions are made globally. Developing countries have demanded to take part in the talks on crucial global agreements because they have realized that if you don't have a seat at the table, you may be on the menu. But having a seat at the table isn't enough. Too often, their microphone has been effectively turned off and no one is listening.

An example: With much hullabaloo, the international community discussed reforms to the system of taxing multinational corporations. Developing countries are obviously in desperate need of funds. As factories moved into their countries, allowing consumers in the more advanced countries to get goods at lower prices, developing countries thought they had secured jobs for themselves *and* a source of funds for education, health care, and other developmental objectives. But multinationals became experts in exploiting globalization. They produced goods where labor was cheap but used global rules to avoid paying taxes anywhere. The process of reforming the system began in the Organisation of Economic Co-operation and Development (OECD), the official think tank of the advanced countries, but after enough criticism from emerging markets and developing countries that their concerns were not getting the attention they deserved, the OECD developed an "inclusive" framework for discussions—or more accurately, it created a façade of inclusiveness.

Representatives from the developing countries continued to criticize the process, saying that their voices were still not being heard—not a surprise, given that the OECD was the club of the advanced countries. The proposed agreement that eventually emerged confirmed the allegations of the developing countries. For instance, while it was good that the agreement called for a minimum tax on corporations, requiring they pay taxes *somewhere*, the minimum tax was set at a very low rate, half the average rate in Latin America.[3] Even as the OECD demanded that countries sign up to the new framework, it refused to release estimates of how the new regime would generate additional revenues for the poor countries. Independent estimates suggested it would be a pittance, and in return for this pittance, countries would have to forgo imposing digital taxes on the likes of Google, Meta, and Amazon—the potential revenue from which would only grow over time.[4] (It was obvious whose interests the restrictions reflected: the digital giants', whose perspectives were well represented by the American negotiators.)

The developing countries were so disappointed with the results they asked to change the venue for the tax discussion to the UN, where they would have a greater voice, even if economic power mattered most in the end. But the US recognized that shifting the venue might curtail its power. The world was already split by vaccine apartheid and two wars, one in the Middle East and one in Ukraine, but the US engineered another, between the developing and advanced countries. As disappointment grew in the developing world over the OECD proposals, the African Union spurred an initiative to begin the process for a tax convention on a range of subjects, possibly including those broached by the OECD but also going well beyond. Rather than acceding to growing global support to discuss these vital matters at the UN, the body created for such purposes, in November 2023, the US voted with 47 other largely advanced countries against a UN agreement to begin the process. The US not only failed in its attempt to stop the historic agreement, which had the support of 125 largely developing countries, it put itself on the wrong side of history and again alienated those whose cooperation would be needed on a host of global problems.[5]

Similar stories could be told about each area of international economic architecture. These problems have preoccupied me over the past quarter century; and while there is now greater recognition of the injustices—the imbalances between constraints (losses of freedom) imposed on the poor countries and the freedoms given to the rich— far too little has been done about them. In the following three sections, I illustrate this by looking at debt, trade, and investment.

The Chains of Debt

Readers of Charles Dickens clearly understand the links between debt and freedom for citizens in the nineteenth century. The punishment for not paying a debt was debtor's prison. Never mind that the prisoner himself, sitting in jail, could do little to repay his debt.[6] Fortunately, we've moved beyond that and look on debtor prisons as part of an almost uncivilized past.

Internationally, things might seem better today, too, than a hundred and some years ago. In the nineteenth century, when countries couldn't repay what they owed, creditor countries used armed force to compel debt payments—as in Egypt in 1882 and Venezuela in 1902– 1903. More recently, countries and provinces have found they can lose meaningful democratic independence, as Newfoundland discovered in the 1930s when it was put in "receivership" and control was substantially turned over to creditors, and Puerto Rico learned in 2016, when its democratically elected government was effectively subjugated to a board assigned to manage the repayment of its debt.[7]

Even without such drastic measures, though, life for a country that has become overindebted is not pleasant. The creditors do what they can to extract as much as they can of what they are owed—paying little, if any, regard to the consequences for the citizens. This is true even if the creditors have played an active role in creating the debt crisis by offering credit at enticing terms, possibly even bribing government officials or private executives to borrow.

In modern society, when a person or a company has borrowed too much, which is the same as when the banks and other creditors have lent too much, there is a formal bankruptcy procedure. The debt is restructured so that people can get on with their lives and corporations can get a fresh start to once again grow and create jobs, if they have the talent and knowledge to do so.

While the creditors highlight the recklessness of borrowers borrowing excessively, the real flaw lies with the creditors. They are supposed to be experts in risk management, knowing how much an individual, firm, or country can borrow without getting in trouble. They are assumed to know far more about the underlying microeconomics and the prevailing macroeconomics than an ordinary person or a poor developing country. Loans are voluntary. If a loan shouldn't have been made, the fault lies as much, or more so, at the feet of the lender as the borrower.

I noted in Part II how the wealthy exert control over the media and have a disproportionate say in our economic system. Nowhere is this more evident than in our discussion here. The bankers in the West tell the story of reckless borrowers, of an Argentina that is a serial defaulter. But they skip over the obvious question: If this were so evident, why lend so much, as they did to Argentina after Mauricio Macri became that country's president in 2015? The obvious answer is that greed overpowered their risk assessment. The banks liked the high interest rates, little thinking that it was not only a sign of high risk but a cause, as the country would find it difficult to meet such onerous terms.

Internationally, there is nothing analogous to a bankruptcy court for sovereigns that can't pay back what they owe. It's extremely important to create a framework for this because resolving cross-border indebtedness is far more complex than resolving domestic debt problems.[8] And what happens as a result is a pure power play, with most of the power in the hands of the creditors. In the past, their demands were amplified and coordinated through the IMF, which acted as the lenders' collection agent.

There was a pattern to what happened when countries got overindebted in the decades after the end of World War II through around
2020. They were threatened with being cut off from all access to
credit if they didn't agree to the terms offered.[9] Without credit and
without foreign reserves, these countries might not be able to buy
food for their people or other imported goods needed for production.
There was a show of bargaining and negotiation, but in the end, it was
little more than a charade. The IMF would draw up an overly optimistic scenario of what the debtor country could afford, and on that
basis, there would be a little debt forgiveness. In return, the country
would do what it could to extract money from its citizens to pay back
the creditors, which meant cutting back spending on health, education, and infrastructure, expenditures necessary for basic livelihoods
and prospects for future growth. The extreme austerity, sometimes
accompanied by increases in taxes, would push the country into a deep
recession. The growth in the rosy IMF scenario would not come to
pass, and there would be another default a few years down the line. It
amounted to a twentieth- and twenty-first-century version of a debtor
prison for the country.[10]

Note the role of the IMF in all this. In the worst cases, the country
assumed the responsibility to pay back the private creditors, the IMF
gave the country the money it needed to do this, and the citizens of
the country were left to pay the bill. While the bankers may *seem* to be
champions of free private enterprise, that's only when it benefits them.
When a large amount of private debt accrues in a developing country,
creditors exert enormous pressure on the government to absorb the
private-sector debt. So those in the private sector, including finance,
in the developed and the developing country share the profits. Meanwhile, the citizens of the developing country bear the downside risk
in this ersatz capitalism. And the IMF is the ringleader that makes
sure it all happens.

More recently, with the crisis in Argentina in 2020—entailing the largest IMF loan in history (about $44 billion)—matters seemed to have improved, much to the chagrin of Wall Street and the US Treasury, which has sometimes been described, not totally unfairly, as a wholly owned subsidiary of Wall Street, even under Democratic administrations. In the 2021 restructuring of Argentina's debt, the IMF played an honest broker role, detailing the level of debt that was sustainable, or would have been had things turned out well (this was before the full force was felt of the global disturbances from the war in Ukraine, the pandemic, and a climate change–induced drought).[11] The rest of the debt would have to be written off, one way or another. Wall Street was livid at the seeming betrayal by the IMF; it wanted to squeeze more dollars out of Argentina than the IMF said was feasible. There were attempts to replace the head of the IMF, which was viewed by some as an attempted coup[12] supported by the US Treasury.

While global debt markets have improved in this way, in others the debt problem has become worse. There are more diverse creditors, with conflicting economic and political agendas. The resolution of debt crises with a few banks at the table was hard enough. Today, it's much more difficult, with hundreds of creditors from multiple countries fighting for their own interests, which typically conflict with others'.[13] The true interests of creditors are also completely obscured by financial markets that allow some to remain at the bargaining table while secretly shifting all the risk of a default to others.[14]

China has become a very important creditor for developing country and emerging market debt,[15] and it has shown very little appetite for debt restructuring. It appears to be as hard-nosed a negotiator as America's private banks.[16] But if one major creditor won't enter meaningfully into debt restructuring, few others will either, because no creditor wants to feel that another creditor is scooping up the money it isn't collecting.[17] Ironically, while China has done much of its lending for geopolitical reasons, its hard-nosed policies have inflicted serious reputational damage, most famously in the case of

Sri Lanka; China took over one of Sri Lanka's major ports when it couldn't repay its debt.

What is clear is that any country that gets excessively in debt to foreigners enters a Faustian bargain. The country gets a little more money today but is at serious risk of losing its freedom later. The countries of East Asia learned that at great cost in the crisis of 1997–1998, when I was chief economist of the World Bank.[18] This was a crisis brought on by East Asian countries opening up their economies

to the free flow of capital, a process called capital market liberalization and a central part of the expanded Washington Consensus agenda—the "reforms" that the World Bank, IMF, and US Treasury foisted on the developing countries.[19] Money flowed freely into the countries as Wall Street saw the region as the new frontier for profits; but then sentiment suddenly changed, partly because Wall Street feared it had lent too much. There was a rush to take money out of the countries, exchange rates plummeted, and borrowers couldn't pay back what they promised. The IMF played its usual role—imposing extreme conditions, providing money that effectively went to the foreign private creditors, and leaving the countries' citizens on the hook. The citizens said, never again. Never again would they risk the loss of their economic sovereignty, a key part of a country's freedom. The East Asian countries reduced their borrowings abroad and increased their reserves (money a country holds in the form of US Treasury bills, gold, or other liquid assets).[20]

Even short of distress, indebtedness has its effects on developing countries and emerging markets. Free capital flows weaken local democratic voices. Capital can give a critical veto power to Wall Street, with international financiers threatening to take out their money if a candidate wins whom they don't like. The threat is sufficiently credible that typically voters are frightened and cast their ballot for a candidate of Wall Street's choice, or at least one it finds acceptable.

This is not hypothetical. It happened the first two times that Luiz

Inácio ("Lula") da Silva ran for the presidency of Brazil. The irony was that when he finally succeeded in getting elected, he led the country to enormous prosperity, quite contrary to the fears of the foreign bankers and the domestic elites.

For years, the international community, spearheaded by Wall Street, the US Treasury, and the IMF, tried to force countries to open up their capital markets, liberalize them, by eliminating restrictions on the flow of money in and out. This move essentially allowed their private firms to be persuaded by Wall Street debt brokers to get into as much debt as possible. Ironically, just as the East Asia crisis was brewing, caused, as I have noted, to a large extent *by these countries' liberalizing their capital markets*, there was a move at the 1997 Hong Kong meeting of the IMF to change the IMF's charter to allow it to push these policies on developing countries and emerging markets. Fortunately, it didn't happen, and a short 15 years later the IMF reversed its position, recognizing that, at times, capital controls that restrict the flow of money in and out of a country (euphemistically called capital account management techniques) could be a useful and desirable tool.[21]

The Charade of "Free and Fair" Trade

The rules governing international trade are a key part of the international economic architecture. Their alleged intent is to expand trade reciprocally, allowing countries to take advantage of economies of scale and comparative advantage, thereby raising living standards. Their objective is to create a "level playing field" by limiting restrictions on imports and subsidies to exports.

Producers and workers in an industry flooded with foreign imports may be unhappy; workers lose their jobs and firms go bankrupt. Property values plummet in the affected communities. But the advocates of these trade agreements say, "Buck up. In the long run, we'll all be better off. As consumers, we all benefit from cheaper imports. We'll shift workers from unproductive sectors trying to compete with more efficient foreign firms to our more productive sectors, and workers will doubly benefit from better jobs and lower prices." But, even in developed countries, too often workers don't move from low-productivity sectors competing with cheap Chinese imports to higher-productivity jobs. Instead, they move to the unemployment rolls, where their productivity is precisely zero. Nor should we be surprised. Neoliberals assumed that moving from one sector and one place to another was costless; it isn't. Consider what happened in the US as globalization unfurled in the past four decades. The old jobs might be in Indiana, the new jobs thousands of miles away in Seattle. The old jobs might be making cars, the new jobs might be for software engineers. Even with ample support, the skills transition would be difficult, not to mention the moving costs involved. But under neoliberal ideology, the focus was on "freeing the market," not levying the taxes that would generate the revenues required to provide adjustment assistance. So, there was little or no help for workers.

The advocates of free trade claimed that everyone would be better off—not just those who benefited from a newfound ability to export—through some kind of mystical trickle-down process. Even standard (neoclassical) economic theory had predicted that without assistance and transfers, trade liberalization would make some groups absolutely, not relatively, worse off.[22] The argument was obvious. By importing unskilled labor–intensive goods from places like China, we reduced the demand for American unskilled labor. If exports created jobs, imports destroyed jobs. The goods the US imported, like textiles and apparel, were more labor intensive—that is, they used more unskilled labor than typical exports. With roughly balanced trade, the increased exports corresponding to the increased imports would not boost unskilled jobs as much as the loss of jobs in the import-competing sectors. Wages of unskilled workers would fall, and unemployment would increase. But when I put this observation before my colleagues in the Clinton administration, they shrugged their shoulders. That work was just the writings of academic scribblers, not to be taken seriously by serious policymakers who *knew* that everyone had to be better off. Ideology and interests—a belief in neoliberalism—trumped theory and evidence.

The consequences are well known: an acceleration of the process of deindustrialization and a depression in the former industrial centers that fed a malaise and contributed, in turn, to a rise in populism, demagogues, and despair.

What interests me most from the perspective of this book is the vocabulary used to advance these agreements, especially in the United States. The trade agreements between countries were, as we have seen, often referred to as free trade agreements, and advocates spoke of "free and fair trade." But they were neither. They were managed for the most part by the interests of the large multinational corporations. A free trade agreement would simply forbid tariffs or subsidies; conceptually, it would be just a few pages long. In practice, trade agreements run to hundreds of pages because of the special treatments given to particular sectors and goods.

While the kinds of industrial subsidies that would enable poor countries to close the gap with rich countries are forbidden, powerful agricultural interests in the US and EU insist on allowing agricultural subsidies. These hurt hundreds of millions of people in the developing world who depend on agriculture by depressing the prices of the goods they sell. It used to be said that the average European cow gets a greater subsidy ($2 a day) than the per capita income of millions in the developing world.

Even the structure of the tariffs—with lower tariffs on basic, low value–added goods (tomatoes versus canned tomatoes)—was designed to discourage the growth of value-added industries in the developing world. And it worked. It's part of the reason that colonial trade patterns persist more than a half century after the formal end of colonialism, with developing countries still largely exporting primary commodities. It's an example of economic neocolonialism, about which the developing countries have long complained. Advanced countries have used their economic power to maintain this old system, which cannot be defended either morally or economically unless considered solely from the perspective of the multinationals.

Trade negotiations occur in "rounds." In each round, all the sides to the negotiations put on the table all the major things they're worried about. They do this in the hope that by putting lots of things on the table, the to-and-fro can result in a grand compromise in which everyone emerges with enough wins for the agreement to be democratically ratified within the country—with the winners outnumbering, and even perhaps compensating, the losers. The Uruguay Round, for instance, began in Punta del Este, Uruguay, in 1986, and was concluded eight years later in Marrakesh, Morocco, in 1994. It led to the establishment of the World Trade Organization (WTO) in 1995. On the table were intellectual property rights, the liberalization of services, agricultural subsidies, tariffs on textiles, and a host of other issues. The last major global trade negotiations that began in November 2001 in Doha, Qatar, in the shadow of 9/11, were in a sense a continuation of the earlier Uruguay Round. In the Uruguay Round, the developed countries got much of what they wanted, and the developing countries signed on in the hope—and with the promise—that in the next round the imbalances of the first would be corrected. This was acknowledged all around, and the new round was accordingly called the Development Round. But it took just a few years for the developed countries to forget their promises, harden their stances, and refuse to compromise. Nothing emerged, and the round was finally abandoned fourteen years later, in December 2015.

Matters worsened as first President Obama, then President Trump, and finally President Biden blocked appointments of judges to the

WTO's appellate court, which adjudicates disputes. The US effectively destroyed the rules-based international trading system. Biden joined Trump in flagrantly ignoring the rules by providing subsidies to chip and other industries and giving preferences to domestic producers in the green transition.[23] The amounts have been enormous and are currently estimated to exceed a trillion dollars, as we noted in chapter 3.[24] And there is now no court of appeals. It seemed clear: the rules are for the weak and powerless, but not for the powerful who made the rules.

In short, the neoliberal rules-based international trade regime increasingly seems like a dangerous farce. It restrained enterprise by taking away the freedom of companies in developing countries to produce critical Covid-19 and AIDS products. At the same time, it expanded the freedom of America's and Europe's drug companies to charge the world high prices. The consequences were equally unbalanced. Millions in the developing world unnecessarily suffered the worst effects of the diseases, and many died.[25] It also restrained the ability of developing countries for decades to move up the value chain and produce more advanced products, by giving their firms small subsidies; it condemned them to remain largely producers of primary products. But now the US, joined belatedly by Europe, is engaged in massive subsidies to grab the new green and high-tech jobs—never mind global agreements.[26]

Investment Agreements: Exploitation in Disguise

Within many trade agreements are investment agreements, which are supposed to protect investors.[27] In addition, there are hundreds of bilateral agreements between different countries. They were originally designed to protect against expropriation—a government taking private property without due compensation.

In practice, expropriation without compensation has become rare, and companies worried about it can usually easily obtain insurance against the risk (from a division of the World Bank Group or from special entities created by the US and other countries for this purpose).

Today, these agreements go well beyond simple expropriation, giving foreign investors rights that are not even afforded to domestic firms. What these agreements typically do is define expropriation expansively. A regulation that might reduce a company's profits—even if the regulation is a perfectly reasonable one like preventing pollution or prohibiting plutonium in baby cereals (an example actually used by one of the lawyers pushing these agreements!)—is viewed as a partial expropriation because it reduces the firm's potential profits. The agreements call for the companies to be compensated by the amount of profits that the company might otherwise have expected to have made if it continued polluting or selling an unsafe product. This is a mythical number, sometimes running into the hundreds of millions of dollars. Rather than forcing companies to pay for the damages they cause, the investment agreements effectively force governments to compensate rich multinationals for *not* harming others.

Four things make these agreements even worse.

First, the treaties introduce a kind of unproductive and unwarranted rigidity into the economic and political system. We never know what the future will bring. We may discover that a good produced by a firm is toxic. If the asbestos industry in the US had been owned by a foreign company when the danger of asbestos was discovered and the product outlawed, under the investment agreement the US government would have had to compensate the asbestos company for the profits they would have made had asbestos continued to be legal.

Similarly, we now recognize the dangers of climate change, but if governments take actions to restrict fossil fuels, under existing investment agreements they might have to pay out as much as $340 billion to compensate the companies for *not* destroying the planet.[28]

The investment agreements restrain the ability of a country to increase taxes on foreign companies whose headquarters are located in one of the countries that's a signatory to the agreement. Circumstances change, and governments must have the right to increase taxes. A country may, for instance, find itself in need of more tax revenue, perhaps because of a pandemic or some other calamity; but the investment agreement implies that while domestic firms and households can have their taxes increased, the foreign investor cannot.[29]

That's the second objection. Foreign companies are treated more favorably, with more protections than domestic companies. It's not a level playing field.

Third, it gives these foreign companies rights without well-specified obligations and responsibilities. They have a right not to have any new regulation imposed on them, but no responsibility not to impose harms on others. Famously, when a city in Mexico wanted to close down a toxic waste dump, the foreign company sued. It claimed, in effect, that it had no responsibility not to pollute.

However, the most noxious part of these agreements is how they are adjudicated. There is no international public court. Instead, a panel of three arbitrators is appointed after the private company sues the state (that's why they're often called Investor-State Dispute Settlement [ISDS] agreements). Each side gets to appoint one arbitrator, and the two appoint the third. Arbitration has become a business. The arbitrators are handsomely paid lawyers who know the game. They get repeat business from the corporations who are suing, so not surprisingly they disproportionately rule in favor of the corporations. And none of the norms we associate with modern judicial proceedings are observed, including transparency. Even the rulings are secret. The arbitrators can have conflicts of interests—a judge in one case can represent a plaintiff in another where similar issues are in dispute— but they don't even have to disclose them. There is no review and no appellate body.

Poor outcomes follow from poor processes. Developing countries have had to pay billions of dollars in cases in which outside objective observers have suggested nothing was due—or at most, the company should have gotten back the money it invested. In one famous case, Philip Morris filed a lawsuit in 2010 against Uruguay for the loss of profits associated with making the company state on its packages that cigarettes are a health hazard, in a manner similar to the warnings on cigarette packages in the US and Europe and dozens of countries around the world. Even then, one of the three arbitrators voted against Uruguay. Had one of the two other arbitrators switched their vote, Uruguay would have had to pay enormous amounts just to warn its citizens about a lethal product.[30] The arbitrator who said that Uruguay should compensate Philip Morris was putting corporate freedom, the "right" of corporations to do as they will—to exploit, in the language of Part I—above all other freedoms.

Countries sign onto such pernicious arrangements because corporations make economic threats—the country won't get any investment unless it signs up—reinforced by lectures, carrots, and sticks from the advanced countries. Again, fear reigns supreme. Developing countries have been cajoled into agreeing, even when there is scant evidence that after signing investment follows.

Interestingly, the US, the advanced country at the forefront of persuading weaker countries to sign on to these agreements, has suddenly reversed course. The country under Trump decided that these investment agreements violated American sovereignty. A major difference between the 1994 North American Free Trade Agreement (NAFTA) (a managed trade regime between the US, Canada, and Mexico) and the United States–Mexico–Canada Agreement (USMCA) that replaced it in 2020 was that the investment agreement provisions were dropped[31] (with a few exceptions). The reason was simple: The US realized that companies in other countries can sue should it want to change taxes or regulations, and this has happened. Canadian companies investing in US pipelines have sued after not getting regulatory approvals. This illustrates the asymmetry noted earlier. American companies cannot sue when they believe they have been hurt by a US regulatory action, but a Canadian company can. This introduces a new complexity: An American company could create a Canadian subsidiary, and if the Canadian subsidiary makes the investment in the US, that subsidiary could sue. The investment treaties have opened up a Pandora's box.

The US, under Trump, saw investment agreements as a violation of US sovereignty, of its freedom to act. But all international agreements restrict a country's actions, just as we saw earlier that all contracts restrict actions. At the same time, the agreements may expand freedoms to act in other ways. Trade agreements reduce a country's freedom to restrict imports, but they expand its freedom to export. That's the nature of most rules and regulations, taxes, and public programs. They expand freedoms in some areas as they contract them in others. The investment agreements fall squarely in the category of rules and regulations designed to expand the "freedom to exploit." They are the result of imbalances of power, and poor countries only sign them based on unfounded fears that if they don't, they'll be left behind. But the result is that corporations get what they want at the expense of other groups within society.

Democracy, Power, and the Global Economic Architecture

In this chapter, we've seen how a central theme of this book—expanding one person's freedom may lead to the unfreedom of others—plays out at the international level. The effects on the economic development of poorer countries have been devastating. Latin America had a lost decade because of its debt crisis. Many countries in Africa experienced a lost quarter century in which they moved backward—there was actually a process of deindustrialization[32] that made these countries more reliant on natural resources and left their economies less diversified and less resilient than they otherwise would be.

But there were equally pernicious effects on democratic development. The conditions placed on these countries in return for receiving financial assistance attempted to impose a version of neoliberal capitalism, with the emphasis on the private sector and privatization. The result was to impair the development of a robust state, undermining the possibility of the kind of concerted collective action necessary for economic success in the twenty-first century. The US, as I noted, has now embraced industrial policies. But the developing countries were told to shun them and so didn't develop the capacity to advance their industries or undertake policies and programs that would help close the gap with the more advanced countries. Moreover, the rules imposed on developing countries exacerbated power imbalances within their countries and in some cases effectively gave veto power to foreigners, the worst possible manifestation of neocolonialism.

An effective democracy requires limiting corporate power and curbing wealth inequalities. But the conditions imposed by the IMF and the World Bank often entailed weakening the power of unions and limiting progressive and corporate taxation. The World Bank for years issued *Doing Business*, a report scoring countries according to whether they had created a business-friendly environment. In defining what they meant, these institutions emphasized low corporate taxes, limited regulation, and pro-business labor relations. In other words, a wholly neoliberal approach. They could have valued good public infrastructure or a well-educated labor force, also necessary for a good business environment. Countries vied to be high on the *Doing Business* list lest they be viewed as an unattractive destination for multinational investment. In effect, the World Bank and the IMF had set up a race to the bottom, in which the only winners were the multinationals. Countries sought to attract them with lower and less-progressive taxes, worse labor conditions, and "better" trade and investment agreements.

Finally, capital market liberalization, which allows capital to move easily in and out of a country, not only exposed countries to greater volatility—for developing countries and emerging markets, often beyond their ability to manage—but also weakened democracy. In some cases, it effectively gave Wall Street and the global financial markets veto power over the choice of leaders. And if the citizens of a country were brave enough to contemplate a more progressive political vision, they would be ruthlessly punished, or at least there would be clear threats. In addition to assistance being withheld, foreign investment and the inflow of capital would slow, and in-country funds would be transferred abroad.

Unfettered markets designed along neoliberal principles have effectively robbed these countries of their political freedom. Where Milton Friedman was right was that economic and political freedoms need to be thought about together; but when you do, you arrive at an answer far different from the one he proposed. Restrictions on free capital mobility, shying away from investment agreements, closely regulating financial institutions, preventing the accretion of excess economic power—these are all ways that the economic system must be constrained if political freedom is to be maintained.

Another world is possible

Today's global economic architecture was largely created in the heyday of neoliberalism. It also, of course, reflected the realities of geopolitical power at that time, as the US emerged dominant after World War II and Russia's power crumbled in subsequent decades.

But there is a new geoeconomics and a new geopolitics. There is polarization not only within countries but between countries. This is different from the borderless world the US worked so hard to create after World War II and the fall of the Berlin Wall—admittedly, a borderless world governed by its rules that worked in its interests, or at least the interests of its large multinationals. Countries and people are now questioning neoliberalism and its rules, both domestically and internationally. People in developing countries and emerging markets are less accepting, for instance, of the right to exploit. They see free markets much as I've characterized them in this book, as giving freedom to some at the expense of others. And they rightly believe that today's system of global governance, in which decisions are made about the trade-offs of freedoms, rights, and responsibilities, lacks fairness and legitimacy. It is not just that the voices of the powerful countries dominate, it is that the voices are, to too large an extent, in line with large corporate and financial interests and not in line with ordinary citizens.

The framework discussed in previous chapters, which carefully balances and weighs the gains of some against the losses of others and shuns neoliberal ideology, provides the foundations for new national economic systems. It also lays the groundwork for a new fair and just global economic architecture that will simultaneously balance freedoms as it apportions rights and responsibilities.

This is not the place to delve into what that architecture would fully look like, but the principles follow closely on those I have already articulated. The discussion in this chapter has mainly focused on some of what should change. For instance, investment agreements should not interfere with a country's right to regulate or tax in the interests of its own citizens, and intellectual property rights provisions should be designed to encourage innovation and promote the health and welfare of everyone everywhere. We need an international framework for resolving excesses of debt, akin to domestic bankruptcy procedures, which considers the well-being of the debtor and broader societal interests. We need an international financial regulatory system that makes the kinds of crises that we repeatedly see less likely to happen and less deep when they do.

Three general principles underlay this alternative framework.

The first principle is that international rules should allow countries to do as they please so long as it does not harm other countries[33]—to use my earlier language, so long as there are not significant externalities on other countries. The US may think it foolish for developing countries to impose restrictions on capital coming into or out of their country, but the restrictions have no global consequence and if the policy is wrong, the country and its citizens alone bear the consequences.[34] As it turned out, the prevalent US view that capital market liberalization promoted growth and stability was wrong;[35] lack of capital controls led to global financial instability, and it was the developing countries that wound up paying the highest price for these flawed ideas.

The second principle is one of fairness or justice. Though we all have an intuitive sense of what that means—or at least what are outrageous violations—it is often useful to think about the matter through the lens provided by John Rawls, not knowing whether one was born in a rich and powerful country or a poor and weak country.[36] Behind the veil of ignorance, how would we respond to the following situation? Assume there is a cure for cancer available, but there is a global shortage of the medicine; a firm in our country is able and willing to produce it at an affordable price, but intellectual property rules prohibit the firm from manufacturing it. And what if 95 percent of the research costs had been publicly funded? Most people have enough empathy to be outraged and would say that a just system would not restrict access to and use of knowledge in such a situation. The freedom to gain access to such knowledge to save lives is more important than the freedom to exploit others through the exercise of market power, enabled by a poorly designed patent system. An intellectual property system that allows this is unfair and unjust. Yet this is the intellectual property system we have. Much of the global economic and financial architecture is like this, too.

What happens if the rich and powerful countries driving today's architecture are unwilling to create a fair or just global architecture and have sufficient power to prevent it? Obviously, we should do what we can to move in the direction of fairness—to fight, for instance, against vaccine apartheid or for tax justice. There have been successes—not as many as I would like, but perhaps more than could have been expected given the power relationships. But there's another option: striving for the *minimal* agreements necessary to keep the global system working, which focus on areas in which cooperation is essential, such as on climate change, but circumscribe the ability of the powerful to impose their will on others. We don't need investment agreements. Trade agreements involving Big Tech and Big Data are more likely to advance the interests of the corporations and limit the ability of governments to regulate them in the public interest.

The third principle is one woven throughout this book: Economic arrangements have societal costs that must be considered. Economics does not stand outside society. We've seen how freeing capital through capital market liberalization comes at a cost, not only an economic cost in the conventional sense but also a cost in economic and political freedom. In an important sense, the countries that turned to the IMF lost their economic sovereignty. And the results of the imposed policies had major societal consequences, with widespread interruptions in education implying that large numbers of people did not have the freedom to live up to their potential. Political freedom is also curtailed, because capital market liberalization effectively gives Wall Street veto power.

The three principles I've just described guide us to quite a different international regime, where power matters less and individuals matter more. There would be more symmetry and, almost surely, less hypocrisy. While it is not a surprise that current arrangements reflect power more than fairness, the perverse treatment of externalities is ironical because externality-like language is often used to defend international actions. IMF bailouts are defended on the grounds of contagion. In the absence of IMF intervention, the thinking goes, a crisis in one country will spread, like an infectious disease, to others. But in reality, the large and powerful countries do as they please, regardless of externalities and regardless of rules. The US talks about the international rule of law in trade, but nothing is done when Trump or Biden violate those rules, whether by imposing unjustified tariffs, by subsidizing its chip industry, or by passing Buy America provisions. And the US, by refusing to allow judges to the WTO's appellate court, ensures that nothing can be done within the rule of law. The US also knows that given the power relationships, nothing can be done outside the rule of law.

Another world is possible, one that expands the freedoms of most countries and the citizens within those countries to act and to live up to their potential. This chapter outlined what such an international order might look like. The next takes a closer look at national policies.

Progressive Capitalism, Social Democracy, and a Learning Society

I hope this is the moment in history in which neoliberalism's failures are so apparent that it will be abandoned. Gabriel Boric, who became Chile's president in 2022, captured the spirit of the moment on the eve of his primary victory when he said, "If Chile was the birthplace of neoliberalism, it will also be its grave!"

Here, I want to discuss an alternative framework, progressive capitalism (or a rejuvenated social democracy), which puts the well-being of all citizens at its center and goes beyond material goods to incorporate a sense of security and freedom. It takes human flourishing as the objective of our economic and social system, which includes citizens leading meaningful and creative lives. Good health, education, and a certain level of material well-being and security are necessary but not sufficient for this. We sometimes forget, but the economy is supposed to serve society, not the other way around.

I've emphasized how all the rules and regulations, laws and programs, shape the economy and society. In a short book like this, I can't lay out the framework of each. In the next few pages, I center my discussion of progressive capitalism around six themes. Several, concerning power, inequality, the importance of collective action, and the role of the economic system in shaping individuals, I've already introduced. Two, concerning creating a learning society and one with a rich ecology of institutions, I've only hinted at, and so I begin my discussion with these.

Creating a Learning Society

The world is ever-changing, and it changes in ways that are unpredictable. This view is markedly different from the equilibrium theory that was so influential in the early years of economics and continues to be today. We need to see institutions and governance structures through evolutionary lenses, where change and learning are always occurring. Our technology is changing. Our tastes are changing. Our understanding of our social and economic systems is changing. And our understanding of the physical world around us is changing. Indeed, one of the important sources of change in our economy and society is from learning—not just from the discoveries of new technologies through advances of science but also from learning more about how our complex political/economic/social system works.[1]

As social scientists, we want to understand the determinants and directions of change; as policymakers and citizens, we want to direct the change while knowing that we never have full control. At best, we may be able to nudge the economy and society one way or another.

Learning is not simply getting a formal education; it occurs throughout life. But there is also institutional learning, where we learn how to redesign institutional arrangements to make them better at achieving the objectives for which they are created and more adept at coordinating with other institutions. We can learn how to design them to transform themselves from within and respond to the ever-changing environments in which they function. Of course, typically there is some learning, but not as much as there could be. Central bankers did a better job in 2008 than they did in the Great

Depression partly because they learned from the failures of that earlier episode. But it was evident in the run-up to the Great Recession that even economists like Federal Reserve chair Ben Bernanke, who claimed to have learned the lessons of the Great Depression, really hadn't. Bernanke supported Alan Greenspan (who preceded him as chair) and most other members of the Fed as they pushed the deregulation that led to the Great Recession. One of the main lessons of the Great Depression was that underregulated financial markets are dangerous.

In recent years, the United States has embraced industrial policies in an attempt to shape the direction of the economy. It now recognizes that markets on their own won't suffice. The US government has also pushed a green economy, supported the development of Covid-19 vaccines, and recognized the US's excessive dependence on chips made abroad. Inevitably, because the US hasn't done much of this type of policy before (outside the military), there will be much to learn. Mistakes will be made. But the discovery of a mistake is no more reason to abandon such policies than recognizing the Fed's failure in the Great Depression and Great Recession is a reason to shut down the Fed. For instance, when the US government lent a half-billion dollars to Elon Musk for Tesla in 2009, it successfully supported the advancement of electric vehicle technology. But it made a mistake. It failed to insist on a share of the upside potential, which it easily could have done by insisting on receiving shares, for instance. If it had, the government (and American taxpayers) would have more than made up for the losses incurred in other technology loans and investments. It will capture some of the profits through taxes on individual income and corporate profits, but far less than if it had included the profit-sharing provision in the contract. The lesson to be learned is that it's important to pick projects well, but it's also important to design contracts well.

A learning society, then, entails both individual and institutional learning—and this learning is indeed part of human flourishing, a basic objective of a good society.[2] Learning is a never-ending process.

Earlier, I contrasted the equilibrium perspective of standard (neoliberal) economics—its assumption of a harmonious world in equilibrium without change—with the ever-changing world we live in often marked by intense conflict. We are finally beginning to understand that we are crashing headlong into our planetary boundaries. We *must* adapt. We have no choice. But the best way forward is almost never obvious. Thus, we take an evolutionary perspective with a focus on adaptation rather than on equilibrium. Progressive capitalism, I believe, will facilitate the evolution of our economy in ways that will help create a good society.[3]

A Decentralized Economy with a Rich Ecology of Institutions

Our economic system has to be decentralized, with a multiplicity of economic units—many enterprises and other entities (of different kinds) making decisions about what to do and how to do it. The world is too complex to be centrally planned, as communism called for more than a hundred years ago.

Having many units generates more learning about their own capabilities, about technology, about what others want. Each unit experiments, with different units having different conceptions about appropriate objectives and how to achieve them.

Much of the debate in recent years has been over the relative role played by public (government) institutions versus private (for-profit) companies. This perspective unnecessarily narrows the discussion. Any well-functioning economy or society requires a mix of types of institutions, not only public and private for-profit, but also cooperatives, private not-for-profit, and so on. And the governmental institutions need to operate at multiple levels, including local, state or provincial, national, and global. These institutions need to exert checks and balances on each other, and the overall governance structures must limit power and its abuse, a topic we will explore further.

I want to emphasize that there must be large parts of the economy that are not and cannot be driven by profits. These include much of the health, education, and care sectors, in which the narrow pursuit of profits often leads to perverse results. The private prison system has failed its core mission of rehabilitating prisoners. In the US, the most successful institutions that explain a lot of the country's overall achievements are its great research universities, which are either foundations, like Harvard and Columbia, or public. In other countries, too, the best universities are not-for-profit foundations, like Oxford and Cambridge, or state institutions, like the *grandes écoles* and the Sorbonne in France. Likewise, the cooperative part of the US financial system (typically referred to as credit unions) was the only segment that, for the most part, behaved in a socially responsible way both before the 2008 financial crisis and after.

But even the profit-making firms would be different under progressive capitalism than under neoliberalism. Their ethos would be different from our current firms hell-bent on maximizing shareholder wealth, whatever the cost to the rest of our society. And these private, profit-making firms wouldn't be revered as they are today. They have no magic potion that allows them to solve problems that others can't; it's just that some problems can be better solved by profit-maximizing firms and others by other kinds of entities.

Power, the Competitive Paradigm, and Progressive Capitalism

Modern economics begins, as I've noted, with a model of perfect competition, in which the economy is in a harmonious equilibrium.

Competition policy isn't even required because the economy will be naturally competitive.

Here, the neoliberals depart markedly from Adam Smith.[4] Earlier, I noted his concern about the proclivity of businesspeople to collude against the public interest. Conservative devotees of Smith champion him only to the extent that he agrees with their views. The fact is, the economy is not naturally competitive, in the narrow sense economists use that term. For economists, a truly competitive economy is one in which no firm has the power to raise prices, impose contractual terms on others, or block the entry of firms so that profits won't be bid away.[5] We've already seen these conditions aren't true in today's world—from the unsavory nondisclosure agreements and compulsory arbitrary provisions, to the persistent profits that are most visible in the digital giants.

Progressive capitalism recognizes that power exists, and that the distribution of power is a central concern; limiting power is crucial. There are power relations within and between the entities that constitute our economy and their interactions with citizens, and some can and do take advantage of others.

Power relations are central to understanding economics, politics, and society. America's economy was built on enslaved labor, hardly a manifestation of a free market. The country's legal structure was designed to enforce slavery and preserve the power relationship.

Power relations are central to understanding the growing inequality and widespread perception that the system is rigged, which have played such an important role in the disillusionment with democracy and its institutions and the growth of populism. Progressive capitalism would achieve a better balance by restraining corporate power, encouraging entry of new firms (by increasing the availability of finance and technology for entrants), and strengthening workers' rights, including through encouraging unionization.

Governance

The term "governance" refers to the rules that determine who makes what decisions and what the objectives are. Corporate governance relates to the rules affecting companies' decisions. Firm managers have enormous power in all the decisions of the company—how it treats workers, customers, shareholders, and stakeholders. Corporate governance laws specify and limit these powers.

Milton Friedman put forward an idea that became a central tenet of twentieth-century neoliberal capitalism, enshrined in the laws of many states: shareholder capitalism. The only goal for managers of firms is to maximize shareholder value. There's no responsibility to pay attention to workers, customers, the community, or even the environment, except to the extent that their actions, with respect to those "stakeholders," affect share prices. On the face of it, there was something noxious about this doctrine. It put Gordon Gekko, the fictional character in the movie *Wall Street*, and his ethos that "greed is good," on a pedestal. Adam Smith may have suggested that the pursuit of self-interest led to the well-being of society, but he rushed to qualify that statement. Not so Friedman.[6]

Even as Friedman enunciated that doctrine in a famous article in the *New York Times* in 1970,[7] economist Sandy Grossman and I, along with others, were analyzing the conditions under which shareholder maximization would lead to societal well-being. We showed that those conditions were extraordinarily restrictive and not satisfied by any real economy. But our articles, published in journals like the *Quarterly Journal of Economics* and the *Journal of Finance*, were far less influential than Friedman's.[8] He was an apostle of the free market and possessed enormous persuasive abilities, putting forward arguments that people like Ronald Reagan and Margaret Thatcher wanted to hear. He was less concerned about whether there were analytics behind these arguments.

Shareholder capitalism may have succeeded in enriching the owners of firms, but it didn't lead to shared societal prosperity.

Rebalancing power relations

Rebalancing power relationships in every aspect of our society (the household, the firm, the economy, politics) is essential for shared prosperity and creating a good and decent society. Today's imbalance of power has expanded the freedom of big corporations even as it constrained the freedom of ordinary citizens. People feel it intensely in the frustrations of day-to-day life. There is no real consumer choice and each company is as exploitive as the next, with awful provisions like mandatory arbitration of disputes and usurious fees. On top of that, there are often two-hour waits to talk to a "service" representative.

We observed in chapter 7 how the Supreme Court has weighed in to tilt the balance even more in favor of expanding the freedom and power of big business at everyone else's expense, ruling out class-action lawsuits in the context of the arbitrations that people have effectively been forced to agree to. This might seem like a small matter, but power relations are created within a system rule by rule, case by case.[9] So today, to achieve a better balance—to replace neoliberal capitalism with progressive capitalism—we have to reconstruct our economic and legal system, rule by rule, regulation by regulation, institution by institution. I've tried to provide multiple examples of what should and can be done throughout this book.

Organizing society

I have repeatedly noted that there are multiple ways to organize society. Some arrangements give more power to some group, less to others; some benefit one group at the expense of others. Traditionally, the rules are set by the powerful for the benefit of the powerful. That should be unacceptable. No real democracy would allow it. I have described an alternative basis for adjudicating among possible arrangements, an application of established philosophical principles underlying what social justice means and what a socially just and fair economic, political, and social system would look like—what would be chosen behind a veil of ignorance. It may be hard to put ourselves into such a mindset and to think through the implications; there may even be dilemmas and quandaries in doing so.[10] And when we complete our exercise, we still may not reach unanimity, or even consensus. But I suspect that the gulf in views we see today would be narrowed, and it would be possible to make compromises to enable us to move forward in the quest for a good and just society.

Checks and balances

One of the arguments for the decentralized economic structure described above, with its rich ecology of institutional arrangements, is the potential that this diversity has for exercising checks and balances. Civil society and the press provide a check against each other and against for-profit entities and the government. In political science, the standard argument for the division of powers within government relates to checks and balances; but equally important, we need checks and balances within society. Indeed, whatever the formal structures, if there is excessive power in the for-profit, private sector, the rich and powerful firms will exercise undue influence in the public sphere.

Economic Divides, Power, and Social Justice

But checks and balances won't work either if there is an excess concentration of wealth and income in society.

If we are to develop a system that works for the common good, an essential ingredient in any system claiming to be a good society, we have to have greater equality in all its dimensions, especially equality of opportunity. (This does *not* mean the elimination of all economic inequality—a system that achieved this would enervate incentives, and even a touch of realism involves recognizing that material incentives will be important for large fractions of the population.)

Particularly problematic is the growing power imbalance, increasing concentrations of wealth and corporate power mirrored by the evisceration of the power and incomes of workers. A social justice agenda is an important part of progressive capitalism. It attempts to reduce levels of inequalities, and not just in income and wealth. It's especially attentive to inequalities that arise from various forms of exploitation.

Access to basic health care is an important part of social justice, and should be a human right (as it is in the Universal Declaration of Human Rights adopted in 1948).[11] Progressive capitalism recognizes this, and most advanced countries have figured out that the fairest and more efficient way to provide health care is some form of public provision, sometimes supplemented by some private provision, especially in any country with a high level of income and wealth inequality.[12] Many people in the US, however, seem to find this hard to accept. The current system, even after the passage of the Affordable Care Act, has left many without adequate health care or no real choice of provider, the opposite of the law's intention. That's why in the US a public option—in which government is one of the providers people can choose—is so important. It enhances choice and competition, which is another way to limit the exploitation by market actors.[13]

Progressive Capitalism, the Role of the State, and Social Democracy

Importantly, progressive capitalism entails a greater role for collective action in all its forms and a better balance between the private sector and collective action, including government at all levels. Communism went too far in one direction, Reagan-Thatcherism went too far in the other, and the Third Way reflected by the triangulation of Clinton,

Blair, and Schröder was an insufficient correction. It embraced neoliberalism, materialism, and free markets, and paid insufficient attention to social justice concerns, to a degree that might not have been acceptable in a world in which communism and market economies were competing for hearts and minds. Indeed, free trade agreements with investment agreements and financial market liberalization experienced their heyday during Clinton's administration. Taxes on capital gains, which overwhelmingly benefited the very rich, were cut.[14]

Collective action can take many forms. Examples of collective action include NGOs, unions, church groups, producer and consumer cooperatives, class-action lawsuits, conservation societies, and a plethora of other groups working to advance causes they believe in.

I began the book with a straightforward observation: *One person's freedom is another's unfreedom.* Externalities are pervasive, and the management of these externalities—including environmental devastation—that are inevitably the direct by-products of unfettered markets requires public actions, including regulations. Indeed, any game needs rules and regulations. I've delineated here the need for regulations to curb the agglomeration of power and the exploitation of some by others.

Another key observation is that people can accomplish together what they cannot accomplish alone. But in many arenas of collective action, free-rider problems arise, so that good (efficient) outcomes require some degree of coercion of the kind that only government can properly impose. It also may be desirable to encourage voluntary collective action, through subsidies, for instance.

Chapter 11 described a plethora of arenas in which collective action was desirable because markets, on their own, were inefficient or failed in some other way. Here, I want to emphasize that the desirability of collective action is broader.

A key component of collective action is more public investments in children and their future, in research, and, more broadly, in social and physical infrastructure. These investments will not just promote growth; they also will enhance the opportunities (the freedoms) of ordinary citizens. A natural empathy toward others should make us averse to the current system, where the fortunes of a child depend so much on the income and education of her parents.

Still another key component is social protection against the vicissitudes of life, including from markets even when they are tempered and tamed.[15] Technologies are always changing, so few workers can be secure in their jobs. And no one can be sure that he won't be struck by a health calamity. Social protection is itself liberating. It frees people to undertake risks that they otherwise wouldn't, lest they fail and be left destitute. That is why societies with better systems of social protection can actually be more innovative.

Government failure

But critics of this perspective emphasizing the role of collective action suggest it pays insufficient attention to government failures. The claim is that as flawed as economic processes may be, political processes—the way decisions are made in government—are worse. This, critics of government action assert, is true even in the absence of outright corruption. Policies and expenditures can be driven more by short-term political gains than by long-term societal interests.

Any American who lived through the Trump administration knows about government and political failures. I am not naive. I know that creating a strong, effective state that advances economic progress and social justice—not special interests—is hard. But I also know that there has been little or no social and economic progress in the absence of a strong and effective state. During my fifty-plus years as an economist, I've seen some economic miracles—per capita incomes in the East Asian countries increasing tenfold, for example—and these successes were directly related to government policies. I've also seen some failures and disappointments. We've not done as good a job at managing the macroeconomy as we could or should have, but things are better than they would have been had they simply been left to the market.[16] We have no choice but to try to make our democracy work in ways that advance the interests of society as a whole. At times, societies have had considerable success in doing just this. We have to learn both from the successes and the failures.

Two of the things we've learned is that an imbalance of economic power translates into an imbalance of political power; and polities in which money dominates inevitably get corrupted. Neoliberalism's dominance in so many places has much to do with the special interests that profit from its ideas and the political power those interests wield.

We know, too, some of the things that contribute to societal and economic success: openness and transparency, adaptive learning institutions, systems of checks and balances—including through an active and diversified press—an active civil society with citizen participation, and a variety of mechanisms for giving citizens a voice.

Shaping People

Finally, the design of our economic, political, and social system has to be cognizant of how it shapes people. As I emphasized in Part II, we are not born fully formed; we are shaped by our parents, our schools, and the environment surrounding us—including the economic, political, and social system in which we are embedded. As we attempt to shape our economic system, we need to be conscious of these effects. As I have noted, cooperative institutions may spur more cooperative behavior. The neoliberal system that we've had for the past half century has failed on its own terms by not producing the shared prosperity it promised, but, more disturbingly, it also bred more selfish and materialistic people who are less honest and trustworthy. What kind of a world is it in which individuals routinely make money by taking advantage of others and don't even feel guilty?

Margaret Thatcher famously said in a 1987 interview, "Who is society? There is no such thing!" But at that very moment as Britain's leader she was trying to shape its society and its citizens. She articulated a vision that's the antithesis of the good society. Neoliberalism's success in moving society in the direction of Thatcher's vision may be its greatest failing.

There is a further set of arguments for the social justice agenda that centers around who we are as individuals and as a society. As I also noted in Part II, inequality leads to the wealthiest citizens feeling a sense of entitlement and the poorest living in despair, without hope or aspirations.

Progressive capitalism's deep aspiration is to construct a society in which there is more empathy, more caring, more creativity and healthy striving, with individuals who are less selfish and more honest—and these attributes will lead to a better-functioning economy and society.[17] I believe that the progressive economy I'm advocating will succeed in doing so.

Concluding Remarks

Some critics have asked, "Can capitalism be progressive? Isn't this an oxymoron?" The system I've described briefly is a significant departure from the current one, even if it shares the term "capitalism." The "capital" that is central to twenty-first-century progressive capitalism is not just physical or financial but includes human capital, intellectual capital, organizational capital, social capital, and natural capital—all the foundations of our economy. Indeed, this broadening of our understanding of the term is essential and corresponds to the changing nature of our economy and society.

We can, I believe, construct an economy and society based on the principles I've outlined. Even if we don't succeed in creating an "ideal" society, we can do much better than the current form of capitalism.

CHAPTER 14

Democracy, Freedom, Social Justice, and the Good Society

A ny discussion of freedom must begin with a discussion of whose freedom we're talking about. The freedom of some to harm others, or the freedom of others not to be harmed? Too often, we have not balanced the equation well: gun owners versus victims of gun violence; chemical companies versus the millions who suffer from toxic pollution; drug companies versus patients who die or whose health worsens because they can't afford to buy medicines. We know whose freedom prevailed. The list of injustices is long.

It is remarkable how, in spite of all the failures and inequities of the current system, so many still champion the free-market economy. This in spite of the daily frustrations of dealing with health insurance companies, telephone companies, landlords, or airlines. It boggles the mind that anyone who lives under twenty-first-century capitalism, let alone reads about the myriad abuses, can believe in unfettered markets or the inevitable efficiency of "free" enterprise.

To put it bluntly, ordinary citizens around the world have been sold a bill of goods. When there's a problem, they've been told to "leave it to the market." They've even been told that the market can solve problems of externalities, coordination, and public goods. That's purely wishful thinking, and I've explained why. A well-functioning society needs rules, regulations, public institutions, and public expenditures financed by taxes.

The other side to this fairy tale that private, profit-seeking firms can do no harm and are perfectly efficient is that government is rapacious and inefficient.

Many people have benefited from this version of the story, including CEOs (and their shareholders), whose freedom to exploit was expanded. Their pockets were enriched, and their powers heightened, especially as public services were privatized. The rich and powerful controlled the media. Political leaders whom they supported repeated and amplified the message, some with memorable lines, like Reagan's "Government is not the solution to our problem; government is the problem."[1]

Mindsets, once created, are hard to change. Many Americans still believe that the United States is the land of opportunity, and they still believe in the American Dream, even though for decades the statistics have painted a very different picture. Of course, America should aspire to be a land of opportunity, but clinging to beliefs that are not supported by today's realities, that hold that markets by themselves are the solution to today's problems, is not helpful. Unfettered markets have created many of the central problems we face, including inequalities, the climate crisis, and America's opioid crisis. And unfettered markets cannot solve any of them; they cannot manage the massive structural changes that we are going through—including global warming, AI, and the realignment of geopolitics—without leaving many behind. Indeed, the private sector on its own cannot address climate change anywhere near adequately, especially with the urgency we need and in a way that equitably shares the costs of the green transition.

And this realization may provide insights into the cultural wars breaking out around the world. Why should the Right so adamantly resist taking the necessary steps to prevent climate change? Why should they refuse to wear masks and get vaccinated during the Covid-19 pandemic? The answer is that climate change and pandemics present inconvenient truths to the free-market mindset. If externalities are important, then collective action is important, and markets by themselves cannot be relied on. Better to ignore reality than change their minds. But change they must if we are to create a society that even roughly corresponds to our aspirations and ideals.

Resolving Disputes over Freedom in a Divided Society

What happens if, even after a society closely examines and extensively debates whose rights are more important, people still don't agree? Almost by definition a society can have only one assignment of rights. Citizens must agree on that assignment collectively by some mechanism of collective decision-making.

We also have to make a collective decision about the regulations that govern our society. We need environmental regulations, traffic regulations, zoning regulations, financial regulations; we need regulations in all the constituents of our economy. In a twenty-first-century economy, a complex set of rules and regulations is necessary.

We would all like to live in a society with like-minded people who, when they reason together, come up with congruent answers to fundamental questions. We would also like to live in a world in which all countries share our views about human rights and democracy. But we don't.

Some small communities can achieve a broad consensus (but typically far from unanimity). But larger societies have a harder time of it. Many of the critical values and presumptions are what economists, philosophers, and mathematicians refer to as *primitives*, underlying assumptions that, while they can be debated, cannot be resolved. Still, given the importance of living together and the need to make at least a limited number of collective decisions, we must ask, is there anything that can be done to find areas of agreement? To answer that it is useful to understand what gives rise to societal divides and why the divides have widened.

The role of income and wealth inequality

I believe a large part of the answer is related to two problems of neoliberalism that I've called attention to: the growing income and wealth divide that marks twentieth- and twenty-first-century neo-liberal capitalism and the polarization caused by the media. Making matters worse is that current rules allow the rich and elites to have a disproportionate voice in shaping both the policies and societal narratives. All of which leads to an enhanced sense by those who are not wealthy that the system is rigged and unfair, which makes it all the more difficult to heal divisions.

As income inequalities grow, people wind up living in different worlds and don't interact. There is a large body of evidence showing that economic segregation is growing and has consequences, for instance, on how each side thinks and feels about the other.[2] The poorest members of society see the world as stacked against them and give up on their aspirations; the wealthiest develop a sense of entitlement, and their wealth helps to ensure that the system *is* rigged. But these individual opinions about the economic divide only increase the societal divide.

The divisive role of the media

The media, including social media, provides another source for this division. Media has immense power to shape societal narratives and has played a role in societal polarization. As I noted, the business model of much of the media entails stoking divides. Fox News, for instance, discovered that it was better to have a devoted right-wing audience attracted by its distorted reporting that watched *only* Fox than to have a broader audience attracted to more balanced reporting.

Social media has discovered that it's profitable to get engagement by enragement, and that it can develop its algorithms to effectively refine whom to target even if the practice leads to societal polarization by providing different information to different users.

Reasoning as a resolution

A premise of this book is that *reasoning*, a core Enlightenment value, and discourse based on that reasoning can enable us to better understand the full complexities of what is at issue and help to reach common ground in the pursuit of the common good. For instance, reasoning about the meaning and nature of freedom leads to the conclusion that the worldview of the libertarian Right is fundamentally incoherent simply because it doesn't recognize that one person's freedom is another's unfreedom. I have attempted to provide a more coherent and meaningful analysis of freedoms within an interdependent modern society.

I believe there is broad consensus on many of the key elements of what constitutes a good and decent society and what kind of economic system supports that society. A good society, for instance, must live in harmony with nature. Our current capitalism hasn't been doing an adequate job of this; progressive capitalism, with a commitment to environmental regulation, would put this front and center.

A good society allows individuals to flourish and live up to their potential. Our current capitalism is failing large portions of the population. Progressive capitalism again addresses this both through predistribution and redistribution.

A good economic system would encourage people to be honest and empathetic, with the ability to cooperate with others. The current capitalist system too often encourages the antithesis; the rich ecology of institutional arrangements under progressive capitalism would do better.

Moreover, when there is no consensus about how to make certain critical decisions, the philosophical traditions of the utilitarians/Benthamites (those who follow the ideas of the nineteenth-century philosopher Jeremy Bentham) and John Rawls can help us think through what set of rules makes sense in a good society; they can also provide at least frameworks for thinking about the sum total of the rules that constitute a society.

Politics is about navigating a world in which there might be large differences in opinion on what should be done collectively. In some cases, there can be horse trading, an agreement on the overall package, with some accepting a set of decisions in one domain that they think is wrong, or at least not ideal, in return for others accepting decisions in another domain about which they are unconvinced. There is harmony in the overall outcome, disgruntlement in the details. There might even be near unanimity in the end, with citizens understanding the benefits from the social cohesion that results from such widespread agreement.

Unfortunately, this is often not the case. Some argue that we should narrow the space of collective decision-making precisely because there are differences that cannot be resolved. I have explained that this comes at a high price. There are enormous benefits from collective actions associated with public goods like research and development, education, and health care. But more fundamentally, we simply can't avoid collective decision-making. We must have a common set of rules to govern us.

What doesn't work typifies the US and a few other places: people who hold the levers of power using them to maintain, amplify, and extend their power while making only limited efforts to find or create a political consensus. The US has a political system created more than 200 years ago that allots disproportionate political weight to some parts of the country and gives the states the ability to partially disenfranchise some citizens through gerrymandering and voter suppression. History has long taught that governments and political systems marked by such disparities between the governing and the governed—even when there is a façade of democracy—cannot survive. Inevitably, trust in the government and belief in its legitimacy will erode.

I still believe that if we could move the discussion out of the realms of ideology, identity, and absolutist positions and into the realm of healthy debate, a consensus might emerge, not on every matter, but on a much broader range of issues, which would allow us to move more easily toward a good society.[3]

Neoliberalism and Sustained Democracy

For a long time, the Right has tried to establish a monopoly over the invocation of "freedom," almost as if they had a trademark on it. It's time to call out the Right and reclaim the word.

Milton Friedman and Friedrich Hayek argued that economic and political freedoms are intimately connected, with the former necessary for the latter. But I've argued that the economic system that has evolved—largely under the influence of these thinkers and others like them—undermines meaningful democracy and political freedom. Meaningful political freedom can only be ensured in the context of an economic system such as progressive capitalism, which ensures a modicum of shared prosperity and where power—money—doesn't have an improper role in the outcomes.

The tenor of both Friedman's and Hayek's argument was that free and unfettered markets on their own are efficient. If only government is kept at a distance, they maintained, competitive markets are self-sustaining and necessary mechanisms to keep democracy running smoothly. To prevent the descent into "serfdom," one needs to keep government small, using it mainly to enforce property rights and contracts, and steering it away from providing public goods, regulating, or redistributing.

I've explained why they (and the myriad others who share their view) are wrong. Markets on their own are essentially never efficient.

Are free markets sustainable without a stronger democracy? Why neoliberal capitalism devours itself

Not only are neoliberal economies inefficient, but neoliberalism as an economic system is not sustainable. There are many reasons to believe that a neoliberal market economy is prone to devour itself. A market economy runs on trust. Adam Smith emphasized the importance of trust, recognizing that society couldn't survive if people brazenly followed their own self-interest rather than good codes of conduct:

> The regard to those general rules of conduct, is what is properly called a sense of duty, a principle of the greatest consequence in human life, and the only principle by which the bulk of mankind are capable of directing their actions. . . . [U]pon the tolerable observance of these duties, depends the very existence of human society, which would crumble into nothing if mankind were not generally impressed with a reverence for those important rules of conduct.[4]

For instance, contracts have to be honored. The cost of enforcing every contract through the courts would be unbearable. And with no trust in the future, why would anybody save? The incentives of neoliberal capitalism focus on self-interest and material well-being and have done much to weaken trust (evidenced so clearly in the financial sector in the run-up to the 2008 financial crisis). Without adequate regulation, too many people, in the pursuit of their own self-interest, will conduct themselves in an untrustworthy way, sliding to the edge of what is legal, overstepping the bounds of what is moral. We've seen, too, how neoliberalism helps create selfish and untrustworthy people. A "businessman" like Donald Trump can flourish for years, even decades, taking advantage of others.[5] If Trump were the norm rather than the exception, commerce and industry would grind to a halt.

We also need regulations and laws to make sure that there are no concentrations of economic power. We've seen not only that business seeks to collude and would do so even more in the absence of antitrust laws, but even playing within current laws there's a strong tendency for the agglomeration of power. The liberal ideal of free, competitive markets would, without government intervention, be evanescent.

And we've also seen that those with power too often do what they can to maintain it. They write the rules to sustain and enhance power, not curb or diminish it. Competition laws are eviscerated, incapable of responding to new technologies and firms' new ways to get and exercise market power. Enforcement is weakened. In this world of neoliberal capitalism, wealth and power are ever ascendant.

Is neoliberalism politically sustainable and consistent with a sustainable democracy?

Neoliberalism is not economically sustainable, and it undermines the sustainability of democracy—just the opposite of what Hayek and Friedman claimed.

We have created a vicious circle of economic and political inequality, one that cements more freedom for the rich and less for the poor, at least in the United States, where money plays such a large role in politics. There are many ways in which economic power gets translated into political power and undermines the fundamental democratic value of one person having one vote. The reality is that some people's voices are much, much louder than others. In some countries, it's as crude as buying votes, with the wealthy having more money to buy more votes. In advanced countries, the wealthy use their influence in the media and elsewhere to create narratives, and they are in the best position to make their narratives become the conventional wisdom. For instance, certain rules and regulations and government interventions that are in the interest of the rich and powerful are in the national interest, they claim—and too often they are successful in persuading others that this is true.

Fear is a key instrument the powerful wield to persuade others to go along with their agenda: If the banks are not bailed out, the economic system will collapse, and *everyone* will be worse off. If the corporate tax rate is not cut, firms will leave and go to other jurisdictions that are more business-friendly.[6]

Is a free society one in which a few dictate the terms of engagement?[7] In which a few control major media and use that control to decide what news the populace sees? People in the West have long criticized the propaganda pumped out by the Nazis and the Communists, but we are embedded in a nightmare realm of Murdochian propaganda and worse, including a Musk- and Zuckerberg-controlled social media allowed to make whatever they want go viral. And we have, as a result, created a polarized world in which different groups live in different universes, disagreeing not only on values but on facts.

A strong democracy can't be sustained with a neoliberal economy for another reason. Neoliberalism has given rise to enormous "rents," the monopoly profits that are a major source of today's inequalities. Much is at stake, especially for many in the top 1 percent, centered on the enormous accretion of wealth that the system has allowed.

Democracy requires compromise if it is to remain politically sustainable, but the middle ground has become increasingly difficult in today's polarized society. And neoliberalism has contributed to this situation in so many ways, not least in the huge economic divides it created. Compromise is also difficult when there is so much at stake in terms of both economic and political power. No wonder then that the Right has adopted a "prisoner take all" attitude. One might have thought that when presidents Bush and Trump came into office with a distinct minority of popular support, they would have sought policies slightly right of center. But no, they took the view that elections

have consequences, and even when there was voter suppression, gerrymandering, and a stacked electoral system, winning provided blanket
permission to do whatever they could get away with.[8] That included
a tax cut for the rich at the expense of ordinary citizens—even as the
country's growing inequality was recognized to be among its central problems. It also included an attempt to cut back health care—
which failed at the national level but succeeded in many Republican
states—in the face of low and declining national life expectancy.

The lack of compromise contributes to instability in politics, policies,
and programs, with large economic and social consequences. Because
large divides in income easily translate into large divides in politics,
the absence of social solidarity and the presence of political divisiveness often lead to instability in policies, like the whiplash over student
debt or the sudden cessation of Covid-era funds for poor families. The
vicissitudes of policies are themselves bad for the economy. Uncertainty
about the economic environment (about regulations and taxes) discourages firms from making the investments required for robust growth.
Economists often criticize the pendulum swing of these policies, but
they don't look at the underlying problem. If societal divisions were
smaller, there would still be changes in policy, but the magnitude of
the shifts would be smaller, and hence the consequences would be less.

Guardrails

To put it differently, a free-market, competitive, neoliberal economy
combined with a liberal democracy does not constitute a stable equilibrium, not without strong guardrails and a broad societal consensus
on the need to curb wealth inequality and money's role in politics.
This kind of strong democracy is necessary to sustain a competitive,
free economy. Whether America's political and economic system today
has enough safeguards to sustain meaningful economic and political
freedoms is questionable.

I've talked about some of the constituent elements of the requisite guardrails, such as competition policy, to prevent the creation, maintenance, and abuse of market power. We need checks and balances, not just within government, as every schoolchild in the US learns, but more broadly within society. Strong democracy, with widespread participation, is also part of what is required, which means working to strike down laws intended to decrease democratic participation like legislation associated with voter suppression.

These guardrails and checks and balances are a core part of progressive capitalism, with its curbs on market power and excessive inequality and with its robust diversity of institutional arrangements. There will certainly be constant pressures to remove the guardrails, weaken the checks and balances, and allow inequalities to grow. We see that today even in the strongest of social democracies.

In the US, the guardrails look pretty shaky. Some, such as Martin Wolf, the *Financial Times*'s chief economic commentator, worry that matters are so bad America might soon no longer be a functioning democracy.[9]

An awareness of the threat posed by the dynamics of any version of capitalism where wealth, power, and inequalities can compound, is part of the answer to how democracy can be sustained. One of the objectives of this book is to enhance that awareness.

The road to populism

Under the very name of freedom, neoliberals and, even more, the radical Right, have advocated policies that restrict the opportunities and freedoms (both political and economic) of the many in favor of the few. All these economic and political failures associated with neoliberalism have hurt large fractions of the citizenry, many of whom have responded by turning to populism, drawn to authoritarian figures like Trump, Bolsonaro, Putin, and Modi. These men search for scapegoats to explain what has gone wrong and provide simplistic answers to complex questions.

We can't help but reach conclusions that are just the opposite of Friedman's and Hayek's. They misread history—I suspect deliberately. The severe bout of authoritarianism—Hitler, Mussolini, Stalin—from which the world was recovering at the time Hayek and Friedman were writing was not caused by governments having played too large a role.[10] Instead, these heinous regimes were brought about by extreme reactions to government not doing enough. It was not then, and it is not today, the case that authoritarianism was arising in social democratic states with large governments, but rather in countries marked by extremes of inequality and high levels of unemployment, where governments have done too little. We've seen that it is the social democracies—the countries that most approximate our vision of progressive capitalism—that have sustained the strongest democracies. The countries that have adopted the tenets of neoliberalism have traveled down the road to populism and serfdom.

In short, Hayek and Friedman were wrong. Unfettered, neoliberal capitalism is antithetical to sustainable democracy. Hayek's famous book *The Road to Serfdom* claimed that a too-big state was paving the way to our loss of freedom. It is evident today that free and unfettered markets advocated by Hayek and Friedman and so many on the Right have set us on the road to fascism, to a twenty-first-century version of authoritarianism made all the worse by advances in science and technology, an Orwellian authoritarianism where surveillance is the order of the day and truth has been sacrificed to power.

With one of the two major parties actively working to suppress votes and doing almost whatever it takes to attain and maintain power, it is understandable that many think the country is now heading toward fascism. Whether this twenty-first-century version will take the ugly turn that some of the worst fascist countries took in the twentieth century is, of course, unknowable. We do know that Trump and some other leaders in the Republican Party have peddled extreme nationalism and made covert, and sometimes almost overt, appeals to racism and authoritarianism.

America may be first in heading down this road, but other countries may not be far behind.

Progressive Capitalism, Social Democracy, and Social Justice

I have laid out an alternative road, simply put, because we have to head somewhere better than where we are going now. And this brings me back to the links between freedom and the progressive capitalism (rejuvenated social democracy) agenda, with its focus on equality, social justice, and democracy.

The freeing role of a liberal education

Educational systems—and our knowledge system more broadly, including research universities and think tanks—play a central role in creating sustainable, free societies by inculcating the kinds of values that are required and by helping free individuals from social coercion and enhancing their autonomy. The lens through which we see the world is influenced by the people around us and the events we experience in ways we usually don't notice. A good liberal arts education helps us to understand these forces. It allows us to see that we don't have to assume the roles in society that our parents and others expect us to play. A better understanding of how our preferences are shaped and how they are affected by peer pressure can be freeing.

Education also plays an important role in shaping our preferences and actions. We may become more cooperative and trustworthy as we better understand how important these traits are for a society to function well.

A liberal education also allows us to see the flaws in current economic arrangements and to understand why, for instance, unfettered markets are the problem and not the solution. And this is why people in favor of continuing current norms (such as restricted gender roles or the primacy of markets) regardless of the merits fight so strongly against a liberal education. They do so even in the US, which has in its foundations of success the very advances in knowledge that rest on a strong educational system based on Enlightenment values.

Democracy

The democracy part of the progressive capitalism/rejuvenated social democracy agenda is crucial, but rejuvenating it necessitates restoring the social justice part, too. This raises critical questions. Besides circumscribing excessive inequalities and the role of money in politics and the media, is there anything else we can do to prevent capitalists' interests from distorting our social, economic, and political system? Is there anything we can do to make democratic progressive capitalism more sustainable, or more likely to be sustained? While there is no magic formula, there are some things we can do. We can attempt to inculcate democratic values more deeply, so people will be suspicious of the agglomeration of power in any form. We can instill a stronger commitment to freedom of the press and the necessity of a diversified press and media, so the wealthy do not have a disproportionate say. We can strengthen systems of checks and balances in our society. It is not just one branch of government checking other branches but the private, public, and civil society spheres checking each other, and the fourth estate checking them all.

And, of course, we have to ensure we have a democracy at all. While earlier concerns were about a majority suppressing minority rights, today the concern in the US is about a minority suppressing majority rights. Voter suppression, extreme gerrymandering, and a host of other antidemocratic actions by Republican extremists have put America's democracy in danger.[11] There are multiple reforms in our political processes that would deepen our democracy and increase the likelihood of its survival.

American exceptionalism

Perhaps we should not be surprised by where the US has landed. It is a country now so divided that even a peaceful transition of power is difficult; where life expectancy is the lowest among advanced nations and where we can't agree about truth or how it might best be ascertained or verified. Conspiracy theories abound, and the Enlightenment has to be relitigated daily.

There are good reasons to worry whether America's form of ersatz capitalism and flawed democracy is sustainable. The incongruities between lofty ideals and stark realities are too great. It's a political system that claims to cherish freedom above all else but in many ways is structured to deny or restrict freedoms of much of its citizenry. The real danger is that the populism to which neoliberalism's failures have given rise will lead to even worse demagogues than those who have already shown up.

We don't have to continue down this road. We are at a moment in which the faults of the current system are apparent, in which a majority are calling for change, and in which most agree with the values, policies, and programs underlying progressive capitalism.

There is a real urgency to the progressive capitalism agenda set forth here and to the progressives recapturing the language of freedom. Progressive capitalism maximizes citizens' real freedoms. But time is not on our side. The climate crisis won't allow us to ignore the way unfettered capitalism has pushed us beyond our environmental limits; and the inequality/populism/democratic crisis won't allow us to ignore how democratic ideals are being torn asunder. The collision of the two represents an especial threat.

When we successfully dismantle the myths about freedom that have been propagated by the Right and arrive at a more nuanced and balanced perspective, we will have taken our first and most important step toward creating a good society, where the freedoms of citizens to flourish, to live up to their potential, and to live in harmony with each other and nature are most expansive. Progressive capitalism will allow us to construct a vibrant democracy in which people cooperate for the common good. It is the truly freeing economic and political system.

ACKNOWLEDGMENTS

This book builds on and extends a lifetime of scholarship on the questions at hand, and so it is impossible to acknowledge all those who have contributed to my understanding of these issues.

Externalities and collective action are the center of attention of any economist working in the economics of the public sector, and that was a field which I began tilling early in my career, inspired by and working with a young cohort of scholars in what was referred to as the New Public Finance, including Jim Mirrlees, Peter Diamond, Agnar Sandmo, and my students Tony Atkinson, Richard Arnott, and Geoff Heal.

Only a few economists have been willing to engage directly in the discussion employing terms like "freedom" and "rights," and two of these are friends whose influence will be apparent: Partha Dasgupta and Amartya Sen.

I have learned a lot from lawyers, too, those more directly concerned with freedoms and rights and the trade-offs that I discuss. Five have been especially important in my understanding of the issues discussed here: Rob Howse at New York University, David Kennedy at Harvard University, Nathalie Bernasconi-Osterwalder at the International

Institute for Sustainable Development, Lori Wallach at Rethink Trade at the American Economic Liberties Project, and Guido Calabresi, who was at Yale University when I taught there. It should also be evident that the issues I discuss here go well beyond standard economics and touch on those that are at the core of political science. Again, I am indebted to a host of thinkers in this arena, not the least Anahí Wiedenbrüg, Edward Stiglitz, Michael Doyle, and Jacob Hacker.

I have benefited, too, from extended discussions with Ravi Kanbur, who has been grappling with many of these same questions. So, too, for my Columbia University colleague Ned Phelps.

No one has had more influence in the shaping of Part II of this book, where I reexamine the concepts of freedom in the context of social coercion and the shaping of individuals by our economic, political, and social system, than Karla Hoff and Allison Demeritt, with whom I have been working on this area, especially as it affects development (in a field called behavioral development economics), for many years. At several points here, I have referred to our forthcoming book, from which I have drawn liberally.

I owe a special thanks to Akeel Bilgrami and Jonathan R. Cole for inviting me to address these issues at their Columbia University seminar on freedom and which provided the genesis for the book; to Akeel for his detailed comments on an earlier draft; to the University of Padua for providing an opportunity to extend that seminar into a larger-scale lecture as part of their 800th anniversary lecture series on freedom; and to Oxford University and Central European University for allowing me to try out these ideas before them. I also am indebted to the Sanjaya Lall Memorial Trust and All Souls College, Oxford, for providing me with the opportunity to spend a month in Oxford, where I had taught some forty-five years earlier, and where I engaged in many a philosophical conversation on issues related to this book. Conversations there with David Vines, John Vickers, and Vincent Crawford were particularly valuable.

As in every book, the influence of my long-term Columbia colleague Bruce Greenwald will be apparent, especially in the understandings of the pervasiveness of externalities and the necessity of creating a learning society.

I am deeply appreciative of Columbia University for providing me for the past quarter of a century with the support and environment within which I could flourish. Good universities are necessary for a free society, and Columbia sets an example.

Columbia has also provided me with first-rate, engaged students with whom I have been able to discuss these issues, several of whom have served as research assistants on this project. But they have been more than ordinary research assistants—they have debated and discussed the ideas. I want to single out Haaris Mateen, Parijat Lal, and Ricardo Pommer Muñoz. Nikhil Basavappa and Gina Markov also contributed, doing research and working on endnotes.

My office at Columbia—Gabriela Plump, Marianna Palumbo, and Caroline Feehan—provided enormous support in every dimension. I want to give an especial thanks for Andrea Gurwitt, who has long been my chief editor, for the enthusiasm and dedication she brought to the project, her insightful comments, and her enormous work in editing, and re-editing, and re-editing again each of the chapters of the book.

I have been blessed by having publishers in both the UK and US with whom I have worked closely now for more than four decades and who've engaged with me on the ideas as they've been formulated and with the writing as it's progressed. At Norton, I've managed to outlast two of my editors (who also served as presidents of Norton), Don Lamm and Drake McFeeley. For the past decade, I've had the great pleasure of working with Brendan Curry, who's been as excited about the ideas of this book as I have; and he's brought on his collaborator, Caroline Adams. Together, they've challenged the ideas, improved the organization, and fine-tuned the language. Their insistence that

I focus on the main messages of the book has meant heaps of pages on the metaphorical cutting-room floor, but I hope and believe it has resulted in a much better book. Thanks also to Laura Sewell for her excellent copyediting. In the UK, at Allen Lane, Stuart Proffitt has again been my editor; his incisive editing is of a detail and quality that one seldom sees today. I also want to thank Fonie Mitsopoulou, who worked with him.

As always, I owe my greatest debt to Anya, with whom I discussed and debated these ideas well before they took the shape of a seminar paper, then a lecture, and now a book. She taught me too how to write in an accessible way. We both believe these ideas are important—they are at the core of our democracy, and if we are to make our democracy work, they have to be widely understood and accepted. If this book succeeds in that mission, it is largely because of her. She again read over the drafts, at each stage helping to hone the message.

Economics is about trade-offs—and thinking about freedoms means thinking about trade-offs. That's a central message of this book. But trade-offs are central to writing this, or any book. There is so much to be said, and so little time and space in which to do so. A book like this should raise questions as much as resolve them. I've had to resist the temptation to delve into every cranny of the subject, qualifying every sentence with the academic footnotes than mark good scholarly work. This, though, is a subject where losing the forest for the trees would be a particular disaster: Indeed, we've grasped onto the freedom language without really understanding the scope of what is at stake. And that, unfortunately, has had consequences.

NOTES

PREFACE

1. And my colleague at All Souls College when I held the Drummond Professorship there in the late 1970s.
2. Isaiah Berlin, *Four Essays on Liberty* (Oxford: Oxford University Press, 1969).
3. In chapter 1, I'll define more precisely what I mean by "the Right."
4. George W. Bush, "President Bush Discusses Financial Markets and World Economy," November 13, 2008, archived George W. Bush White House website, https://www.archives.gov/presidential-records/research/archived-white-house-websites.
5. Ronald Reagan, "Remarks Announcing America's Economic Bill of Rights," July 3, 1987, Ronald Reagan Presidential Library and Museum, https://www.reaganlibrary.gov.
6. At this point, he seems to claim, without proof, that these economic freedoms were "envisioned by those Americans who went before us." This is an illustration of the Right's rewriting of history and reinterpretation of the Constitution to serve their current agenda.
7. Ron Paul, "Concurrent Resolution on the Budget for Fiscal Year 2005," Congressional Record, vol. 150, no. 39 (March 25, 2004): H1561.
8. Rick Santorum, "Concurrent Resolution on the Budget for Fiscal Year 2005," Congressional Record, vol. 150, no. 39 (March 9, 2004): S2383.
9. Ted Cruz, "Five for Freedom," *National Review*, November 11, 2015.
10. There were many aspects of this deregulation, the details of which need not detain us here. Deregulation included allowing commercial banks to

engage in the same kinds of activities that investment banks did, issuing shares and bonds—something that had been forbidden since the Great Depression.

11. Each was an economist at the beginning of his career but might rightly be thought of as going well beyond the confines of that discipline by the end. Still, the ways of thinking of economics greatly influenced their thinking and argumentation, even as they became philosophers and political scientists and political activists. To say that they went beyond economics is meant as a compliment, not as a criticism.

12. Most importantly, these are subjects dealt extensively within the philosophical literature, but not, to my knowledge, as much through the lens of economics. See, for instance, Robert Nozick, *Philosophy, Science, and Method: Essays in Honor of Ernest Nagel*, Sidney Morgenbesser, Patrick Suppes, and Morton White, eds. (New York: St. Martin's Press, 1969); and Isaiah Berlin, "Two Concepts of Liberty," in *Four Essays on Liberty*, and the large literature associated with it. I make no pretense of engaging with that literature.

There is also a large legal literature dealing with how to reconcile conflicting rights (freedoms). I note the large literature—for instance, Ronald Dworkin, *Taking Rights Seriously* (Cambridge, MA: Harvard University Press, 1977) and Hurst Hannum, *Autonomy, Sovereignty, and Self-Determination: The Accommodation of Conflicting Rights* (Philadelphia: University of Pennsylvania Press, 1990)—associated with constitutional law in the US and human rights more broadly, which has dealt thoughtfully and deeply about these topics.

13. Another ambition for this book is disciplinary—to make the discipline of economics a more capacious cognitive enterprise. This will be particularly evident in the introduction to Part III.

14. Friedrich A Hayek, *The Road to Serfdom* (London: Routledge, 1944).

15. I'll provide a more extensive definition of neoliberalism in chapter 1.

16. Milton Friedman, *Capitalism and Freedom* (Chicago: University of Chicago Press, 1962).

17. We correctly identified the seriousness of the problem. Our only mistake was to underestimate the pace with which climate change would proceed and the magnitude of its consequences.

18. There is now a broader Wellbeing Economy Alliance, a civil society alliance of organizations promoting these ideas.

CHAPTER 1: INTRODUCTION: FREEDOM IN DANGER

1. I also believe that the authoritarian regimes cannot *sustainably* deliver what citizens desire, even if in the short run they may have some successes—that is, even if there is a "benevolent" dictator who succeeds in enhancing the country's well-being, there is no assurance that his successor will do

so; quite the contrary. But this critique of authoritarian regimes would take me beyond this short book. There is a huge literature on the subject. My own contributions include Raaj Sah and J. E. Stiglitz, "The Quality of Managers in Centralized versus Decentralized Organizations," *Quarterly Journal of Economics* 106, no. 1 (1991): 289–95, identifying the tendency of problematic succession in authoritarian regimes, and my 1994 book, written as the Soviet empire collapsed, *Whither Socialism?* (Cambridge, MA: MIT Press). Later, I will argue at some length that the prevailing neoliberal regime is also not sustainable.

2. "Legum denique idcirco omnes servi sumus ut liberi esse possimus," M. Tullius Cicero (66 B.C.), Pro Cluentio, trans. W Ramsay and G. Gilbert Ramsay, 3rd ed. (Oxford: Clarendon Press, 1876) pg. 121.

3. Or charity. But as I explain below, because of the free-rider problem, one cannot rely on charity. There are further objections to the reliance of one person's freedom on the charity of another, which would take us beyond the confines of this book.

4. And especially those sometimes called the right-libertarians, who have appropriated the label of libertarianism in the US. The ambiguities in the term are illustrated by the fact that while many American libertarians think of themselves as followers of Ayn Rand (the influential author of *The Fountainhead* and *Atlas Shrugged*, who claimed among her followers Alan Greenspan, chair of the Federal Reserve from 1987 to 2006), she distanced herself from libertarianism, writing (in *Ayn Rand Answers, the Best of Her Q & A* [New York: New American Library, 2005]): "Libertarians combine capitalism and anarchism. That's worse than anything the New Left has proposed. It's a mockery of philosophy and ideology. . . . Anarchists are the scum of the intellectual world of the Left, which has given them up. So the Right picks up another leftist discard. That's the libertarian movement." She goes on to say, "Libertarians are a monstrous, disgusting bunch of people." In the text, when I use the terms "libertarians" and "libertarianism," I refer to the variant that has been dominant in the US.

5. There is ample evidence that even Southern slaveowners recognized the moral outrageousness of slavery. For instance, President Jefferson, in his 1806 annual message to Congress, looking forward to the prohibition of the importing of slaves, referred to "those violations of human rights which have been so long continued on the unoffending inhabitants of Africa, and which the morality, the reputation, and the best interests of our country have long been eager to proscribe."

6. The difference between mis- and disinformation is simple. They're both incorrect information, but with disinformation, the false information is deliberate.

7. By "options," economists mean the full specification of, say, the set of goods and services that the individual could enjoy, *including a full specifi-*

cation of the quality of those goods and services. See also the discussion in the next notes.

8. Isaiah Berlin and others have made a distinction between positive and negative freedoms, the former being freedom *to do*, the latter being freedom from being constrained about *what to do*. See Isaiah Berlin, *Liberty* (Oxford: Oxford University Press, 2002). But the two are so intertwined that this distinction is of limited use. Many of the constraints, instances of government coercion, are justified because they are necessary to expand (or prevent from being limited) the freedom of others.

9. Many changes affect the opportunity set in complex ways, eliminating some possibilities while opening up others. In such cases, we cannot say whether there is more freedom to act in one case than in the other. We may be able to evaluate the losses in comparison to the gains, to say whether the individual is better off in one situation than in the other. Below, I discuss a methodology of doing so systematically.

10. Many economists would also argue that all that matters are outcomes, not the processes by which they are arrived at. Modern behavioral economists suggest that this is not the case. Individuals may care whether they have chosen a particular bundle of goods or whether that bundle of goods has been given to them. But it may also be the case that individuals care about the process because they are thinking that, while in this particular instance, the outcomes are the same, it is likely that when circumstances change, the outcomes will be better if I can make the choices than if someone makes those choices for me. There is, moreover, the question of human agency. Many would argue that making one's own decisions is inherently a good thing, and a good society should be structured to allow that—subject to the limitations we note throughout the book, such as harms done to others.

Some have worried that if an individual is *seemingly* given the freedom of choice, but there is someone, such as a parent, who can override that choice if it is not to their liking, or even impose further constraints in the future such as the withdrawal of the right to make a choice, then the person is not really free to choose. Such concerns can easily be brought into our framework once we recognize (as modern economic theory standardly does) that what is relevant is not just the opportunities at the moment but both those now and in the future, recognizing that choices today can affect future opportunity sets. If there are known potential adverse consequences of the individual making the "wrong" choice, the individual's opportunity set recognizes this. Her opportunity set is more constrained than it would be if there were not that potential intervention. This analysis, in turn, can be extended to consequences where they *might* be adverse consequences, but whether there were and what they were was uncertain.

11. Modern behavioral economics, discussed extensively in Part II, argues

that this is not quite right: the way we describe (or frame) an issue can have real consequences. See, in particular, the review article by Samuel Bowles, "Endogenous Preferences: The Cultural Consequences of Markets and Other Economic Institutions," *Journal of Economic Literature* 36, no. 1 (1998): 75–111.

12. Of course, matters are more complex than this discussion suggests; on many of the issues discussed below, different libertarians may take somewhat different views.

13. Extreme "free market" economists have argued that the economy is *naturally* competitive, that even when there is a single firm in an industry, competition *for* the market is an effective replacement for competition *in* the market. But such assertions, like many other tenets of "free market" economics, did not withstand scrutiny, as I explain in the next chapter.

14. By analogy, the income individuals or corporations get from the largesse of government, or by corruption, whether private or public, getting paid a price on a government contract above the competitive price or getting a natural resource at a price below the competitive price, is referred to as rents, and the efforts individuals put into getting these rents are naturally referred to as rent-seeking. Such expenditures of time and effort are not only unproductive but they can even be counterproductive.

15. Though typically, the exploiter has higher income and more power than the exploited. But we are equally disturbed by a poor trickster scamming a rich old person.

16. And more broadly, with any reasonable welfare criterion.

17. Garrett Hardin, "The Tragedy of the Commons," *Science* 162, no. 3859 (1968): 1243–48.

18. Traditional economists often make a distinction between preferences (which are "deep" and immutable) and beliefs, which can change with information. But twenty-first-century behavioral economics emphasizes that preferences—what we like and want—too can change, not just by "information" but by experiences—even by a simple experience of watching a soap opera and identifying with a character. See Demeritt, Hoff, and Stiglitz, *The Other Invisible Hand* (forthcoming) and the works cited there, including Eliana La Ferrara, Alberto Chong, and Suzanne Duryea, "Soap Operas and Fertility: Evidence from Brazil," *American Economic Journal: Applied Economics* 4, no. 4 (2012): 1–31.

19. There is a small literature in economics on nonrational persuasion. See, e.g., the review article by Andrew Kosenko and Joseph E. Stiglitz, "Robust Theory and Fragile Practice: Information in a World of Disinformation," in *The Elgar Companion to Information Economics*, Daphne R. Raban and Julia Wlodarczyk, eds. (Cheltenham, UK: Edward Elgar Publishing, 2024).

20. For a broad treatment, see Demeritt, Hoff, and Stiglitz, *The Other Invisible Hand*.

21. See Joseph E. Stiglitz and Bruce C. Greenwald, *Creating a Learning Society: A New Approach to Growth, Development, and Social Progress* (New York: Columbia University Press, 2014); and Joel Mokyr, *The Enlightened Economy* (New Haven, CT: Yale University Press, 2009).

22. Portugal, Ireland, Greece, and Spain.

23. The recent growth of populist groups in Scandinavia has to do with the perception that the governments have not done enough to protect their citizens against immigrants and the crime that some perceive as having come as a result; again, the complaint is not that government has done too much. See Jens Rydgren, "Radical Right-Wing Populism in Denmark and Sweden: Explaining Party System Change and Stability," *The SAIS Review of International Affairs* 30, no. 1 (2010): 57–71.

CHAPTER 2: HOW ECONOMISTS THINK ABOUT FREEDOM

1. Adam Smith, IV:II in *The Wealth of Nations*, 1776.

2. Smith, *Wealth of Nations*, I:X.

3. Of course, Hobbes was writing before the modern era of regulation and before John Maynard Keynes, simply to argue for the need for a government to maintain order.

4. Charles Dickens's pictures of nineteenth-century industrial England suggested that not all was well, that markets had not, after all, been uplifting for all. Poverty, squalor, and environmental degradation abounded: "In the country, the rain would have developed a thousand fresh scents, and every drop would have had its bright association with some beautiful form of growth or life. In the city, it developed only foul stale smells, and was a sickly, lukewarm, dirt-stained, wretched addition to the gutters" (*Little Dorrit* [London: Bradbury & Evans, 1857], 30–31). And: "Every repulsive lineament of poverty, every loathsome indication of filth, rot, and garbage; all these ornament the banks of Folly Ditch" (*Oliver Twist* [London: Richard Bentley, 1838], 56).

5. John Stuart Mill was among them; David Ricardo and William Stanley Jevons were two other influential English classical economists.

6. Politics curbed the size of New Deal expenditures, especially after 1936, so that it was only with World War II and the public expenditures to which it gave rise that the economy fully recovered. The war also accomplished something that the market on its own had trouble doing—moving the economy from a rural, agrarian economy to an urban, manufacturing one.

7. As a rough indicator, growth measured by real GDP increased at an annual rate of 3.9 percent during the 1950–80 period, and real per capita income was growing at 2.5 percent (see U.S. Bureau of Economic Analysis, Real Gross Domestic Product, retrieved from FRED, Federal Reserve Bank of St. Louis, and U.S. Bureau of Economic Analysis, Real Dispos-

able Personal Income: Per Capita retrieved from FRED, Federal Reserve Bank of St. Louis). In contrast, various estimates put the US per capita income growth rate during the period 1800–1960 in the range of 0.94 to 1.29 percent per year, half to two-thirds of the later number. See Thomas Weiss, "U.S. Labor Force Estimates and Economic Growth, 1800–1860," in *American Economic Growth and Standards of Living Before the Civil War*, Robert E. Gallman and John Joseph Wallis, eds. (Chicago: University of Chicago Press, 1992), 19–78.

8. In PPP (purchasing power parity), China's economy became larger than the US economy around 2015. Perhaps it's not an accident that bipartisan criticism of China seems to have markedly accelerated since then. For a popular discussion of the different reactions inside China and the US to the news that the US had—at least in this widely used measure—become number two, see Joseph E. Stiglitz, "The Chinese Century," *Vanity Fair*, January 2015.

9. This turned out to be both controversial (as I described in my book *Globalization and Its Discontents*) and unsuccessful, with the privatized company going into bankruptcy less than sixteen years after privatization—but not before the US Nuclear Regulatory Commission had investigated it for "failure to control components with uranium deposits, inadequate maintenance, testing and operation of safety valves on equipment, and exceeding the possession limit for uranium enriched greater than 20 percent" (US Nuclear Regulatory Commission, May 29, 1998, press release).

10. The reasons for this have to do more with politics than economics. In the US, the New Democrats wanted to distance themselves from the New Deal of FDR, which seemed a thing of the past. The Republicans had done an excellent job of tarnishing that brand and Keynesian ideas along with it, following the inflationary bouts of the 1970s. In Europe, the center-left strove to distinguish itself from the Socialists and Communists; the failure of the Soviet Union left that perspective in tatters. On both sides of the Atlantic, center-left parties attempted to find a "third way," between the extremes of communism and unfettered capitalism. A major strand of economic theory bolstered these efforts. This theory argued that markets by and large delivered efficient outcomes. There were limited instances where markets failed to do so, and only limited interventions were needed to remedy these market failures. My own work built off these ideas, showing, however, that these market failures were far more pervasive and far harder to correct.

11. As I note in Part III, the policy agenda pushed on developing countries also included opening up their financial markets (capital market liberalization), even in the face of evidence that such liberalization contributed to instability and inequality, but not to growth.

12. "Statement of Aims," Mont Pelerin Society, https://www.montpelerin.org.

13. Over the years, its leaders have included not only Hayek and Friedman

but other leading conservative economists like George Stigler, Gary Becker, James Buchanan, and John Taylor.

14. "Statement of Aims," Mont Pelerin Society.

15. See Francis Fukuyama, *The End of History and the Last Man* (New York: Free Press, 1992).

16. Robert Reich (the secretary of labor; now a professor at the University of California, Berkeley) and I represented the former group; Robert Rubin and Larry Summers the latter. But the divisions were complicated—Rubin was against the proposed welfare reform, though Summers favored cutting the capital gains tax, a provision which correctly was predicted to increase inequality enormously. For a fuller telling of this story, see my 2003 book on the Clinton administration: *The Roaring Nineties: A New History of the World's Most Prosperous Decade* (New York: W. W. Norton, 2003).

17. The term was used consciously by early proponents of the idea, such as Milton Friedman in "Neo-Liberalism and Its Prospects," *Farmand* (1951): 89–93. But today, it is used most prominently by critics. Here, I use it just as a descriptive label for a set of ideas, though I go on to discuss the limitations of this viewpoint.

18. The use of the term "liberal" to describe progressive Democrats in the US runs counter to the prevailing usage in the rest of the world. In many countries, the "Liberal" political party is one that advocates policies more aligned with neoliberalism, though typically they are strong advocates of competition policies and distance themselves from the special interests of big business.

19. That is, market dysfunctions so evident in massive unemployment are present, typically in less visible form, even when the economy is near full employment. The problems posed by market coordination, information imperfections and asymmetries, imperfect capital and risk markets, and so on, are ever present.

20. I used the term "market fundamentalism" in my 2002 book *Globalization and Its Discontents* for all the reasons to be discussed shortly. I had also used the term extensively in my earlier writings and speeches, including my Nobel Memorial Prize lecture. There were a host of others who used the term even earlier, including George Soros. See Richard Kozul-Wright and Paul Rayment, *The Resistible Rise of Market Fundamentalism: Rethinking Development Policy in an Unbalanced World* (London: Zed Books, 2008).

21. Actually, the beginnings can be traced earlier, for instance, to the deregulation movement that began in the late 1970s with President Carter in the US.

22. Opportunity Insights, "National Trends," April 2, 2018, https://opportunityinsights.org/national_trends/.

23. *PBS NewsHour*, "Majority of Americans Doubt Young People Will Be Better Off Than Their Parents, AP-NORC Poll Finds," October 4, 2022.

24. For an overview on the origins of inequality and its consequences, see

Joseph E. Stiglitz, *The Price of Inequality: How Today's Divided Society Endangers Our Future* (New York: W. W. Norton, 2012).

25. Some have attempted to defend the Washington Consensus policies, arguing that the poor performance of the countries adopting these policies in the years before 2000 has been at least partly offset by strong performance since 2000. But, at least in many cases, the growth that occurred in the early part of this century was short-lived, often based on high resource prices. As this book goes to press, there is a broad consensus that especially sub–Saharan African countries have paid a high price for the premature deindustrialization foisted on them by Washington Consensus policies.

26. A Harvard team chosen by the US government to assist in the transition played a particularly invidious role—for which the key player was eventually held accountable in a US court. For a fuller telling of this tale, see David Warsh, *Because They Could: The Harvard Russia Scandal (and NATO Enlargement) After Twenty-Five Years* (CreateSpace Independent Publishing Platform, 2018).

27. It was shown that markets are only efficient if there was perfect competition, where there were so many firms that no firm believed it had any effect on prices. If a firm charged ever so much more than the market price, it would lose *all* its customers. There are few markets in which that is the case. In most arenas, there are sufficiently few firms—sufficiently limited competition—that any large firm can affect prices.

28. The paper I presented there was subsequently published as "On the Optimality of the Stock Market Allocation of Investment," *Quarterly Journal of Economics* 86, no. 1 (1972): 25–60. The results were then generalized in a series of papers, including Joseph E. Stiglitz, "The Inefficiency of the Stock Market Equilibrium," *Review of Economic Studies* 49, no. 2 (1982): 241–61; and Bruce C. Greenwald and Joseph E. Stiglitz, "Externalities in Economies with Imperfect Information and Incomplete Markets," *Quarterly Journal of Economics* 101, no. 2 (1986): 229–64.

Interestingly, when interviewed in his later life by Michael Hirsh, a columnist at *Foreign Policy Magazine*, on some of the critical issues Friedman came to agree we me. For instance, Hirsh quotes Friedman on Russia's policy post Communism: "I said, privatize, privatize, privatize. I was wrong. He [Joe] was right." *Capital Offense: How Washington's Wise Men Handed America's Future over to Wall Street* (Hoboken, NJ: Wiley, 2010).

29. In the context of economics, these ideas were explored by Karla Hoff and Joseph E. Stiglitz, "Modern Economic Theory and Development," in *Frontiers of Development Economics: The Future in Perspective*, Gerald Marvin Meier and Joseph E. Stiglitz, eds. (Oxford: Oxford University Press, 2001), 389–459.

30. This was a key idea in my 1994 book, *Whither Socialism?* See also Joseph E. Stiglitz, *Selected Works of Joseph E. Stiglitz: Volume V, Rethinking Welfare*

Economics and the Economics of the Public Sector (Oxford: Oxford University Press, forthcoming).

31. I saw that vividly in the East Asia crisis, especially among Korean firms going bankrupt. See Stiglitz, *Globalization and Its Discontents* (2002). The influential economist Joseph Schumpeter, in his book *Capitalism, Socialism and Democracy* (New York: Harper & Brothers, 1942), argued that the process of creative destruction associated with business cycles promoted economic growth. Theory and evidence show that Schumpeter was wrong. See, e.g., Joseph E. Stiglitz, "Endogenous Growth and Cycles," in *Innovation in Technology, Industries, and Institutions: Studies in Schumpeterian Perspectives,* Yuichi Shionoya and Mark Perlman, eds. (Ann Arbor: University of Michigan Press, 1994), 121–56.

32. Sanford Grossman and I showed theoretically that markets couldn't be informationally efficient (Sanford J. Grossman and Joseph E. Stiglitz, "On the Impossibility of Informationally Efficient Markets," *American Economic Review* 70, no. 3 [1980]: 393–408; and Sanford J. Grossman and Joseph E. Stiglitz, "Information and Competitive Price Systems," *American Economic Review* 66, no. 2 [1976]: 246–53), a result confirmed empirically by Rob Schiller, who received the Nobel Memorial Prize in Economics for his work in 2009.

33. A strong recent proponent of this view is Harvard economics professor (and chair of President George W. Bush's Council of Economic Advisers [2003–2005]) Gregory Mankiw, who wrote, "People should receive compensation congruent with their contributions. If the economy were described by a classical competitive equilibrium without any externalities or public goods, then every individual would earn the value of his or her own marginal product, and there would be no need for government to alter the resulting income distribution." See N. Gregory Mankiw, "Spreading the Wealth Around: Reflections Inspired by Joe the Plumber," *Eastern Economic Journal* 36, no. 3 (2010): 285–98; and N. Gregory Mankiw, "Defending the One Percent," *Journal of Economic Perspectives* 27, no. 3 (2013): 21–34.

34. In contrast to, say, income taxes, where the more the individual works, the higher her income, and therefore the more she pays in taxes.

35. Robert E. Lucas, "The Industrial Revolution: Past and Future," 2003 Annual Report Essay, Federal Reserve Bank of Minneapolis, https://www.minneapolisfed.org/article/2004/the-industrial-revolution-past-and-future. Lucas went on to say: "The potential for the lives of poor people by finding different ways of distributing current production is nothing compared to the apparently limitless potential of increasing production." But he failed to show that achieving a better distribution of income was antithetical to growth, and a key argument in my book *The Price of Inequality*, and an immense body of subsequent research, including that mentioned in the next note, is that the opposite is true:

America's excessive inequality is adverse to growth. In addition, Lucas failed to show that much, if any, of the fruits of the growth that he cited "trickled down" to those below in a relevant time span. Growth in the US over the past four decades has left those at the bottom even worse off.

36. See Federico Cingano, "Trends in Income Inequality and Its Impact on Economic Growth," OECD Social, Employment, and Migration Working Papers no. 163, Organisation for Economic Co-operation and Development, 2014; Jonathan D. Ostry, Andrew Berg, and Charalambos G. Tsangarides, "Redistribution, Inequality, and Growth," IMF Staff Discussion Notes (2014); and Jonathan D. Ostry, Prakash Loungani, and Andrew Berg, *Confronting Inequality: How Societies Can Choose Inclusive Growth* (New York: Columbia University Press, 2019).

The claim that issues of distribution could be separated from those of efficiency is referred to as the Second Fundamental Theorem of Welfare Economics and only holds under very restrictive conditions, not satisfied by any real-world economy. (The First Fundamental Theorem provided the highly restrictive conditions under which an economy is efficient.)

37. Friedman, *Capitalism and Freedom*, 32.

38. There was a dramatic decline in life expectancy in the US associated with the Covid-19 pandemic, reflecting both the poor state of public health and the poor response. The Centers for Disease Control and Prevention reported in 2023 that US life expectancy had declined to 76.4 years, the lowest it had been in nearly two decades. For a fuller discussion, see Harvard School of Public Health, "What's Behind 'Shocking' U.S. Life Expectancy Decline—and What to Do About It," April 13, 2023. There is a vast literature detailing the increase in inequality in most advanced countries. A 2020 Pew Research Center report summarized the research for the US by saying, "Income inequality may be measured in a number of ways, but no matter the measure, economic inequality in the U.S. is seen to be on the rise" (Juliana Menasce Horowitz, Ruth Igielnik, and Rakesh Kochhar, "Trends in Income and Wealth Inequality," Pew Research Center's Social and Demographic Trends Project, January 9, 2020).

The OECD details the increase in inequality in most countries around the world over the quarter century beginning with the mid-1980s, with the US having the highest level and among the largest increases (OECD, "Focus on Inequality and Growth – December 2014" [2014]). A couple of statistics convey the magnitude of the inequality: the top 1 percent in the US have roughly 20 percent of the income and 40 percent of the wealth, and someone at the 10th percentile in income in 2020 had 13.53 times the income of the person at the 90th percentile. There are also large disparities in life expectancy.

CHAPTER 3: ONE PERSON'S FREEDOM IS
ANOTHER PERSON'S UNFREEDOM

1. Defined as events where four or more individuals are killed. See "Mass Shootings," Gun Violence Archive, https://www.gunviolencearchive .org/mass-shooting.
2. The majority of gun violence comes from suicide and homicide. See "Past Summary Ledgers," Gun Violence Archive, https://www .gunviolencearchive.org/past-tolls.
3. For comparisons on gun ownership and gun deaths between the US and UK, see the Institute for Health Metrics and Evaluation, "Global Burden of Disease Database"; GOV.UK, "Statistics on Firearm and Shotgun Certificates, England and Wales: April 2020 to March 2021"; and Violence Policy Center, "Gun Ownership in America: 1973 to 2021," November 2021. Among World Bank high-income countries in 2021, the US ranked seventh in rates of gun homicides and first among countries with populations over 10 million—nineteen times greater than France, which was ranked second. Gun violence also accounts for 8 percent of US deaths among those under 20, more than double any other high-income country with a population over 10 million. See "On Gun Violence, the United States Is an Outlier," The Institute for Health Metrics and Evaluation, https://www.healthdata.org/.
4. *District of Columbia v. Heller*, a landmark Supreme Court case in 2008, changed earlier interpretations, in which gun rights were far more restricted. See Justia Law, US Supreme Court, District of Columbia v. Heller, 554 U.S. 570 (2008).
5. With Lord Nicholas Stern and Charlotte Taylor, I have provided a detailed critique of the analyses put forward by some economists (like Nobel Prize winner William Nordhaus) suggesting that we should allow climate change to proceed apace, so long as we stay below 3.5 degrees Celsius. We explained why the global consensus of 1.5 to 2 degrees C is correct, especially once risk is taken into account. See Nicholas Stern, Joseph Stiglitz, and Charlotte Taylor, "The Economics of Immense Risk, Urgent Action and Radical Change: Towards New Approaches to the Economics of Climate Change," *Journal of Economic Methodology* 29, no. 3 (July 3, 2022): 181–216.
6. "US & Allied Killed and Wounded," Costs of War, 2021, Watson Institute for International and Public Affairs, Brown University.
7. A number estimated between 4.5 and 4.6 million. Miriam Berger, "Post-9/11 Wars Have Contributed to Some 4.5 Million Deaths, Report Suggests," *Washington Post*, May 15, 2023.
8. See J. E. Stiglitz and Linda J. Bilmes, *The Three Trillion Dollar War* (New York: W. W. Norton, 2008).
9. Qi Zhao et al., "Global, Regional, and National Burden of Mortality

Associated with Non-Optimal Ambient Temperatures from 2000 to 2019: A Three-Stage Modelling Study," *Lancet Planetary Health* 5, no. 7 (July 1, 2021): e415–25.

10. See, for example, David W. Eyre et al., "Effect of Covid-19 Vaccination on Transmission of Alpha and Delta Variants," *New England Journal of Medicine* 386, no. 8 (February 24, 2022): 744–56; and Stella Talic et al., "Effectiveness of Public Health Measures in Reducing the Incidence of Covid-19, SARS-CoV-2 Transmission, and Covid-19 Mortality: Systematic Review and Meta-Analysis," *BMJ* 375 (November 18, 2021): e068302. However, many on the Right deny the existence of a relationship between these practices and the incidence of the disease, just as they deny the relationship between greenhouse gases and climate change. The world is complex, and multiple factors simultaneously play a role in both cases; disentangling effects is not easy. Climate deniers, for instance, point to cold spells—but that ignores the fact that global warming is associated with climate *variability*, and indeed, some climate scientists point to Arctic warming as contributing to the vortex that brought record cold weather to Texas in 2021. So, too, while there are myriad factors affecting the spread of Covid-19, since it is an airborne virus, ventilation, masking, and social distancing matter, *keeping other things constant*, as the above-cited studies show.

11. More precisely, 74.3 percent, from table 4 in "Population: 1790 to 1990," in Population and Housing Unit Counts, US Census Bureau, US Department of Commerce, August 1993.

12. United Nations, Department of Economic and Social Affairs, Population Division, "2018 Revision of World Urbanization Prospects," 2019.

13. Sarah Manavis, "How a Lack of Zoning Messed Up Houston in More Ways Than One," *City Monitor*, June 19, 2017, updated July 19, 2021.

14. Janet Currie and Reed Walker, "Traffic Congestion and Infant Health: Evidence from E-ZPass," *American Economic Journal: Applied Economics* 3, no. 1 (January 2011): 65–90.

15. With one financial institution effectively betting on the bankruptcy of its rivals through some of these complex financial products, the financial system became intertwined in a world of such complexity that it could only be understood through recent advances in mathematics (in a branch of the subject called network theory), which demonstrated the fragility of the resulting systems. See, for instance, Stefano Battiston, Guido Caldarelli, Co-Pierre Georg, Robert May, and J. E. Stiglitz, "Complex Derivatives," *Nature Physics* 9, no. 3 (March 2013): 123–25; and Stefano Battiston, Guido Caldarelli, Robert M. May, Tarik Roukny, and J. E. Stiglitz, "The Price of Complexity in Financial Networks," *Proceedings of the National Academy of Sciences* 113, no. 36 (September 6, 2016): 10031–36. For an account of how this played out in 2008, see J. E. Stiglitz, *Freefall: America, Free Markets, and the Sinking of the World Economy* (New York:

W. W. Norton, 2010). Well before the crisis, those of us working in this area warned of how this interdependence had made the financial system more fragile—there were significant systemic fragilities. Remarkably, except for Andy Haldane and his research team at the Bank of England, this work was largely ignored by central bankers, as they focused on the more conventional models that effectively *assumed* self-interested behavior of the bankers would lead them to caution—that self-regulation would largely suffice to protect the economy. See Joseph E. Stiglitz and Bruce Greenwald, *Towards a New Paradigm in Monetary Economics* (Cambridge: Cambridge University Press, 2003).

16. Economists used to think that pecuniary externalities, in which one person's or group's actions affected prices (and it was through these effects on prices that others are affected), didn't impede the efficiency of the market. One of the contributions of the 1986 work of Greenwald and Stiglitz, "Externalities in Economies with Imperfect Information and Incomplete Markets," was to show that such pecuniary externalities did, in general, result in inefficiency.

17. There are, of course, other possibilities: taxes to fund public health programs could increase, or resources could be diverted from treating other diseases. In each of these cases, increased smoking has consequences for others—that is, there are still externalities.

18. Adam Smith, *The Theory of Moral Sentiments* (London: Printed for A. Millar, A. Kincaid, and J. Bell, 1759).

19. See Smith's introduction to *The Theory of Moral Sentiments.*

20. These empirical findings are perfectly consistent with our understanding of how the disease spreads. As the Centers for Disease Control and Prevention put it, "COVID-19 spreads when an infected person breathes out droplets and very small particles that contain the virus. Other people can breathe in these droplets and particles, or these droplets and particles can land on their eyes, nose, or mouth." See "COVID-19 and Your Health," Centers for Disease Control and Prevention, February 11, 2020, https://www.usa.gov/agencies/centers-for-disease-control-and-prevention.

    Many on the Right did not want to accept these scientific findings, perhaps because it would have forced them to recognize that there were important externalities.

21. So, too, we debate whether an abortion is killing, and if so, when? From the point of conception, or later in the pregnancy?

22. There are subtle interactions between financial and real variables, which would take us beyond this simple exposition. For instance, an increase in public indebtedness may crowd out private investment, leading to a lower level of real capital. There is then a cross-generational externality but it is limited by the extent to which this crowding out occurs.

23. This is an example of a macroeconomic externality, a notion discussed briefly earlier in the chapter. The tendency for excessive private borrow-

ing may be particularly grave because, in crises, governments have a tendency to bail out private corporations, with the IMF providing the dollars necessary to repay private creditors and facilitating rich individuals and corporations taking their money out of the country—leaving the country greatly indebted to the IMF, but with nothing to show for it. This historical pattern, noted in Stiglitz, *Globalization and Its Discontents*, was repeated on a grand scale in 2019, as the IMF lent Argentina $44 billion.

24. Though many of the University of Chicago's economists belonged to the Chicago School (including Gary Becker, Robert Lucas, and George Stigler, whom I referred to earlier), not all the economists at the university belonged to the Chicago School, and many Chicago School economists were located elsewhere.

25. Coase won the Nobel Memorial Prize in Economics in 1991. His classic paper was R. H. Coase, "The Problem of Social Cost," *Journal of Law and Economics* 3 (1960): 1–44.

26. Alternatively, one person could buy all the apple orchards and beehives.

27. That is, even if they are not *perfectly selfish*, as economists tend to assume, neither do they typically weigh the well-being of others as much as that of themselves.

28. See Hardin, "The Tragedy of the Commons."

29. Though they didn't simply take the land—there was legislation enabling it—those who lost their rights to use the land (essentially *their* property rights) had no say in the political process.

30. Except there, those who had formerly grazed were forcefully removed from the land. See the later discussion.

31. Coase's (largely irrelevant) response might have been that there were alternative assignments of property rights—ways of dividing up the common land—in which efficiency could have been obtained and everyone could have been made better off.

32. To make sure that everyone was better off, the shares of the monopolists would have to be appropriately distributed to everyone in the world.

The cap-and-trade system for carbon emissions allocates tradable *rights to pollute*, limiting the pollution to the desired amount (the "cap") and ensuring that pollution is done, as it were, in an efficient manner; in that sense, it can be thought as implementing a Coasian property rights scheme. It's turned out harder to implement than many originally thought, partly because the value of those property rights is in the trillions of dollars, and with so much money at stake, politics inevitably plays an important role.

33. There is no simple way to elicit how much each individual values the public good, i.e., how much each would be willing to pay the owner of the atmosphere to keep the level of pollutants low. Thus, whenever this is a public good, the benefits of which an individual cannot be excluded from, the Coase solution will not work. See Joseph Farrell, "Information

and the Coase Theorem," *Journal of Economic Perspectives* 1, no. 2 (December 1987): 113–29; and Eric S. Maskin, "The Invisible Hand and Externalities," *American Economic Review* 84, no. 2 (1994): 333–37.

On the other hand, in the public regulatory framework discussed next, the government can undertake a statistical analysis, e.g., calculating the societal benefits of reduced health-care costs and increased life expectancy, without having to ascertain the magnitudes for any particular individual.

34. The problem is ameliorated to some extent if some individuals are other-regarding (that is, they take into account their effects on others), as some, perhaps many, individuals are—though Coase, along with the other economists of his school, argued in terms of perfectly selfish individuals. Still, as long as all individuals are not perfectly altruistic, there was be a free-rider problem, at least to some extent.

35. More generally, the transaction costs associated with Coase's solution may be high, e.g., there are costs to privatization. In practice, many privatizations have not gone well. Other limitations have been discussed in Daniel Kahneman, Jack L. Knetsch, and Richard H. Thaler, "Experimental Tests of the Endowment Effect and the Coase Theorem," *Journal of Political Economy* 98, no. 6 (1990): 1325–48; and Robin Hahnel and Kristen A. Sheeran, "Misinterpreting the Coase Theorem," *Journal of Economic Issues* 43, no. 1 (2009): 215–38.

36. I should be clear: Friedman was not the originator of this idea (or many of the others that he pushed). Using prices to "correct" externalities is associated with the Cambridge economist A. C. Pigou in *The Economics of Welfare* (London: Macmillan, 1920). William Baumol and Agnar Sandmo provided early formal expositions in William J. Baumol, "On Taxation and the Control of Externalities," *American Economic Review* 62, no. 3 (1972): 307–22, and Agnar Sandmo, "Optimal Taxation in the Presence of Externalities," *Swedish Journal of Economics* 77, no. 1 (1975): 86–98.

37. Milton Friedman, interview by Phil Donahue, *The Phil Donahue Show*, 1979.

38. For instance, with credit rationing, some individuals simply can't borrow, and with imperfect risk markets, individuals can't purchase insurance against all the risks they face. Not only is it obvious that such imperfections exist and are important, economic theory over the past forty years has explained why that is so. See, for instance, J. E. Stiglitz and A. Weiss, "Credit Rationing in Markets with Imperfect Information," *American Economic Review* 71, no. 3 (1981): 393–410.

39. Martin Weitzman showed this forcefully in the context of a simple model with uncertainty and incomplete risk markets: If a government had to choose between just a price intervention and a quantity regulation, he demonstrated that there were a wide range of circumstances in which quantity regulation was preferred. More generally, a mix of price and

quantity regulations may be preferred. See M. Weitzman, "Prices vs. Quantities," *Review of Economic Studies* 41, no. 4 (1974): 477–91.

In the context of climate change, I showed this in "Addressing Climate Change Through Price and Non-Price Interventions," *European Economic Review* 119 (October 2019): 594–612.

40. Technically, economists refer to this as instrument uncertainty.

41. See, for instance, Elinor Ostrom, *Governing the Commons: The Evolution of Institutions for Collective Action* (Cambridge: Cambridge University Press, 1990): 90, 91–102.

42. Estimates suggest that about a sixth of the area of England was involved in the enclosure movement. See Gilbert Slater, "Historical Outline," in *The Land: The Report of the Land Enquiry Committee*, 3rd ed., vol. 1 (London: Hodder and Stoughton, 1913). Indeed, "many [of the commons] were managed according to very detailed rules set by the local manorial court regulating stocking levels (or "stints"), manuring, disease control and so forth; but these rules varied considerably from one village to another," Simon Fairlie, "A Short History of Enclosure in Britain," Hampton Institute, February 16, 2020. Fairlie's conclusion about the enclosures was poignant: "It was downright theft. Millions of people had customary and legal access to lands and the basis of an independent livelihood was snatched away from them through what to them must have resembled a Kafkaesque tribunal."

Interestingly, in Scotland (where not only were there enclosures but the farmers were forcibly removed from the land they had traditionally tilled or used for grazing, in what was called the clearances), in some cases, the level of grazing increased. While the new set of property rights forcibly imposed on the poor may or may not have increased efficiency, it clearly increased inequalities.

43. See Megan Hernbroth, "IRA Costs Could Balloon over $1 Trillion," Axios, March 30, 2023; Leslie Kaufman, "A Year into Biden's Climate Agenda, the Price Tag Remains Mysterious," Bloomberg, August 16, 2023; and John Bistline, Neil Mehrotra, and Catherine Wolfram, "Economic Implications of the Climate Provisions of the Inflation Reduction Act," Brookings Papers on Economic Activity Conference Draft, Spring 2023.

44. All of this depends, of course, on the evolution of technology. It's now relatively easy to measure the carbon emissions of an electric power plant or to measure a car's pollutants (of course, that assumes that car manufacturers don't deliberately misrecord the pollutants, as Volkswagen did a few years ago in what came to be called the Dieselgate scandal).

45. This is the central message of the 2017 High-Level Commission on Carbon Prices, which I co-chaired, along with Nicholas Stern. See Joseph E. Stiglitz, Nicholas Stern, Maosheng Duan, et al., "Report of the High-Level Commission on Carbon Prices," International Bank for Recon-

struction and Development and International Development Association/ The World Bank, May 29, 2019.

46. An analogous set of issues arises at the global level: developing countries are loath to accept carbon taxes or regulations that might impede their development—they focus on equity, emphasizing the fact that most of the increased level of carbon in the atmosphere is the result of the actions of advanced countries and that advanced countries are far better able to bear the costs of carbon taxes and regulations. They've been resistant to global carbon rules, even though they are among those that will suffer the most from global warming. A package analogous to that just described is the appropriate response. Chapter 12 delves more deeply into these international issues.

CHAPTER 4: FREEDOM THROUGH COERCION: PUBLIC GOODS AND THE FREE-RIDER PROBLEM

1. One of the reasons for the critical role of government in transformative investments like this is their cost. As former *Scientific American* editor Michael Moyer put it, "In truth, no private company would have been capable of developing a project like the Internet, which required years of R&D efforts spread out over scores of far-flung agencies, and which began to take off only after decades of investment. Visionary infrastructure projects such as this are part of what has allowed our economy to grow so much in the past century," in "Yes, Government Researchers Really Did Invent the Internet," *Scientific American,* July 23, 2012. See also Marianna Mazzucato, *The Entrepreneurial State* (London: Anthem Press, 2013).

2. Organisation for Economic Co-operation and Development (OECD), "Life Expectancy at Birth," in *Health at a Glance 2023: OECD Indicators* (Paris: OECD Publishing, 2023).

3. BioNTech received $445 million in funding from the German government to assist with COVID-19 vaccine development. See Hussain S. Lalani, Jerry Avorn, and Aaron S. Kesselheim, "US Taxpayers Heavily Funded the Discovery of COVID-19 Vaccines," *Clinical Pharmacology and Therapeutics* 111, no. 3 (2022): 542–44.

4. Even if government is necessary for supporting and paying for the collection of sewage, the questions is, should the government contract out that service to a private firm? The results of privatization and private contracting have often been disappointing and, in some cases, disastrous. US prisons are a case at point: cost savings, if present at all, were minimal, recidivism was increased, and the overall well-being of prisoners reduced in the quest for cost savings.

In some cases, after several decades under privatization, services are back in the government's hands, such as a large portion of the British railway system.

5. Not all public goods are "pure" in the sense that their benefits are fully accessible to all (without cost); but the argument holds even if much of the benefits are broadly available. The concept of pure public goods was first formalized by economist Paul Samuelson in 1954. See Paul A. Samuelson, "The Pure Theory of Public Expenditure," *Review of Economics and Statistics* 36, no. 4 (1954): 387–89. While most publicly provided goods are not pure in the sense defined by Samuelson, the central result that without government intervention, there will be under-provision holds. For a discussion of these more general cases, see Anthony B. Atkinson and Joseph E. Stiglitz, *Lectures in Public Economics* (New York: McGraw-Hill, 1980; Princeton, NJ: Princeton University Press, 2015).

6. See Joseph E. Stiglitz, "Toward a General Theory of Consumerism: Reflections on Keynes' *Economic Possibilities for Our Grandchildren*," in *Revisiting Keynes: Economic Possibilities for Our Grandchildren*, Lorenzo Pecchi and Gustavo Piga, eds. (Cambridge, MA: MIT Press, 2008), 41–87.

7. The term "prisoner's dilemma" relates to one of the early settings in which this breakdown of cooperation was studied. Consider two criminals who committed a crime together. If they both remain silent, they remain in jail for six months, until trial, but they won't be convicted. But the prosecutor offers them both a deal: if you confess, I'll let you out right away if I use your confession to convict the other (that is, if the other prisoner doesn't confess). In that case, the non-squealing prisoner gets 10 years. If both confess, they both go to prison for two years. It would be best for both to remain silent, but that's not an equilibrium. If one prisoner believes the other is going to be silent, he squeals. But if he squeals and the other doesn't, the other prisoner really gets punished, so it's better for the other prisoner to squeal, too. So both squeal, and both go off to prison for two years.

8. In some circumstances, there might be a better equilibrium in which stores that are open on Sunday charge a higher price on Sunday, compensating store owners for having to work that day. But this may not be possible: changing the price labels may be costly, or customers may feel this is unfair, a form of price gouging against those who have to shop on Sunday. More generally, the decentralized market equilibrium will not be efficient, and some government intervention to govern which stores are open may be welfare enhancing. An example is the rotation among pharmacies that are open each Sunday in some European countries.

9. Elsewhere, I have shown that flash trading in the stock market—where speculators try to garner information a microsecond before others, spending millions of dollars to get this informational advantage—is of precisely this form, as seen in Michael Lewis, *Flash Boys: A Wall Street Revolt* (New York: W. W. Norton, 2015). A more formal analysis is presented in Joseph

Stiglitz, "Tapping the Brakes: Are Less Active Markets Safer and Better for the Economy?" Presented at the Federal Reserve Bank of Atlanta Financial Markets Conference: Tuning Financial Regulation for Stability and Efficiency, April 15, 2014.

10. It still might be the case that with optimal public provision, speculators might try to take advantage of others, in which case some additional anti-speculation coercive measure might have to be taken.

11. This discussion of situations where cooperation is beneficial yet cannot be sustained in the absence of public intervention is not meant to be exhaustive. For instance, an important class of situations is referred to as the stag hunt. In simplified form: A hunter can either hunt a hare or a stag. Stags are much more valuable, but it is assumed that hunting stags requires cooperation. In the absence of cooperation, hunters will have to be satisfied with a hare. But in the absence of enforced cooperation, any hunter may worry that the other hunter, uncertain about the arrival of the stag, will leap to kill a hare because something is better than nothing, thereby scaring off any stag in the vicinity. In the absence of a high degree of trust, enforced cooperation (coercion) may make both better off.

12. See Kenneth J. Arrow, "An Extension of the Basic Theorems of Classical Welfare Economics," in *Proceedings of the Second Berkeley Symposium on Mathematical Statistics and Probability*, Jerzy Neyman, ed. (Berkeley: University of California Press, 1951), 507–32; Kenneth J. Arrow, "The Role of Securities in the Optimal Allocation of Risk-Bearing," *Review of Economic Studies* 31, no. 2 (1964), 91–96; Gerard Debreu, "Valuation Equilibrium and Pareto Optimum," *Proceedings of the National Academy of Sciences* 40, no. 7 (1954), 588–92; and Gerard Debreu, *The Theory of Value* (New Haven, CT: Yale University Press, 1959).

13. As I noted in chapter 2, market fundamentalism refers to the almost religious belief that markets were efficient—an unshakable belief, even in the presence of evidence and theory to the contrary. See note 20, chapter 2, for a discussion of the history of the use of the term.

14. Arrow and Debreu had provided *sufficient* conditions for the efficiency of markets. There followed a long, and unsuccessful, attempt to find weaker conditions. For instance, they had assumed a full set of risk markets. The studies cited above, in chapter 2, note 28, and in chapter 5, note 16, showed that in the absence of a full set of risk markets, the economy was essentially never efficient. Matters were even worse than Arrow and Debreu envisaged. They had assumed perfect information. Greenwald and I showed that whenever there was imperfect/asymmetric information, markets were not efficient. See Greenwald and Stiglitz, "Externalities in Economies with Imperfect Information and Incomplete Markets." Similarly, we showed that, in general, economies where there is endog-

enous innovation are not efficient. See Stiglitz and Greenwald, *Creating a Learning Society.*

15. Putting aside for the moment the fact that markets are typically not competitive, especially not in the way that these theorists had assumed, which I address in chapter 7.

16. This is confirmed by a host of experiments in behavioral economics and is discussed further in Part II.

17. See the discussion in chapter 3.

18. Finnish Tax Administration, "Finnish Citizens Understand the Significance of Paying Taxes—Young People Are a Bit Divided," *Tax Administration Bulletin*, May 11, 2021.

19. Just as a national public good benefits anyone within the country, global (or international) public goods benefit anyone in the world. I first introduced this now widely used concept in "The Theory of International Public Goods and the Architecture of International Organizations," Background Paper No. 7, Third Meeting, High-Level Group on Development Strategy and Management of the Market Economy, UNU/WIDER, Helsinki, Finland, July 8–10, 1995, and then elaborated on it in a series of papers over the subsequent years: "IFIs and the Provision of International Public Goods," *Cahiers Papers* 3, no. 2, European Investment Bank (1998): 116–34; "Knowledge as a Global Public Good," in *Global Public Goods: International Cooperation in the 21st Century*, Inge Kaul, Isabelle Grunberg, and Marc Stern, eds., United Nations Development Programme (New York: Oxford University Press, 1999), 308–25; and "Global Public Goods and Global Finance: Does Global Governance Ensure That the Global Public Interest Is Served?" in *Advancing Public Goods*, Jean-Philippe Touffut, ed. (Cheltenham, UK: Edward Elgar Publishing, 2006), 149–64.

    The concept was a natural parallel to one I had explored a couple of decades earlier—public goods the benefits of which were limited to a small locality—called local public goods, which had first been investigated by Charles Tiebout. See J. E. Stiglitz, "Theory of Local Public Goods," in *The Economics of Public Services*, Martin S. Feldstein and Robert P. Inman, eds. (London: Macmillan, 1977), 274–333; and Charles Tiebout, "A Pure Theory of Local Expenditures," *Journal of Political Economy* 64, no. 5 (1956): 416–42.

20. That they made voluntary commitments in the Paris meeting shows that countries did not fully free ride, as standard economic theory suggests. Note, however, that many countries have not lived up to the commitments they made in Paris.

21. US Department of State, Office of Environmental Quality, "The Montreal Protocol on Substances That Deplete the Ozone Layer," https://www.state.gov.

CHAPTER 5: CONTRACTS, THE SOCIAL CONTRACT, AND FREEDOM

1. Much of the early discussion of social contracts discussed it in terms of the relationship between the sovereign (king) and his subject. Modern usage thinks of the social contract more broadly: among citizens, with each other, as they contemplate what powers to devolve upon their government.
2. Adam Smith, *The Theory of Moral Sentiments*.
3. The problem, of course, is that when individuals vote on policies, they know what their position in society is or is likely to be. Still, individuals, in thinking about what is a just society, might reason along the lines put forward by Rawls.

   Rawls combined this approach of assessing justice by looking behind the veil of ignorance with a more stringent criterion, that a just distribution of income and wealth should maximize the well-being of the worst-off individual. That view is not widely accepted.

   I agree with Rawls that looking for a fair and just resolution requires that one think about such matters behind a veil of ignorance. There are many subtleties in this idea that we will not be able to follow up on. Behind the veil of ignorance, individuals may not only not know what their endowments are (whether they will be rich or poor), but also what they will like or how risk averse they will be, all of which may lead to differences in views about desirable social arrangements. Matters get still more complicated in Part II of the book, where preferences are endogenous.
4. We don't have to go as far as Rawls and argue that we should only accept inequalities to the extent that they enhance the well-being of the worst-off individual (for instance, lower tax rates on the rich can be justified if and only if they raise additional revenues, which can be used to improve the well-being of the worst-off individual) to accept the notion that a central concern in designing rules should be their effect on the distribution of income, wealth, and power.
5. Even behind the veil of ignorance, we cannot be sure that there will be unanimity, except under some special circumstances; but at least the extent of differences is likely to be reduced.
6. Smith, I:X in *The Wealth of Nations*.
7. Smith, *Nations*, I:VIII.
8. "Justice Department Requires Six High Tech Companies to Stop Entering into Anticompetitive Employee Solicitation Agreements," US Department of Justice, Office of Public Affairs, September 24, 2010.
9. For instance, with legal provisions giving shareholders limited liability in the event of bankruptcy. Over the past two decades, the trade-offs in freedoms have played out in ways that have diminished debtors' freedoms,

as those of the creditors expanded, and that of some creditors more than others. Derivatives were given priority over other claimants, a hidden kind of "subsidy" to those banks issuing the derivatives at the expense of other creditors. Student loans could not be forgiven, even if the schools failed to provide an education that did anything to enhance the students' life prospects. Provisions of the 2005 bankruptcy act pushed by the banks, ironically titled the Bankruptcy Abuse Prevention and Consumer Protection Act, introduced a form of indentured servitude, with banks being able to garnish a quarter of a worker's wages, charging such usurious rates on the remaining balances that no matter how hard the worker tried, his indebtedness simply increased over time.

10. Through what are called class action suits. See the discussion below.

11. I should emphasize, they typically don't use the language we employ here. They make these assertions seemingly on the basis of some natural law, or as an implication of (their reading of) the Constitution. Sometimes, their assertions are based on a half-baked economic analysis that such rules are necessary for the economy to work, or to work well.

12. For instance, whether direct public production is preferable to public procurement from private companies or a public-private partnership. Regrettably, these partnerships are often distinguished by a structure where the government bears any losses and private parties receive any gains.

13. Richard M. Titmuss, *The Gift Relationship: From Human Blood to Social Policy* (London: George Allen and Unwin, 1970).

14. The book and movie *He Said, She Said* provide a vivid description of how these NDAs work.

15. For a recent book describing such discrimination, see Emily Flitter, *The White Wall: How Big Finance Bankrupts Black America* (New York: Atria/ One Signal Publishers, 2022).

16. Kenneth Arrow and Gerard Debreu, in their pathbreaking proof that competitive markets were efficient, *assumed* that there was insurance for every risk. It was a *sufficient condition* for market efficiency. They were unable to establish whether markets were or were not in general efficient when insurance markets were incomplete. There ensued over the next quarter century a debate about whether it was necessary; that is, whether markets might, under plausible conditions, still be efficient if there were not a full set of risk markets. Then, in 1986, John Geanakoplos and Heracles M. Polemarchakis, and Bruce C. Greenwald and I, independently proved that markets without a full set of insurance markets were essentially never efficient. See J. Geanakoplos and H. M. Polemarchakis, "Existence, Regularity, and Constrained Suboptimality of Competitive Allocations When the Asset Structure Is Incomplete," in *Uncertainty, Information and Communication: Essays in Honor of K. J. Arrow*, vol. 3, W. P. Hell, R. M Starr, and D. A. Starrett, eds. (New York: Cambridge Uni-

versity Press, 1986), 65–95; and Greenwald and Stiglitz, "Externalities in Economies."

17. Consider an important risk facing American investors contemplating putting money into China for an investment to produce goods to be exported to the US. Any thoughtful investor, aware of the vagaries of politics, might want insurance against the risk that the US takes an anti-China stance and imposes tariffs—something that actually happened during the Trump administration. For instance, an investor in 1985 would want such insurance, and for a long-term investment, the insurance would have to cover the risk of such a tariff well into the future. The standard theory requires that such insurance exist. But this kind of insurance is not offered, so it is just one of multiple risks that investors have to bear themselves and that can't be transferred to an insurance firm. The fact that investors must bear these risks themselves because there is no insurance obviously has real consequences.

18. My earlier work with Andrew Weiss—see Stiglitz and Weiss, "Credit Rationing in Markets with Imperfect Information"—explained why that is so. The analysis is now well accepted, and more than forty years after presenting it, no holes have been poked in it. The empirical literature has also provided overwhelming support. But the Right ignores this reality and its strong implications.

19. The general theory establishing that that was the case was set out in two of my earlier papers with Michael Rothschild. See Michael Rothschild and Joseph E. Stiglitz, "Increasing Risk: I. A Definition," *Journal of Economic Theory* 2, no. 3 (1970): 225–43, and Michael Rothschild and Joseph E. Stiglitz, "Increasing Risk II: Its Economic Consequences," *Journal of Economic Theory* 3, no. 1 (1971): 66–84.

20. See Jacob Hacker, "Economic Security," in *For Good Measure: Advancing Research on Well-Being Metrics Beyond GDP*, Joseph E. Stiglitz, Jean-Paul Fitoussi, and Martine Durand, eds. (Paris: OECD Publishing, 2018).

21. And because of the lack of income, individuals are often forced to accept almost any job offered, when by continuing to search, they might have found one much better matched to their skills. Thus, the lack of adequate unemployment insurance contributes to inefficiency.

The Right worries that the provision of unemployment insurance contributes to another inefficiency—individuals will loaf around, collecting unemployment benefits, rather than working. This argument was central to their opposition to the provision of better unemployment benefits during the Covid-19 pandemic. The pandemic provided a good opportunity to test the significance of this effect, because different states made different decisions concerning providing unemployment benefits. Overall, the conclusion is unambiguous: there is little, if any, effect discouraging work. See Kyle Coombs, Arindrajit

Dube, Calvin Jahnke, Raymond Kluender, Suresh Naidu, and Michael Stepner, "Early Withdrawal of Pandemic Unemployment Insurance: Effects on Employment and Earnings," *AEA Papers and Proceedings* 112 (May 2022): 85–90.

22. Part of the reason that transaction costs are so low is that these programs are *universal*; the government doesn't have to spend any money on advertising. And the government doesn't need to earn an exorbitant profit. Moreover, the Social Security contributions can be collected with one's taxes, so the incremental administrative costs are remarkably low.

23. There is a large and somewhat controversial literature assessing the efficiency of the public sector. Australia's student loan program is far more efficient than any private program in any country—with better provisions and more tailored to the needs of the borrowers.

While there are multiple examples of inefficient government programs, Australia's student loan program and the US retirement program show that there can be efficient government programs. And there are multiple instances of private-sector inefficiency. The losses from the misallocation of capital in the run-up to the 2008 financial crisis, and the losses from that privately induced crisis, were enormous.

24. Of course, some individuals might feel that they want to save less than they are required by public programs, or that they would prefer to put their money into a high-risk, high-return financial asset. Their loss of freedom must be set against the increase in freedom of everyone else. And there's one more dimension: when these individuals come to retire, there is a real risk that they won't have sufficient income to have a decent life; they will be below the poverty line. A decent society can't allow that to happen. So behind the veil of ignorance a good society must ensure that all have set aside sufficient money and invested safely to live with a modicum of decency in retirement.

25. In a 2009 town hall, in the context of pushing for Obamacare, President Obama said, "And I got a letter the other day from a woman; she said, I don't want government-run health care, I don't want socialized medicine, and don't touch my Medicare." ("Remarks by the President in AARP Tele-Town Hall on Health Care Reform," July 28, 2009). Katrina vanden Heuvel in her article "Keep Your Hands Off My Medicare!" (*The Nation*, May 3, 2011) describes Rep. Daniel Webster (D-FL) arriving at his town hall to be greeted with signs that said: "Hands Off Medicare."

26. At any one moment, policymakers have only a few levers they can pull. It's obvious that we can't change everything at once, though we should think of a sequence of related changes, considering how the changes we make today will affect the country's future course—including the possibility of future changes in policy.

27. Smith, *Nations*, I:XI.

CHAPTER 6: FREEDOM, A COMPETITIVE ECONOMY, AND SOCIAL
JUSTICE

1. Nassau William Senior was the first holder of the Drummond Chair in Economics at All Souls College, Oxford, in 1825. I became the fifteenth holder of the chair in 1976. He wrote in opposition to Karl Marx.
2. In most countries, when slavery was abolished, it was the "property rights" of the slaveowners—even though their property could rightfully be viewed as stolen—rather than the enslaved that were paramount. When Britain abolished slavery, it generously compensated slaveowners with a 20-million-pound debt issuance, amounting to some 5 percent of the country's GDP; it provided no compensation for the formerly enslaved. See Michael Anson and Michael D. Bennett, "The Collection of Slavery Compensation, 1835–43," Bank of England Staff Working Paper No. 1,006 (November 2022). GDP numbers from Gregory Clark, "Debt, Deficits, and Crowding Out: England, 1727–1840," *European Review of Economic History* 5, no. 3 (2001): 403–36.

   America's promises were better—40 acres and a mule—but it never lived up to its promises. See William A. Darity Jr. and A. Kirsten Mullen, *From Here to Equality: Reparations for Black Americans in the Twenty-First Century*, 2nd ed. (Durham: University of North Carolina Press, 2022).
3. Many indigenous people also had the view that if you weren't using a particular piece of land, *of course* you would let someone else who wanted to use the land do so, with the understanding that if you did need the land, it would be returned. The colonialists didn't understand this kind of magnanimity.
4. Many other aspects of our legal system help define and limit property rights and define the rights of some relative to others. Bankruptcy laws specify which claimants get paid when a borrower cannot meet fully her debt obligations—and the conditions under which debtors can walk away from the debts. Changes in those laws may strengthen the property rights of some but weaken those of others, as I've already noted in note 9 of the previous chapter. Corporate governance laws typically are for the protection of minority shareholders—restricting what majority shareholders can do.
5. There are further complexities that are not so central to the messages of this book, except to illustrate further the sense in which property rights are social constructions. Typically, we think of the ownership of an asset as entailing control rights (rights about how to use the asset) and income rights (the rights to the income derived from the asset); but sometimes those are separated. Some companies sell shares, for instance, in which one gets an assigned portion of the profits, but limited, or no, control rights.
6. Based on a 2020 study by the RAND Corporation: "The study revealed

that the manufacturer price for any given type of insulin averaged five to ten times higher in the U.S. ($98.70 USD) than in all other OECD countries ($8.81 on average)." See Andrew W. Mulcahy, Daniel Schwam, and Nathaniel Edenfield, "Comparing Insulin Prices in the United States to Other Countries: Results from a Price Index Analysis," RAND Corporation, October 6, 2020.

7. Not surprisingly, the landowners may resist the redistribution with claims that it was acquired legally, that there is a statute of limitations on theft that has expired, and so on.

8. See, e.g. World Economic Forum, *The Global Social Mobility Report* (2020), and Stiglitz, *The Price of Inequality*, and the references cited there.

9. OECD, *A Broken Social Elevator? How to Promote Social Mobility* (Paris: OECD Publishing, 2018).

10. See Michael Sandel, *The Tyranny of Merit: What's Become of the Common Good?* (New York: Farrar, Straus and Giroux, 2020); and Daniel Markovits, *The Meritocracy Trap: How America's Foundational Myth Feeds Inequality, Dismantles the Middle Class, and Devours the Elite* (New York: Penguin Press, 2019).

11. Describing this vicious circle was a central contribution of my book *The Price of Inequality*. An implication was that societies could get trapped in a bad equilibrium—high economic and political inequality.

12. Achieving a better overall distribution of income by increasing equality of market incomes is referred to as pre-distribution. See, in particular, Stiglitz, *The Price of Inequality,* and Jacob S. Hacker and Paul Pierson, *Winner-Take-All Politics: How Washington Made the Rich Richer—and Turned Its Back on the Middle Class* (New York: Simon & Schuster, 2011). I led two projects, one in Europe, the other in the US, asking how the rules and regulations might be rewritten to produce more equitable (and in many cases more efficient) outcomes. See Joseph E. Stiglitz, with Nell Abernathy, Adam Hersh, Susan Holmberg, and Mike Konczal, *Rewriting the Rules of the American Economy: An Agenda for Growth and Shared Prosperity* (New York: W. W. Norton, 2015); and Joseph E. Stiglitz, with Carter Daugherty and the Foundation for European Progressive Studies, *Rewriting the Rules of the European Economy: An Agenda for Growth and Shared Prosperity* (New York: W. W. Norton, 2020).

13. Country of citizenship explains almost 60 percent of variability in global income. Citizenship and parental income class combined explain about 80 percent. See Branko Milanovic, *The Haves and Have-Nots: A Brief and Idiosyncratic History of Global Inequality* (New York: Basic Books, 2010). Conversely, some with low income under current rules might have had higher incomes had they been born in an alternative environment; their relative strengths may have been more amply rewarded.

14. And, again, even more so when it arises out of inheritances that them-

selves were based on exploitation or the advantages of privilege and power.

15. Rawls argued that inequalities were justified only to the extent that they enhanced the income/well-being of the worst-off individuals, i.e., the tax on the rich should be such as to maximize the revenue collected to redistribute (or to spend on public goods that might benefit the poor). Even with such taxation, there may be some inequalities. The view I take is somewhat less extreme.

16. The question of whether taxes reduce savings or work is highly controversial, with those on the Right claiming large effects and progressives suggesting that the effects are, at best, limited. So-called supply siders under President Reagan claimed that taxes were so high that lowering taxes on the rich would enable *greater* help for the poor. They were empirically wrong. Research on the responsiveness of labor supply, for instance, to taxation suggests that with "reasonable" evaluations of the gains of the poor versus the losses of the rich, there should be a high marginal tax rate on income at the top. For a discussion of the nature of the trade-offs in a simple model with a linear income tax, see Joseph E. Stiglitz, "Simple Formulae for Optimal Income Taxation and the Measurement of Inequality," in *Arguments for a Better World: Essays in Honor of Amartya Sen, Volume I, Ethics, Welfare, and Measurement*, Kaushik Basu and Ravi Kanbur, eds. (Oxford: Oxford University Press, 2009), 535–66. For optimal marginal tax rates at the top, see Emmanuel Saez, "Using Elasticities to Derive Optimal Income Tax Rates," *Review of Economic Studies* 68 (2001): 205–29; and Peter Diamond and Emmanuel Saez, "The Case for a Progressive Tax: From Basic Research to Policy Recommendations," *Journal of Economic Perspectives* 25, no. 4 (Fall 2011): 165–90.

17. That is, losses one year can be used to offset profits another year.

18. The original argument was due to Evsey Domar and Richard Musgrave (one of the great public finance economists of the middle of the twentieth century) in their famous 1944 paper, "Proportional Income Taxation and Risk-Taking," *Quarterly Journal of Economics* 58, no. 3 (1944): 388–422. One of my earlier papers developed a more general formulation: "The Effects of Income, Wealth and Capital Gains Taxation on Risk-Taking," *Quarterly Journal of Economics* 83, no. 2 (1969): 263–83.

19. Theory and evidence show that the effect of tax rates on corporate profits has little effect on investment, employment, or innovation. The 2017 corporate income tax cut is emblematic: only dividends, share buybacks, and CEO pay seem to have increased.

20. See Cingano, "Trends in Income Inequality and Its Impact on Economic Growth"; Ostry, Berg, and Tsangarides, "Redistribution, Inequality, and Growth"; and Ostry, Loungani, and Berg, *Confronting Inequality: How Societies Can Choose Inclusive Growth*.

21. Part II discusses at greater length how the nature of our economy shapes individuals.

22. Seven separate studies done at Berkeley, for instance, showed that children from rich families are "more likely to break the law and social customs." Yasmin Anwar, "Affluent People More Likely to be Scofflaws," *Greater Good Magazine*, February 28, 2012.

23. And that would be especially so if one believes that everyone has a moral claim to have sufficient income to provide basic necessities. Behind the veil of ignorance, most would agree with this.

24. Today, residents of both Puerto Rico and Washington, DC, face taxation without representation. Every visitor to Washington is constantly reminded of this, as most DC license plates bear the words "Taxation without Representation."

CHAPTER 7: THE FREEDOM TO EXPLOIT

1. See, e.g., Gustavo Grullon, Yelena Larkin, and Roni Michaely, "Are US Industries Becoming More Concentrated?" *Review of Finance* 23, no. 4 (2019): 697–743; David Autor, David Dorn, Lawrence F. Katz, Christina Patterson, and John Van Reenen, "The Fall of the Labor Share and the Rise of Superstar Firms," *Quarterly Journal of Economics* 135, no. 2 (2020): 645–709; and Thomas Philippon, *The Great Reversal: How America Gave Up on Free Markets* (Cambridge, MA: Belknap Press, 2019).

2. Mike Konczal, "Inflation in 2023: Causes, Progress, and Solutions," Testimony before the House Committee on Oversight and Accountability, Subcommittee on Health Care and Financial Services, March 9, 2023; and Mike Konczal and Niko Lusiani, *Prices, Profits, and Power: An Analysis of 2021 Firm-Level Markups* (New York: Roosevelt Institute, 2022).

3. The 9th Circuit Court of Appeals in San Francisco "approved a $25 million settlement . . . with students who said they were duped by Donald Trump and his now-defunct Trump University." Tom Winter and Dartunorro Clark, "Federal Court Approves $25 Million Trump University Settlement," NBC News, February 6, 2018.

4. In the aftermath of the global financial crisis, a rash of suits against the big banks showed systematic patterns of fraud. The firms originating the mortgages and passing them on to others typically issued a form of "money-back guarantee" that if the mortgage was not as described (e.g., a rental property rather than owner-occupied) or if the mortgage originating process was not as described (e.g., that there were a set of checks to make sure the information about the mortgage was accurate and that the mortgage lived up to certain standards), then the originator or the "securitizer" (the investment bank putting a bundle of such mortgages together) would cover any losses or replace the mortgage with an equiva-

lent "good" mortgage. The banks systematically reneged on these contracts. In almost all cases, the banks were found guilty (or settled), paying tens of billions of dollars. See, for example, Matthew Goldstein, "UBS to Pay $1.4 Billion to Settle Financial-Crisis Fraud Case," *New York Times*, August 14, 2023; and "Bank of America to Pay $16.65 Billion in Historic Justice Department Settlement for Financial Fraud Leading Up to and During the Financial Crisis," Office of Public Affairs, US Department of Justice, August 21, 2014.

5. See, for example, Liza Featherstone, *Selling Women Short: The Landmark Battle for Workers' Rights at Wal-Mart* (New York: Basic Books, 2009).

6. These were called the Opium Wars (1839–1842; 1856–1860). For a discussion of those who made their fortunes from this trade, see Amitav Ghosh, *Smoke and Ashes: Opium's Hidden Histories* (New York: Farrar, Straus and Giroux, 2023).

7. The economics were simple: The West wanted tea, porcelain, and other goods produced by China; China wanted little produced by Europe. There was a trade deficit. The opium trade "solved" that problem: the UK, which controlled India, could export opium from there to China.

8. "Inflation-Adjusted Earnings in Motor Vehicles and Parts Industry Down 17 Percent from 1990 to 2018," Bureau of Economic Analysis, January 6, 2020.

9. In Ceylon, the colonial authorities imposed a capitation tax, and if people didn't earn enough to pay the tax, they had to work for the government for a day.

10. See Jonathan Crush, "Migrancy and Militance: The Case of the National Union of Mineworkers of South Africa," *African Affairs* 88, no. 350 (1989): 5–23.

11. Some apologists for the drug companies say that the high profits are necessary to induce research that is necessary for innovation. But the US allows these exorbitant profits even when there is no such "innovative" justification—for example, when there is not even a patent involved. And there is little evidence that exorbitant profits have any significant effect on innovation—but they can have a significant effect on the health of individuals who cannot acquire the drug.

12. There is a possible rational "market" explanation: market participants did not expect the war to last long and assumed that prices would soon fall. But after the initial months of the conflict, it seemed likely that it would be protracted. Future prices reflect only modest declines.

13. In competitive markets, each small firm would take the price as given, and this effect would not arise. But as we noted, markets are far from perfectly competitive. Collectively, they understood that rapidly expanding production would simply erode those profits. See Anton Korinek and Joseph E. Stiglitz, "Macroeconomic Stabilization for a Post-Pandemic World," Hutchins Center Working Paper No. 78, Brookings Institution

(August 2022), for a brief discussion of the role of tacit collusion in the context of the post-pandemic inflation.

Of course, there are marked differences in how rapidly different kinds of production can be expanded, especially taking into account limitations on infrastructure. But by most accounts, there were ample opportunities to expand, say, fracking in some places in the US. Not surprisingly, the oil companies used the occasion of high prices to lobby for more long-term leases, the increased oil and gas from which would likely appear long after the temporary spike in energy prices was over.

14. This is, in fact, often true in times of crisis: markets respond too slowly. In 1950, the US government enacted the Defense Production Act (DPA) to commandeer resources at critical times. The Trump administration invoked the law during the pandemic. Other countries have similar laws, and similarly used these laws in the pandemic. The US could, and argu-ably should, have invoked the DPA in response to the shortages created by the war in Ukraine.

Still another, more limited action might have been effective: simply guaranteeing the price of oil or gas for a few years, removing the risk that the war would be short-lived and prices would fall back to more normal levels.

15. I laid out the case a half century ago in "Taxation, Corporate Financial Policy and the Cost of Capital," *Journal of Public Economics* 2 (1973): 1–34, and subsequently provided a less mathematical and more accessible ver-sion of the argument in "The Corporation Tax," *Journal of Public Economics* 5 (1976): 303–11. The idea is simple: because the cost of capital is deduct-ible (either directly, through expensing, as is the case in the US now, or indirectly, through depreciation allowances), the tax is essentially a tax on *pure* profits (for instance, monopoly returns), and whatever a firm does to maximize that is the same as it does to maximize (1-t) times that, where t is the corporate tax rate. The one situation where the tax may be distor-tionary is that where firms are capital constrained—i.e., their investment is constrained by a lack of funds. But in the case of a windfall profits tax, the oil and gas companies have not been so constrained: they've been paying out tens of billions of dollars to shareholders. Moreover, the tax system can be designed to allow the deduction of *new* investment. It can even be designed to discourage inflationary price increases, by taxing those who increase their markups at a higher rate.

16. There are many reasons for this, and for the ability of these firms to sus-tain their dominant power for long periods of time. In some cases, for instance, there are network externalities—the more individuals on the network (using a platform), the more valuable it is for an individual to join the network. Once a network has established itself, it may be hard to dislodge it.

17. A limited number of firms can afford these up-front costs—especially

not small potential competitors. Moreover, taking into account the large up-front costs, it may be desirable to have only a few firms, as in the case of a natural monopoly, where efficiency entails a single firm (e.g., a single electricity firm).

There are some significant complexities to this story: cloud computing—which benefits startups in that they don't have to build their own data centers—has paradoxically reduced overhead for startups while at the same time handing more power to Amazon, Google, and Microsoft.

18. I was an expert witness in a case against Sabre, the dominant airline reservation system in the US, where the jury found Sabre guilty of monopolization through a wide range of techniques, including lying about the availability of seats on airlines that tried to challenge their monopoly power. *US Airways, Inc., for American v. Sabre Holdings Corporation*, 938 F.3d 43 (2d Cir. 2019).

19. This doctrine was called contestability. See William J. Baumol, "Contestable Markets: An Uprising in the Theory of Industry Structure," *American Economic Review* 72, no. 1 (1982): 1–15. But even with arbitrarily small fixed sunk costs, potential competition could not replace actual competition. See Stiglitz, "Technological Change, Sunk Costs, and Competition"; and Stiglitz and Greenwald, *Creating a Learning Society*.

20. See Partha Dasgupta and Joseph Stiglitz, "Uncertainty, Industrial Structure and the Speed of R&D," *Bell Journal of Economics* 11, no. 1 (1980): 1–28. If the incumbent were to simply issue a guarantee that he would match the price of any competitor—better, more than match, undercutting them by 5 percent—then any entrant would know that trying to grab market share by undercutting prices simply wouldn't work.

21. John Kenneth Galbraith, *American Capitalism: The Concept of Countervailing Power* (Boston: Houghton Mifflin, 1952).

22. See *AT&T Mobility LLC v. Concepcion*, 563 U.S. 333 (2011); *Epic Systems Corp. v. Lewis*, 584 U.S. (2018); *Am. Express Co. v. Italian Colors Rest.*, 570 U.S. 228 (2013); *Lamps Plus, Inc. v. Varela*, 587 U.S., 139 S. Ct. 1407; 203 L. Ed. 2d 636 (2019).

23. A similarly unjust exercise of market power, and in many ways even more societally corrosive, are nondisclosure provisions put into contracts, discussed in the previous chapter.

24. In his testimony before Congress in the aftermath of the financial crisis, Blankfein seemed to see nothing wrong with Goldman not disclosing what it had done, in a standard evocation of "buyer beware." While the firm claimed it did nothing wrong, in response to a complaint by the Securities and Exchange Commission it agreed that it had made a "mistake" and paid what, at the time, was a record fine for a Wall Street firm.

25. This idea is akin to that of Guido Calabresi, who argued that the most efficient system of liability (e.g., responsibility for an accident) is to put

the burden on the "least cost accident avoider." See Guido Calabresi, *The Costs of Accidents: A Legal and Economic Analysis* (New Haven, CT: Yale University Press, 1970).

26. James Boyle, *The Public Domain: Enclosing the Commons of the Mind*, New Haven: Yale University Press, 2008. For a more extensive discussion, see J. E. Stiglitz, *Making Globalization Work* (New York: W. W. Norton, 2006); and J. E. Stiglitz, "The Economic Foundations of Intellectual Property," sixth annual Frey Lecture in Intellectual Property, Duke University, February 16, 2007; *Duke Law Journal* 57, no. 6 (2008): 1693–724.

27. *Association for Molecular Pathology v. Myriad Genetics, Inc.*, 133 S. Ct. 2107 (2013); also see Regulatory Transparency Project, podcast, Roger D. Klein and Chayila Kleist, "Explainer Episode 55 —10 Years On: The Impact and Effects of AMP vs. Myriad," June 12, 2023, for a discussion on the broad consequences of the decision. Defenders of these patents say that without them, the knowledge wouldn't have been generated in the first place. In the case at hand, that claim is unambiguously false: the Human Genome Project was analyzing *all* the human genes. At most, the knowledge would have been produced a few months later.

28. Michael Cavna, "Mickey Mouse Is Finally in the Public Domain. Here's What That Means," *Washington Post*, January 1, 2024.

29. Chapter 6 argued against there being any innate moral legitimacy with the incomes and wealth generated even by a well-functioning competitive economy. Some have argued for an exception for innovators, saying that there is something just about rewarding them for their enormous contributions. There are a host of objections to this view, but even if one thought they should be rewarded, the argument says nothing about the magnitude. In particular, there is no philosophical or economic argument for an entitlement to the exercise of monopoly power over the innovation for 20 years. The justification, if there is any, relates to the balancing of societal costs of monopoly with the societal gains from the induced innovation.

Even ascertaining an individual inventor's marginal contribution is difficult. As Isaac Newton famously put it: "If I have seen further, it is by standing on the shoulders of giants." Ascertaining who should receive credit for the Covid-19 vaccine illustrates this: Among the list typically cited are Katalin Kariko and Drew Weisman at the University of Pennsylvania; Paul Krieg, Douglas Melton, Tom Maniatis, and Michael Green at Harvard University; and Robert Malone at the Salk Institute for Biological Studies. See, for instance, Elie Dolgin, "The Tangled History of mRNA Vaccines," *Nature* 597, no. 7876 (September 14, 2021): 318–24. But, of course, none of them reaped the financial rewards: those went to Pfizer and Moderna.

30. For a fuller discussion of the prize and other systems for motivating and financing innovation, see Stiglitz, *Making Globalization Work*.

PART II: FREEDOM, BELIEFS, AND PREFERENCES, AND THE CREATION OF THE GOOD SOCIETY

1. Philosopher David Hume famously distinguished between preferences and cognition (or beliefs). The latter he argued is subject to reason—although (to use modern terminology), when the world is ever changing, we may have no way of being sure that our judgments of relative frequencies are "correct." He argued that preferences, however, are not. As George J. Stigler and Gary S. Becker argued, in "De Gustibus Non Est Disputandum," *American Economic Review* 67, no. 2 (1977): 76–90, following Hume: preferences are just given, not subject to reason. Hume's famous slogan was "Reason is the slave of the passions," a view not inconsistent with modern behavioralist theories of confirmation bias, and with its implication of "equilibrium fictions." See Karla Hoff and Joseph E. Stiglitz, "Equilibrium Fictions: A Cognitive Approach to Societal Rigidity," *American Economic Review* 100, no. 2 (May 2010): 141–46. Beliefs that are *objectively* wrong can be sustained, because we discount information that is contrary to those beliefs and we seek out only information that is consistent with those beliefs. It is partly this that leads to polarization in society, a subject I discuss further below.

2. It is not that economists *discovered* this reality—as I've already suggested, it's almost obvious. It's that, at last, they began to incorporate this insight into their analyses.

3. See Robert H. Frank, Thomas Gilovich, and Dennis T. Regan, "Does Studying Economics Inhibit Cooperation?" *Journal of Economic Perspectives* 7, no. 2 (1993): 159–71. More recent work of Ifcher and Zarghamee supports this relationship in the context of brief exposure in a lab. See John Ifcher and Homa Zarghamee, "The Rapid Evolution of Homo Economicus: Brief Exposure to Neoclassical Assumptions Increases Self-Interested Behavior," *Journal of Behavioral and Experimental Economics* 75 (2018): 55–65. On the other hand, research done at the University of Massachusetts–Amherst suggests that while those who study economics are more conservative, studying economics does not make them more selfish. This may have to do with the way economics is taught there; the university has a reputation for having a very progressive economics department, suggesting that it may not be inevitable that studying economics makes one more conservative. See Daniele Girardi, Sai Madhurika Mamunuru, Simon D. Halliday, and Samuel Bowles, "Does Economics Make You Selfish?" University of Massachusetts Amherst Economics Department Working Paper Series 304 (2021).

4. Their pathbreaking technical article was published in 1979, but had been circulating for years. Daniel Kahneman and Amos Tversky, "Prospect Theory: An Analysis of Decision Under Risk," *Econometrica* 47, no. 2 (1979): 263–91. I had the good fortune to begin discussions on these

issues after a Social Science Research Council seminar at the University of Michigan in 1973.

5. Daniel Kahneman, *Thinking, Fast and Slow* (New York: Farrar, Strausand Giroux, 2011).

6. There is one way in which cognitive limitations matter for our analytic approach: making choices is more difficult when one has a more expansive opportunity set, and accordingly, some individuals prefer a more constrained one (contrary to our view that expanding opportunity sets, giving individuals more freedom to choose, is always better). Of course, what individuals typically really want is a restaurant or store that knows the preferences of people like them and has therefore stripped away those things that would not in the end have been chosen, thereby reducing decision costs.

There is another complexity that can arise even in situations in which individuals have fixed preferences, related to what economists call time consistency. I know today that I will be tempted to eat too much tomorrow, or to take an addictive drug, so I want my choice set tomorrow to be reduced, to constrain me to act tomorrow in a way that is consistent with my preferences today. Ulysses tying himself to the mast to resist the Sirens is an early example. This book does not delve into either of these complexities.

7. See Demeritt, Hoff, and Stiglitz, *The Other Invisible Hand.*

CHAPTER 8: SOCIAL COERCION AND SOCIAL COHESION

1. This was emphasized, for instance, by the French sociologist Emile Durkheim.

2. Human capital was at the center of economists' traditional discussion of the role of education. And schools do more than screen and signal abilities, as emphasized in more recent literature. This role in shaping individuals was ignored in the standard treatments because the economists' standard model simply *assumed* that individuals' preferences were fixed and given at birth.

3. I noted earlier that economics also seems to attract those who are disproportionately selfish and that the longer students study economics, the more selfish they seem to become. See note 3 in the introduction of this part.

4. Akeel Bilgrami, "The Philosophical Significance of the Commons," *Social Research: An International Quarterly* 88, no. 1 (2021): 203–39.

5. Smith acknowledged that there was something almost miraculous about it, describing what happened as if it were done by an invisible hand. In some interpretations of Smith, that invisible hand takes on a theological meaning. As we noted in Part I, however, modern economics has explained that there is a presumption that the pursuit of self-interest does

not lead to the well-being of the entire society. Prices provide a coordinating mechanism; it works, but works imperfectly.

6. See Demeritt, Hoff, and Stiglitz, *The Other Invisible Hand*.

7. He argued this in a famous article in 1970 in the *New York Times Magazine*: "The Social Responsibility of Business Is to Increase Its Profits," September 13, 1970.

8. Uri Gneezy and Aldo Rustichini, "A Fine Is a Price," *Journal of Legal Studies* 29, no. 1 (2000): 1–17.

9. See Haesung Jung et al., "Prosocial Modeling: A Meta-Analytic Review and Synthesis," *Psychological Bulletin* 146, no. 8 (2020): 635–63, for a review.

10. Gary S. Becker, *The Economics of Discrimination* (Chicago: University of Chicago Press, 2010).

11. Modern game theory has shown how such equilibria, advantaging one group at the expense of others, can be sustained. For a discussion of social capital and a critique of some of its impacts, see Ismail Serageldin and Partha Dasgupta, eds., *Social Capital: A Multifaceted Perspective* (Washington, DC: World Bank Publications, 2001), including the chapter by J. E. Stiglitz, "Formal and Informal Institutions," pp. 59–68.

12. Famously illustrated by Singapore's war against gum chewing.

13. Demeritt et al., in *The Other Invisible Hand*, further discuss the way that established norms give rise to societal rigidities, impeding the ability to adapt to changing circumstances and sometimes sustaining dysfunctional social practices like foot binding. They also explore how norms change and can be changed, and how, at least in some instances, they get established in the first place. These are important questions, especially as one considers the effects of social coercion on individuals' freedom, but I cannot pursue them within the confines of this book.

14. A 2013 novel by Dave Eggers, *The Circle* (New York: Knopf), depicts an Orwellian corporate dystopia inside the world's largest internet company.

15. Or at least most of us are. Questions may be raised about those with limited cognitive capacities and social disorders, like sociopaths.

16. Amartya Sen in his 2009 book, *The Idea of Justice* (Cambridge, MA: Harvard University Press), argues that not only do we have the capacity to reason about such matters but we have an innate empathy and understanding of fairness that are incorporated in our reasoning. But even so, this does not fully resolve the free-rider problem.

17. Personal correspondence.

18. This is a central criticism that Karla Hoff and I, in "Equilibrium Fictions: A Cognitive Approach to Societal Rigidity," provide of, say, the work of those who model individuals as choosing a set of preferences or beliefs or an identity that maximizes a meta-utility function, such as Roland Bénabou and Jean Tirole, "Incentives and Prosocial Behavior," *American Economic Review* 96, no. 5 (2006): 1652–78; and Roland Bénabou and Jean

Tirole, "Identity, Morals, and Taboos: Beliefs as Assets," *Quarterly Journal of Economics* 126, no. 2 (2011): 805–55.

19. This skepticism of our ability to transcend our lenses is reinforced by recent research showing that the introspection required to understand lens formation is difficult to maintain even among those who have the most capacity for it. Mohsen Javdani and Ha-Joon Chang, "Who Said or What Said? Estimating Ideological Bias in Views Among Economists," *Cambridge Journal of Economics* 47, no. 2 (March 1, 2023): 309–39, found through an RCT that changing source attributions from mainstream to less-mainstream sources reduces economists' reported agreement with statements (with meaningful variation by gender, research area, and undergraduate major— consistent with ideological bias), despite 82 percent professing one should only pay attention to content. The finding seems reflective of subconscious biases that the participants do not recognize.

20. While *some* individuals within a group are able to come to understand that the lens through which they see the world has been given to them, and decide to accept it or not, for many it is unthinkable to think outside those lenses; the lens is a part of their identity, and it is unthinkable that they have another identity.

21. While (with a few exceptions) the banks were not "convicted," there were multiple out-of-court settlements, with the financial institutions paying fines sometimes in the hundreds of millions. See Sewell Chan and Louise Story, "Goldman Pays $550 Million to Settle Fraud Case," *New York Times*, July 15, 2010; and Charlie Savage, "Wells Fargo Will Settle Mortgage Bias Charges," *New York Times*, July 12, 2012.

22. See Wenling Lu and Judith Swisher, "A Comparison of Bank and Credit Union Growth Around the Financial Crisis," *American Journal of Business* 35, no. 1 (January 1, 2020), and Stiglitz, *Freefall*, for a more extensive discussion.

23. Brian M. Stecher et al., "Improving Teaching Effectiveness: Final Report: The Intensive Partnerships for Effective Teaching Through 2015–2016," RAND Corporation, June 21, 2018. A more recent popular survey summarized similar results but was more hopeful about programs that combined incentive pay with other features. See Matthew Stone and Caitlynn Peetz, "Does Performance-Based Teacher Pay Work? Here's What the Research Says," *EducationWeek*, June 12, 2023.

24. Four out of the top five state education systems (New Jersey, Connecticut, Vermont, and Massachusetts) are also among the top ten states in terms of public-school teacher unionization rates. For education rankings, see Scholaroo, "States Ranked by Education—2023 Rankings," January 23, 2023, and for unionization rates, see "Public School Teacher Data File, 2017–18," National Teacher and Principal Survey, National Center for Education Statistics, US Department of Education.

25. There is a large literature on the subject of this subsection. See Yann Algan, "Trust and Social Capital," chapter 10 in Stiglitz, Fitoussi, and Durand, *For Good Measure: Advancing Research on Well-Being Metrics Beyond GDP*, J. E. Stiglitz, Jean-GDP.

26. Thus, as we noted earlier, parents and schools try to shape individuals in this way, with some success overall. We are reminded of how successful when we encounter someone like Donald Trump, who is not so inculcated.

27. As Stefano Battiston of the University of Zurich and I put it in the title of a recent working paper (forthcoming), "Unstable by Design."

28. Advocates of neoliberal capitalism argue that there are corrective forces, like reputation, that curb these excesses and ensure the system's long run viability. In chapter 11, we explain why, while present, they are too weak.

CHAPTER 9: THE CONCERTED SHAPING OF INDIVIDUALS AND THEIR BELIEFS

1. They have, for instance, vociferously opposed the repeal of current provisions that give them preferential treatment with respect to liability for what they transmit across their platforms compared to other media (see the below discussion). They sometimes take a disingenuous stand with respect to moderating content on their platform, suggesting that it is up to government to define standards—but simultaneously quietly lobbying against the imposition of any standards.

2. This section contains ideas from and is partially borrowed from Anya Schiffrin and J. E. Stiglitz, "Facebook Does Not Understand the Market-place of Ideas," *Financial Times*, January 17, 2020; and Joseph E. Stiglitz and Andrew Kosenko, "Robust Theory and Fragile Practice: Information in a World of Disinformation," *The Elgar Companion to Information Economics,* Daphne R. Raban and Julia Włodarczyk, eds. (Northampton, MA: Edward Elgar Publishing, 2024).

3. Those making this mistake are in good company: One of the early researchers in this area, George Stigler of the University of Chicago, made the same mistake. He wanted to believe that markets for information were just like ordinary markets; and just like he (mistakenly) believed that the latter were efficient, he believed the former were, too. See, e.g., George J. Stigler, "The Economics of Information," *Journal of Political Economy* 69, no. 3 (1961): 213–25.

4. There is still another reason that competition in information markets is imperfect. Typically, when there is imperfect information, markets are imperfectly competitive. Inherently, marketplaces for information will themselves be characterized by information imperfections. But we know that marketplaces that are not perfectly competitive are, in general, not efficient.

5. While in simple models where the acquisition, dissemination, and processing of information is costless, and where consumers are perfectly rational, firms have incentives to be honest and there would be no need for disclosure requirements, these assumptions never hold, e.g., when there is costly verification, and most well-functioning governments impose at least some disclosure requirements. The original theoretical analyses were due to Stiglitz (1975) and Milgrom (1981). See J. E. Stiglitz, "The Theory of 'Screening,' Education, and the Distribution of Income," *American Economic Review* 65, no. 3 (1975): 283–300; and P. R. Milgrom, "Good News and Bad News: Representation Theorems and Applications," *Bell Journal of Economics* 12, no. 2 (1981): 380–91.

6. The US Consumer Financial Protection Bureau (CFPB) likewise requires lenders to state their terms transparently.

7. See, for example, Jack Ewing, "Inside VW's Campaign of Trickery," *New York Times*, May 6, 2017.

8. See, inter alia, Shlomo Benartzi and Richard Thaler, "Heuristics and Biases in Retirement Savings Behavior," *Journal of Economic Perspectives* 21, no. 3 (2007): 81–104.

9. Even when companies arise to vet the quality of the information, there is a cost to doing so, which somebody must bear.

10. Even with a free-rider problem, there may still be *some* efforts at providing some information to offset mis- and disinformation, but such efforts won't suffice. NewsGuard is a commercial attempt to provide "transparent tools to counter misinformation for readers, brands, and democracies." See "About NewsGuard," https://www.newsguardtech.com/about -newsguard/. It has had more limited success than was at first hoped.

11. Of course, there may be large areas where this is not the case— metaphysical issues where the principles of tolerance discussed in the next chapter are crucial.

12. This is, of course, inconsistent with the view of many on the Right who insist on their right to have *their* interpretation of the facts, even within science—to claim, for instance, that climate change isn't real.

13. This may be too narrow a reading of history: there have long been episodic efforts to undermine an independent judiciary and, in some circles, to question expertise, including that embraced by educational and research institutions. Under Trump, these efforts became emboldened and more widespread.

14. Similarly, for workers in disputes with their employers in the absence of unions. Making matters worse: the Supreme Court has undermined the ability for individuals to engage in class actions, making redress against corporations all the more difficult, as we saw in chapter 7. The conservative Supreme Court has been engaged in a subtle process of rewriting the rules of the economy in ways which favor corporations at the expense of workers and consumers.

15. Schiffrin and Stiglitz, "Facebook Does Not Understand the Marketplace of Ideas."

16. Sometimes their profits come from more explicit scurrilous activities, exemplified by click fraud, where platforms extract cash from other firms for no benefit.

17. In a perfectly competitive market, prices convey all relevant information. Formally, economists say prices are a sufficient statistic for all the relevant information.

18. This is called the first welfare theorem. Although efficiency can also be sustained by *perfect* price discrimination, the information generated by platforms and employed by firms engaged in price discrimination is far from sufficient to enable perfect price discrimination (although modern algorithms can come much closer than before). In Joseph E. Stiglitz, "Monopoly, Non-Linear Pricing and Imperfect Information: The Insurance Market," *Review of Economic Studies* 44, no. 3 (1977): 407–30, I showed that, in the presence of imperfect information, there are large welfare losses associated with monopoly arising from the attempt to engage in imperfect price discrimination.

19. This is true even though, indirectly, there may be side benefits from the attempt to build, say, a better advertising engine to extract more profits out of consumers. It has, for instance, been a major spur to AI. Still, the relentless drive for profits repeatedly results in the degradation of product quality, as we have already noted.

20. Research has shown that platforms are incentivized to show toxic content (which is often polarizing) because it increases ad and content consumption. See George Beknazar-Yuzbashev, Rafael Jiménez Durán, Jesse McCrosky, and Mateusz Stalinski, "Toxic Content and User Engagement on Social Media: Evidence from a Field Experiment," November 1, 2022, http://dx.doi.org/10.2139/ssrn.4307346.

21. Even with fully rational individuals, there can be polarization, and polarization may be increased by what and how the media provides information. In our fragmented world, individuals differ in their judgments about the accuracy of information provided by different media outlets. Given the scarcity of time, even if information were free, citizens would turn to suppliers of information that are, from their perspective, "better." This reinforces societal polarization. And even in the absence of different information, *rational* individuals confronted with the same information— but in possession of different worldviews—will interpret that information differently.

22. Or that they had deliberately made it more addictive, or that a succession of Marlboro Men had died of lung cancer.

23. See, e.g., Karla Hoff and Joseph E. Stiglitz, "Striving for Balance in Economics: Towards a Theory of the Social Determination of Behavior,"

Journal of Economic Behavior and Organization 126, Part B (2016): 25–57; and Demeritt, Hoff, and Stiglitz, *The Other Invisible Hand.*

24. The literature on polarization is multifaceted and complex. There is some evidence, for instance, that being exposed to other views also increases polarization. See Christopher A. Bail, Lisa P. Argyle, Taylor W. Brown, John P. Bumpus, Haohan Chen, M. B. Fallin Hunzaker, Jaemin Lee, Marcus Mann, Friedolin Merhout, and Alexander Volfovsky, "Exposure to Opposing Views on Social Media Can Increase Political Polarization," *Proceedings of the National Academy of Sciences* 115, no. 37 (2018): 9216–21.

25. See, for instance, Kevin Quealy, "The More Education Republicans Have, the Less They Tend to Believe in Climate Change," *New York Times*, November 14, 2017.

26. Because the public "owns" the airwaves, it was (reasonably) thought they had especially the right to make sure that the airwaves were used in ways that enhanced societal welfare—and did not lead to the polarization seen today. There was a widespread view that the fairness doctrine was not only constitutional but essential for democracy. In the 1969 Supreme Court case upholding the doctrine, Justice Byron White argued, "It is the right of the viewers and listeners, not the right of the broadcasters, which is paramount." See Justia Law, *Red Lion Broadcasting Co., Inc. v. FCC*, 395 U.S. 367 (1969).

27. Dan Fletcher, "A Brief History of the Fairness Doctrine," *Time*, February 20, 2009. See also Victor Pickard, "The Fairness Doctrine Won't Solve Our Problems—But It Can Foster Needed Debate," *Washington Post*, February 4, 2021. For a broader discussion of these issues, see Victor Pickard, *America's Battle for Media Democracy: The Triumph of Corporate Libertarianism and the Future of Media Reform* (Cambridge: Cambridge University Press, 2014).

28. It has long been known that there is a correlation between watching conservative media and having conservative beliefs, but the direction of causality has been unclear. Does watching Fox News actually make individuals more conservative? That question has been answered in some natural experiments that have identified Fox News' effect as significantly causal. See Stefano DellaVigna and Ethan Kaplan, "The Fox News Effect: Media Bias and Voting," *Quarterly Journal of Economics* 122, no. 3 (2007): 1187–234.

29. In the United States, there has been considerable success in convincing individuals that bequest taxes are taxes on death, rather than a means of preventing the perpetuation of wealth inequality.

30. We enter here into difficult philosophical terrain discussed briefly in the previous chapter. Individuals have human agency—they don't have to be "fooled" by the media; they don't have to trust Fox News. With evidence that Fox News propagates lies, one might have thought that there would be more circumspection in giving Fox credence. But the reality,

uncovered by behavioral science, is that individuals *are* affected, and that the media does shape the lens through which significant portions of the population see the world.

31. As earlier chapters have explained, how we see our laws and regulations is affected by such lenses. For instance, property rights and the freedom to contract are both social constructions and every society defines and constrains those rights, and hopefully does so in ways to promote societal welfare. They are not based on any "natural law." The metanarrative through which the consequences of alternative rules governing property and contracts are seen obviously affects the rules we adopt.

32. As I noted in chapter 1, there is a long tradition of seeing our particular shared ideology (shared views about the world) as both necessary for the smooth working of society and for sustaining the power of the elites (see the discussion of Antonio Gramsci in the preface).

33. Social media platforms sometimes claim they are just a neutral transmitter of information (or misinformation) from others. But that's not true. Their algorithms determine how information is received—and affect the extent to which there may be differences in what different individuals see. The legacy media obviously takes a more active role in creating stories.

34. I should emphasize: our current dysfunction is not the result of just today's distorted media landscape. For instance, neoliberalism's rise, some half a century ago, can't be attributed to it. There are other forces at play. Populism might have risen even had all the reforms to make the media more democratic and accountable been done long ago.

35. Just two years after the loan, it became clear to the financiers that Argentina couldn't pay what it owed. Capital fled the country; Macri went to the IMF and got a $44 billion loan in a futile attempt to sustain the economy, with the dollars simply used to facilitate the capital flight, leaving the country massively in debt without anything to show for it.

36. For a definition of media power and an application to the case of the US, see Andrea Prat, "Media Power," *Journal of Political Economy* 126, no. 4 (August 2018): 1747–83.

37. Some claim that all that is required is "informed" consent. But this won't suffice for two reasons: individuals aren't, in general, fully apprised of the consequences of such assent (part of the limitations of information and rationality noted elsewhere in this book), and firms present the choices in ways that bias the outcomes. I was at a dinner at which the head of one of the large telecommunications firms boasted how it could get informed consent for a pittance, small amounts compared to the profits derived from the information gleaned.

38. To the contrary, until recently, US trade negotiators have tried to force other governments to adopt pro-tech regulations; as is so often the case, in its trade negotiations, the US government (and in particular, the US

Trade Representative) reflects producer interests, not the interests of the country as a whole—a central message of my books *Globalization and Its Discontents* and *Globalization and Its Discontents Revisited*, as well as my book with Andrew Charlton, *Fair Trade for All* (Oxford: Oxford University Press, 2005).

39. In particular, the General Data Protection Regulation (GDPR) of 2018 that attempts to protect privacy, and the Digital Services Act (DSA) of 2022.

40. See Stiglitz, *The Price of Inequality* and *People, Power, and Profits.*

41. For instance, the oil monopoly was attacked by breaking it up. But when there are large network externalities, this may not be a good solution. Regulating a large number of platforms to ensure they are moderating content appropriately and not causing social harms may be more difficult than regulating a few. Still, stronger enforcement of existing regulations would help a great deal, e.g., restraining the platforms from engaging in their anticompetitive practices (as the EU and the Federal Trade Commission have been trying to do with Google and Amazon) and not allowing mergers and acquisitions that would reduce competition either now or in the foreseeable future (Meta/Facebook's acquisition of Instagram should almost surely have been blocked).

42. Not surprisingly, those who seek financial wizardry don't just evaporate when one magic elixir—securitization—shows itself to be flawed; they look for another: this time, Bitcoin and other cryptocurrency. The collapse of FTX shows that advances in technology can combine with finance to produce ever more fraudulent outcomes.

CHAPTER 10: TOLERANCE, SOCIAL SOLIDARITY, AND FREEDOM

1. There is an indirect impact: the *knowledge* that there are others who are acting in a particular way may affect an individual's well-being. The notion of tolerance discussed in this section gives no weight to this, as the next paragraph makes clear.

2. This is an arena in which Enlightenment perspectives often failed to dominate, even in seemingly enlightened societies, with many countries having strong laws specifying what was unacceptable and meting out severe punishments.

3. Other countries have similarly introduced institutional features to help ensure state secularism; in France, this is embedded in a set of principles referred to as *laïcité*, and it includes prohibitions against religious symbols (like headscarves) in schools.

4. See Will E. Edington, "House Bill No. 246, Indiana State Legislature, 1897," Proceedings of the Indiana Academy of Science 45 (1935): 206–10. The bill passed in the Indiana House of Representatives but was rejected in the Indiana Senate.

5. One could justify this intolerance of thought with the logic that thinking such thoughts increases the likelihood of actions that induce social harms (analogous to the argument of the previous chapter that what is disseminated over the internet can induce social harms). The Bible is explicit, warning about being "ensnared." The logic here is similar to that presented earlier in the case of gun control: allowing guns increases the likelihood that an individual will be shot. The Right often responds that "people kill, not guns," i.e., there is always human "agency," and if individuals *choose* to exercise that agency through shooting and killing someone, the gun shouldn't be blamed, but the individual; and those who act responsibly shouldn't have their freedom to carry a gun decreased because of the existence of those who can't control themselves appropriately. But there is an obvious difference between taking that view in the case of guns and the view that one should not *think* about committing certain acts. Guns provide an *instrument* of harm.

6. Of course, one can only know a person's thoughts by observing her actions, or her speech; and as I noted in the last chapter, even speech can be viewed as an "action," particularly when it is directed at affecting others' actions.

7. Though, again, in each of these instances, there are important externalities.

8. For instance, a humane society will not allow an elderly person to go homeless or starve simply because he has not saved enough. Thus, if an individual does not provide adequately for his retirement, there are costs imposed on others—an externality.

9. So, too, the tolerance of the climate deniers seems limited: in some places in the US, there is a ban on teaching climate science, presumably because of their concern that such teaching will lead to actions (in the next generation) that run counter to their beliefs.

10. For example, fiscal policies in which governments cut back spending are contractionary, so national income falls as a result. It has been true virtually *always*, so I feel a high degree of confidence about it. But sometimes something else also happens—for instance, exports increase because of growth in a neighboring economy, and one has to disentangle the two effects. Yet as strong as the evidence is in this area, there are disputes. Some conservative economists claim that the reduced deficit from reduced spending will so increase confidence that the economy will grow in what is called, in seemingly contradictory language, expansionary contraction. This just isn't true. Reducing budget deficits, *contracting* spending, is essentially always contractionary. The wrong view leads to wrong policies—austerity—with great harms to the economy and especially unskilled workers.

11. "The Codrington Legacy," All Souls College, University of Oxford, https://www.asc.ox.ac.uk/codrington-legacy.

12. And that is why it is such a mistake to assess market power in the media by looking just at market power in the market for advertising.

PART III: WHAT KIND OF ECONOMY PROMOTES A GOOD, JUST, AND FREE SOCIETY?

1. This agenda was closely related to a broader philosophical strand of thought, dating at least back to Auguste Comte. Those views have now been generally discredited, including by some, like Ludwig Wittgenstein, who originally were among its advocates. The physicist Werner Heisenberg put it nicely: "The positivists have a simple solution: the world must be divided into that which we can say clearly and the rest, which we had better pass over in silence. But can anyone conceive of a more pointless philosophy, seeing that what we can say clearly amounts to next to nothing? If we omitted all that is unclear, we would probably be left with completely uninteresting and trivial tautologies." See Werner Heisenberg, "Positivism, Metaphysics and Religion," in *Physics and Beyond: Encounters and Conversations*, translated by Arnold J. Pomerans (New York: Harper & Row, 1971), 213. My thesis supervisor, Paul Samuelson, played a central role in pushing the positivist agenda within economics.

2. Nineteenth-century utilitarians like Jeremy Bentham had argued that society should be arranged so as to maximize the sum of the utilities of all individuals. The positivists said that that was meaningless since there was no way to objectively or scientifically measure the level of utility of each person, no way to compare utilities. There was no way to assess whether the enjoyment I received from eating a strawberry was greater or less than the enjoyment you receive. Thus, the positivists focused on the concept of Pareto efficiency.

3. Economists might advise on *how* best to manage any required redistribution, but even then there was an abdication of responsibility, as they talked about mythical, nondistortionary lump-sum redistributions. The claim was that, with these redistributions, one could still rely on the market and that one should, in any case, not interfere with economic efficiency. This was referred to as the second fundamental theorem of welfare economics. With imperfect information this is not, in general, true, which I showed in a series of papers. For a popular exposition, see Stiglitz, *Whither Socialism?*

   One of the important advances in economics in the second half of the twentieth century was analyzing trade-offs between efficiency and distribution more precisely, in a world in which there were not lump-sum redistributions.

4. Sometimes, economists focus on reforms that are such that the economic gains of the winners are large enough to compensate the losers, so all *could* be better off; but typically, such compensations are not made. Whether

such changes represent welfare increases accordingly depends crucially on who are the winners and the losers.

5. Whether such interventions were a Pareto improvement is no matter.

6. In practice, the technocratic economists' refusal to take moral stances and judgments is a charade: they often take implicit moral stances when engaging with public policy but hide them behind the glow of "technical impartiality."

7. The endogeneity of preferences—the fact that they are changeable—poses a challenge to both the utilitarian and Rawlsian frameworks. With *given* preferences and with risk-averse individuals, thinking about what a good society would be behind the veil of ignorance helps us to think about why an egalitarian society is desirable. But what if it is possible that we create a society of gamblers who love risk, who would willingly undertake an unfair gamble entailing a small chance of winning a lot and a high probability of living in poverty? If everyone were of that nature, then behind the veil of ignorance, all would choose economic and social arrangements that led to higher inequality.

8. Twentieth-century economics posited that we can say nothing about the relative merits of two societies in which preferences were different. We can only ascertain how good an economic system is in delivering well-being *given those preferences*. I believe that is wrong. While endogenous preferences make it more difficult to make unambiguous statements about individual well-being than is the case with fixed preferences, one can still say some things about an individual's behavior related to ultimate well-being. One can ascertain, for instance, whether particular actions are consistent with stated objectives—whether, for instance, certain actions, appearing to reflect our preferences *today*, are consistent with our seeming long-term well-being; one can similarly uncover other instances of possible dissonance. Time inconsistency (which means that if, today, one makes a plan for, say, savings and consumption for the coming years, when next year arrives, one will want to actually behave as the plan envisioned, consuming and saving the amounts in the plan) has, in fact, been a major theme in behavioral economics. But even here there is an ambiguity. While tomorrow we may regret that we did not save yesterday as much as we wish *today* we had saved, acting on our tastes (preferences) *as they were then* was not in any sense wrong. There is a sense in which we should not even feel regret. We may even know that we will have different preferences in the future. Still, we act today in terms of what gives us pleasure today, and that may well "rationally" take into account some notion of regret tomorrow that our behavior today had not been different. Only if we are not fully cognizant of what is going on can we be said not to be rational. (There is much more that could and should be said on these topics but addressing them adequately would take us beyond the confines of this book.)

9. For fuller discussions and references, see chapters 3 and 4.

10. I am not claiming that they take the same form in all societies or are given the same weight. Thus, I do not endorse the universalist agenda that there is a single set of natural values, waiting to be discovered. At the same time, as the above remarks should make clear, though I recognize that there might arise societies with different values, I am skeptical of the extreme relativist position, which says that anything goes. This is partly because of the arguments put forward in chapter 10: a good society needs to have a certain level of social cohesion, and there are some perspectives (values, rules, and regulations) that are antithetical to the possibility of that. I emphasize, though, that here I am taking a pragmatic approach: given where our society is today, the values I've listed are those on which there is general assent; these should be fostered.

Chapter 11: Neoliberal Capitalism: Why It Failed

1. Robert Bork was nominated by President Reagan to be on the Supreme Court, but the nomination was rejected because of his extreme views. That rejection gave rise to the slang term "borked." He articulated his views on competition in *The Antitrust Paradox* (New York: Free Press, 1978).

2. Chapter 2 explained why that is so.

3. See, for example, the work of Ed Prescott, who received the Nobel Prize in 2004.

4. This has been well described by Mariana Mazzucato in her insightful book *The Entrepreneurial State*.

5. In *Creating a Learning Society*, Bruce Greenwald and I explain why markets misdirect innovation resources. See also Daron Acemoglu, "Distorted Innovation: Does the Market Get the Direction of Technology Right?" *AEA Papers and Proceedings* 113 (May 2023): 1–28.

6. There is considerable evidence of widespread misperceptions of others—and that those matter. See Leonardo Bursztyn and David Y. Yang, "Misperceptions About Others," *Annual Review of Economics* 14 (August 2022): 425–52.

7. Where these provisions led to vaccine apartheid, with large parts of the world's population deprived of access to vaccines. See the discussion in the next chapter.

8. Many of the societal rigidities are thus associated with beliefs and preferences, which themselves are affected by the beliefs and preferences of others—a central message of Part II of this book and of Demeritt et al., *The Other Invisible Hand*.

9. Though to be fair, this seems more of a ruse than a principle of law, since their references to historical precedence and interpretation seem to be highly selective. They discard the principle when it proves inconvenient.

10. As I noted earlier in the discussion of market fundamentalism, I call it a religion in part because belief in free markets continues, in spite of contrary evidence and theory. For those who hold on to it, it is hard, if not impossible, to refute.

11. See, e.g., the work of Joseph Henrich, Robert Boyd, Samuel Bowles, Colin Camerer, Ernst Fehr, Herbert Gintis, and Richard McElreath, "In Search of Homo Economicus: Behavioral Experiments in 15 Small-Scale Societies," *American Economic Review* 91, no. 2 (May 2001): 73–78; and an early overview of the relevant literature in volumes 1 and 2 of the *Handbook of the Economics of Giving, Altruism and Reciprocity*, eds. Serge-Christophe Kolm and Jean Mercier Ythier (Amsterdam: Elsevier, 2006).

12. For discussions on this in the political science literature, see, e.g., Elizabeth Rigby and Gerald C. Wright, "Political Parties and Representation of the Poor in the American States," *American Journal of Political Science* 57, no. 3 (January 2013): 552–65; and Matt Grossman, Zuhaib Mahmood, and William Isaac, "Political Parties, Interest Groups, and Unequal Class Influence in American Policy," *Journal of Politics* 83, no. 4 (October 2021).

13. Making matters still worse is the fact that the US Constitution, giving every state two senators, underweighs the political power of some and overweighs that of others.

14. At the same time, one does not need crises to produce positive social innovations and reforms. The provision of health care to the aged (Medicare) in 1965 occurred in an era of relative prosperity. See Robert Haveman, "Poverty and the Distribution of Economic Well-Being Since the 1960s," in *Economic Events, Ideas, and Policies: The 1960s and After*, George L. Perry and James Tobin, eds. (Washington, DC: Brookings Institution Press), 243–98.

15. Anne Case and Angus Deaton, *Deaths of Despair and the Future of Capitalism* (Princeton, NJ: Princeton University Press, 2020).

16. In some of these cases, it was not just an "intellectual wave" that moved around the world. America directly intervened in countries to move them along in the direction that the US wanted. In other cases, however, our soft power has played a more important role.

17. Absolute mobility in the US has experienced a sharp decline. More than 90 percent of Americans born in 1940 ended up making more, in real terms, than their parents, but for those born in 1984, this figure had fallen to 50 percent. Relative intergenerational mobility is also much lower in the US than in similarly advanced economies. The probability that a child born to parents in the bottom fifth of the income distribution reaches the top fifth is 7.5 percent, which is a little over half the rate in Canada. Moreover, this rate has not improved in the US, remaining fairly flat for Americans born between 1970 and 1986.

For more on these trends, see work by Raj Chetty, Nathaniel Hendren, Patrick Kline, Emmanuel Saez, and Nicholas Turner, "Is the United States Still a Land of Opportunity? Recent Trends in Intergenerational Mobility," American Economic Review 104, no. 5 (May 2014): 141–47; Raj Chetty, Nathaniel Hendren, Patrick Kline, and Emmanuel Saez, "Where is the land of Opportunity? The Geography of Intergenerational Mobility in the United States," The Quarterly Journal of Economics 129, no. 4 (November 2014): 1553–1623; Raj Chetty, David Grusky, Maximilian Hell, Nathaniel Hendren, Robert Manduca, and Jimmy Narang, "The fading American dream: Trends in absolute income mobility since 1940," Science 356, no. 6336 (April 2017): 398–406; and Miles Corak and Andrew Heisz, "The Intergenerational Earnings and Income Mobility of Canadian Men: Evidence from Longitudinal Income Tax Data," Journal of Human Resources 34, no. 3 (Summer, 1999): 504–33.

18. But to throw a little cold water on this slightly optimistic note, some recent elections, such as in Sweden, have evidenced large numbers of young people voting for extreme right-wing parties.

CHAPTER 12: FREEDOM, SOVEREIGNTY, AND COERCION AMONG STATES

1. See, for instance, Stiglitz, *Globalization and Its Discontents, Globalization and Its Discontents Revisited,* and *Making Globalization Work*; and Charlton and Stiglitz, *Fair Trade for All.*

2. There is much debate about why the IMF has pushed such policies, especially when the inflation is not caused by an excess of aggregate demand so is not likely to be cured by higher interest rates, outside of a calamitous effect on output and employment. Higher interest rates serve well the interests of financial markets, whose interests are strongly reflected in the US Treasury, whose perspectives have traditionally dominated at the IMF.

3. Officially, the rate was 15 percent, but carve outs are expected to reduce revenues substantially.

4. Part of the problem was that the formula that was used to allocate taxing "rights" was one which reflected the interests of the advanced countries. See Julie McCarthy, "A Bad Deal for Development: Assessing the Impacts of the New Inclusive Framework Tax Deal on Low- and Middle-Income Countries," Brookings Global Working Paper #174 (May 2022); and Independent Commission for the Reform of International Corporate Taxation, "ICRICT Response to the OECD Consultation on the Pillar One and Pillar Two Blueprints," December 13, 2020.

5. See, e.g., Joanna Robin and Brenda Medina, "UN Votes to Create 'Historic' Global Tax Convention Despite EU, UK Moves to 'Kill' Proposal," International Consortium of Investigative Journalists, November 22, 2023, https://www.icij.org.

6. That debtor prisons were an accepted part of the order of the day should remind us of how social views of what is acceptable and desirable change markedly over time. The injustices of such a system seem obvious, yet it was justified as a warning to individuals not to get overindebted, and it served financiers' interests—the threat of prison enabled them to extract money from the debtor's relatives.

7. The PROMESA (Puerto Rico Oversight, Management, and Economic Stability Act) Board was appointed by the federal government, which had denied the island its right to have its own bankruptcy process.

8. That means that "contractual approaches"—designing contracts which enable a quick resolution of bankruptcies—are even more difficult. At one time, in the early part of the century, many were optimistic that such contractual approaches would nonetheless work for sovereign debt, even though no country internally relied on them. With Argentina's crisis, it became clear that better contracts helped, but they did not fully address the problems of debt resolution.

9. Earlier chapters have shown the role fear has played in the adoption of the neoliberal agenda domestically.

10. Sprinkled in with this inhumane harshness was a dose of humanity, evidenced, for instance, by the HIPC (Highly Indebted Poor Country) Initiative, involving substantial debt write-offs from the IMF and multilateral and bilateral donors to restore debt sustainability. Countries had to comply with an array of conditionalities. It was launched in 1996, with an estimated $76 billion in present discounted value of debt write-offs. But a quarter century later, the debt problem has returned. See International Monetary Fund, "Debt Relief Under the Heavily Indebted Poor Countries (HIPC) Initiative," https://www.imf.org/en/About/Factsheets/Sheets/2023/Debt-relief-under-the-heavily-indebted-poor-countries-initiative-HIPC.

11. In the end, political dysfunctionality in Argentina compounded the problems. As this book goes to press, it is not clear how Argentina will be able to repay the *restructured* debts; it is almost inevitable that there will be another restructuring.

12. To be sure, the "official" grounds were different, and many things were at play. The efforts seemed to be spearheaded by the US. See my op-ed, "A Coup Attempt at the IMF," Project Syndicate, September 27, 2021, https://www.project-syndicate.org/commentary/coup-attempt-against-imf-managing-director-georgieva-by-joseph-e-stiglitz-2021-09.

13. Debt securitization itself has almost surely exacerbated the debt problem—just as it did in the 2008 financial crisis that began in the US. Banks and bankers get rewarded on the basis of the origination of loans, with insufficient attention to the countries' capacity to repay.

14. Through what are called CDSs, credit default swaps, a special kind of derivative, acting like an insurance policy, that would pay off the credi-

tor if, and only if, the debtor defaulted. These played an important role in the 2008 financial crisis.

15. Diwan and Wei use the World Bank's International Debt Statistics (IDS) database to estimate that as of 2020, China held 15.1 percent of the total long-term external debt stocks (public and publicly guaranteed) of low-income countries and 9.4 percent of the stocks for lower-middle-income countries. Ishac Diwan and Shang-Jin Wei, "China's Developing Countries Debt Problem: Options for Win-Win Solutions," Finance for Development Lab Policy Note 3 (December 2022). Horn et al. use raw data based on public commitments to estimate debt stocks and find that after accounting for "hidden" debt (i.e., Chinese loan commitments not reported to the World Bank), China owned upward of 30 percent of external debt for the 50 countries most indebted to China in 2016. See Sebastian Horn, Carmen M. Reinhart, and Christoph Trebesch, "China's Overseas Lending," *Journal of International Economics* 133 (November 2021): 1–32. In a *Forbes* article, Katharina Buchholz claims that "in 2022, 37% of debt service payments by low-income countries went to China." "The Countries Most in Debt to China," *Forbes*, August 19, 2022.

16. In some cases, it has even used comparable rhetoric, claiming that it has, in effect, a fiduciary duty to its citizens to collect as much as it can, just as the financial institutions claim they do, on behalf of their investors.

17. Because of internal politics, it seems difficult for China to just write off debt; it can more easily restructure the debt, allowing the postponement of payments in ways which lower the present discounted value of what is owed—an effective haircut. But comparing this form of debt reduction with a more straightforward reduction is often difficult, partly because of controversy over the appropriate discount rate to use in assessing the value of debt postponement.

18. For a fuller telling of this story, see Stiglitz, *Globalization and Its Discontents*. For a discussion of the aftermath, see Stiglitz, *Globalization and Its Discontents Revisited*.

19. The Washington Consensus was a consensus between the World Bank, the IMF, and the US Treasury (i.e., between the three institutions located between Fifteenth and Nineteenth Streets in Washington, DC), not a consensus about development policy among the rest of the world, about what reforms countries needed to undertake to achieve growth. Capital market liberalization wasn't included in the original tenets as articulated by John Williamson in his summary of the policy framework pushed by the Bretton Woods institutions in Latin America: "What Washington Means by Policy Reform," in John Williamson, ed., *Latin American Readjustment: How Much Has Happened* (Washington, DC: Peterson Institute for International Economics, 1989), but it quickly became part of the standard package foisted on developing countries and emerging markets. For a broader discussion of the issues, see the edited volume by

Narcis Serra and Joseph E. Stiglitz, *The Washington Consensus Reconsidered: Towards a New Global Governance* (New York: Oxford University Press, 2008).

20. See Bruce Greenwald and Joseph E. Stiglitz, "A Modest Proposal for International Monetary Reform," *Time for a Visible Hand: Lessons from the 2008 World Financial Crisis*, eds. Stephany Griffith-Jones, José A. Ocampo, and Joseph E. Stiglitz, Initiative for Policy Dialogue Series (Oxford: Oxford University Press, 2010), 314–44; and "Towards a New Global Reserves System," *Journal of Globalization and Development* 1, no. 2 (2010), Article 10.

21. Though even then, they argued for limiting both the tools and the circumstances in which they would be employed. The analytic foundations and even empirical evidence for their long-term opposition to capital controls was at best weak. In Joseph E. Stiglitz, "Capital Market Liberalization, Globalization, and the IMF," in *Capital Market Liberalization and Development*, José Antonio Ocampo and Joseph E. Stiglitz, eds. (Oxford: Oxford University Press, 2008), 76–100, I showed how capital controls could enhance economic stability and well-being. See also Jonathan D. Ostry, Atish R. Ghosh, and Mahvash Saeed Qureshi, *Capital Controls* (Cheltenham, UK: Edward Elgar Publishing, 2015). (Ostry was formerly deputy head of research at the IMF.)

22. That theory assumed perfectly competitive markets, including labor markets. But markets are not perfectly competitive and globalization undermined the bargaining power of workers, making matters for them even worse than predicted by the standard theory.

23. The question of whether the US has undermined the international rules-based system stands apart from the question of whether, net, the Inflation Reduction Act was positive, given the importance of the actions it induced for reducing climate emissions.

24. See, in particular, note 44 in chapter 3.

25. A major exception to the hoarding of intellectual property and Covid-19–related products was the AstraZeneca vaccine, developed jointly with Oxford University, where there was a commitment to make it available on a not-for-profit basis to developing countries. Unfortunately, the vaccine's safety and efficacy were established later than was the case for the mRNA vaccines of Pfizer and Moderna, and it was less effective. Some in the developing countries shunned the vaccine, claiming that a second-rate product was being foisted on them.

26. The US has largely couched its actions as a response to China not playing by the rules, but this is somewhat disingenuous. For an articulation of the US position by National Security Advisor Jake Sullivan, see "Remarks by National Security Advisor Jake Sullivan on Renewing American Economic Leadership at the Brookings Institution," The White House, April 27, 2023.

27. I develop some of the ideas in this section further in Joseph E. Stiglitz, "Regulating Multinational Corporations: Towards Principles of Cross-Border Legal Frameworks in a Globalized World Balancing Rights with Responsibilities," *American University International Law Review* 23, no. 3 (2007): 451–558, Grotius Lecture presented at the 101st Annual Meeting of the American Society for International Law, Washington, DC, March 28, 2007; and Joseph E. Stiglitz, "Towards a Twenty-first Century Investment Agreement," preface in *Yearbook on International Investment Law and Policy 2015–2016*, Lise Johnson and Lisa Sachs, eds. (Oxford: Oxford University Press, 2017), xiii–xxviii.

28. Kyla Tienhaara, Rachel Thrasher, B. Alexander Simmons, and Kevin P. Gallagher, "Investor-State Disputes Threaten the Global Green Energy Transition," *Science* 376, no. 6594 (May 13, 2022): 701–3.

29. Still another example: The price of oil may skyrocket, generating wind-fall profits. The country legitimately might want to impose a windfall profits tax, but because of the investment agreement, may not be able to do so. A well-designed contract would not have allowed a foreign oil company to walk off with the entire bonanza, but contracts are usually not well designed, and no contract can fully anticipate the future.

30. See, for instance, Malena Castaldi and Anthony Esposito, "Philip Morris Loses Tough-on-Tobacco Lawsuit in Uruguay," Reuters, July 9, 2016.

31. The provisions of chapter 11 of NAFTA.

32. What Dani Rodrik has called "premature deindustrialization." See Dani Rodrik, "Premature Deindustrialization," *Journal of Economic Growth* 21, no. 1 (2016): 1–33.

33. This is much in the spirit of the classical view of liberty, as espoused by Mill. My discussion in earlier chapters has emphasized that externalities are far more prevalent than Mill seemed to suggest, and so, too, for situations where collective action might improve the welfare of all. As I noted above, there are important externalities arising from the action of *large* countries such as the US, and regulations on their behavior which lead to their taking into account the effects of their externalities would be desirable.

34. Consider capital market regulations restricting the inflow of foreign capital. Capitalists in the US are only harmed to the extent that they are denied an opportunity for investment (or exploitation), and this should not be sufficient grounds for interference. Of course, the West took the opposite stance in the Opium Wars; I think that's wrong, and it has had long-lasting, deleterious effects in relations between the West and China.

35. Almost surely, their strong advocacy of capital market liberalization had more to do with their view that it would open up vast new opportunities for profits than for their deep concern for the well-being of developing countries.

36. We can also approach these issues from the perspective of a Smithian "impartial spectator."

    Rawls himself was reluctant to apply his analytic framework in such a cross-cultural context. He outlined a vision for fairness in a global context in "The Law of Peoples," *Critical Inquiry* 20, no. 1 (1993): 36–68. However, these attempts triggered well-argued critiques of cultural relativism. See Patrick Hayden, "Rawls, Human Rights, and Cultural Pluralism: A Critique," *Theoria: A Journal of Social and Political Theory*, no. 92 (1998): 46–56. A large literature has been spawned on these issues, beyond that which we can delve into here, raising issues analogous to those discussed in note 3, chapter 5, note 10 in the next chapter, and notes 7 and 10 in the introduction to Part III. For example, behind the veil of ignorance, we don't know how risk averse we will be, and without knowing that, we can't assess well alternative risky situations. In looking here, at international *economic* agreements, I am putting fewer demands on the theory than Rawls did, i.e., I do not discuss issues either of human rights or international obligations of rich countries to provide assistance to the poor.

CHAPTER 13: PROGRESSIVE CAPITALISM, SOCIAL DEMOCRACY, AND A LEARNING SOCIETY

1. That is, a change in knowledge, or even beliefs, about how the economy functions affects how the economy functions. This is true whether or not those beliefs are true. Neoliberalism was a set of (wrong) ideas about how the economy worked; but as neoliberal ideas spread, laws and behavior changed, and with them so did the economic system. Ideas matter. In that case, they mattered for the worse.
2. For a more extensive discussion of what is entailed in a learning society, see Stiglitz and Greenwald, *Creating a Learning Society.*
3. I've described extensively how neoliberalism has pushed us in the opposite direction. While advocates of neoliberalism championed how it pushed for changes in technology and policies that would advance growth, it was weak in constructing mechanisms that would facilitate the ability of those adversely affected to cope with these changes, giving rise to the growth of populism among affected populations. The backlashes against "advances" like trade liberalization and even to science and universities being seen in so many parts of the world suggest that even the pace of change in technology and standards of living, more narrowly defined, may slow.
4. Consider, for instance, the following quote from *The Wealth of Nations*: "Our merchants and masters complain much of the bad effects of high wages in raising the price and lessening the sale of goods. They say nothing concerning the bad effects of high profits. They are silent with regard

to the pernicious effects of their own gains. They complain only of those of other people."

5. There are many explanations for this. See Joseph E. Stiglitz, "Technological Change, Sunk Costs, and Competition," Brookings Papers on Economic Activity, Economic Studies Program, Brookings Institution, vol. 1987, no. 3 (1987): 883–947. I discuss there how even small sunk costs enable the persistence of high monopoly profits—what matters for entry is not profits now but what profits will be if there is entry. Incumbent profit-making firms can take actions that make it clear that ex post competition will be tough and profits low. There are a variety of such entry deterrent strategies. Even without active deterrent policies, high financial costs of entry may deter entry.

6. Friedman's view was that if there were externalities, then government should have done something to mitigate them (he didn't like regulations, preferring price interventions). It was wrong, he thought, for firms to take on board any responsibility for externalities if the government failed to do so. But there was a deep intellectual inconsistency. Shareholder value maximization by powerful companies lobbying against regulations resulted in inadequate government policies.

7. Friedman, *"The Social Responsibility of Business Is to Increase Its Profits."*

8. See Joseph E. Stiglitz, "On the Optimality of the Stock Market Allocation of Investment," *Quarterly Journal of Economics* 86, no. 1 (1972): 25–60 (presented to the Far Eastern Meetings of the Econometric Society, June 1970, Tokyo); Sandy Grossman and Joseph E. Stiglitz, "On Value Maximization and Alternative Objectives of the Firm," *Journal of Finance* 32, no. 2 (1977): 389–402; and Sandy Grossman and Joseph E. Stiglitz, "Stockholder Unanimity in the Making of Production and Financial Decisions," *Quarterly Journal of Economics* 94, no. 3 (1980): 543–66.

9. Transaction costs, typically ignored in economic analyses, can play a large role in affecting how the economic system works, including the existence and persistence of power relations. The reason class-action suits are so important is that the cost of getting redress for a wrongful action by a corporation is prohibitive for a single individual.

   As I noted earlier, advances in economic theory in recent decades have shown that even very small costs can dramatically change outcomes.

10. Such as, behind the veil of ignorance, we don't know how risk averse we will be. Without knowing that, we can't assess well alternative risky situations. We could, of course, approach this problem from the perspective of being behind the veil of ignorance—for instance, assuming that we were equally likely to have utility functions of different degrees of risk aversion. Here, we ignore this and other related refinements of the analysis. See also the discussion in note 3 of chapter 5, note 36 of chapter 12, and notes 7 and 10 of the introduction to Part III.

NOTES

11. That declaration recognized many of the other rights and attributes of a good society that this book has focused on. It was a global agreement about a "common standard of achievement for all peoples and all nations."

    Unfortunately, Conservative governments over a long period have underfunded the UK's National Health Service, impairing its ability to deliver the health services needed.

12. There are many other areas in which the public option could enrich choice and competition—for instance, in the provision of mortgages or retirement annuities. The public option seems particularly relevant for a country like the US, in which many remain wedded to the notion that the private sector is more efficient and more responsive to individual needs and wants. To the extent that's true, the public option won't be taken up; to the extent that it's not true, it will.

13. The public option illustrates that the details of the institutional and legal structures that define progressive capitalism will differ across countries, depending on their history and culture. There is no single form of progressive capitalism. Fleshing out these details also illustrates the magnitude of the challenge ahead.

14. The Clinton administration did try to take strong actions on climate change and to reform the health-care system, to provide better access to health care, but these efforts were beaten back. On the other hand, it followed the neoliberal orthodoxy by emphasizing balancing the budget—it even achieved a surplus—and in financial market deregulation. For a fuller account, see my 2003 book, *The Roaring Nineties*, or Nelson Lichtenstein and Jill Stein, *A Fabulous Failure: The Clinton Presidency and the Transformation of American Capitalism* (Princeton, NJ: Princeton University Press, 2023).

15. This is an example of an arena where the presumption of efficient markets needs to be reversed: it should be obvious that markets do not provide insurance against many of the most important risks individuals face.

16. And indeed, the macroeconomic failures themselves owed much to the ideology that markets were self-correcting; thus one didn't need strong bank regulations.

17. I want to emphasize, though, that the success of progressive capitalism does not depend on any rosy fantasy that all individuals be transformed. Rather, it takes off from the reality that individuals shape and are shaped by the economic system. There has to be a congruence, and not only in a mythical "long-run equilibrium," if only it could be obtained. It must be achievable, *given where we are today*, through an evolutionary process. Progressive capitalism works well even if individuals are as selfish as standard economics assumes they are; but it may work even better if more people are more other-regarding.

CHAPTER 14: DEMOCRACY, FREEDOM, SOCIAL JUSTICE, AND THE GOOD SOCIETY

1. He was slightly more qualified in what he said in his 1981 inaugural address, "*In this present crisis*, government is not the solution to our problem; government is the problem" (italics added); but his message was intended to be broader.

2. See Jonathan J. B. Mijs and Elizabeth L. Roe, "Is America coming apart? Socioeconomic segregation in neighborhoods, schools, workplaces, and social networks, 1970–2020," *Sociology Compass* 15, e12884 (2021).

3. In the end, when the basic disagreements about the rules that constitute a good society are deep enough and important enough, it becomes hard for a society to function well, if at all. When there is a large correlation between geography and beliefs, it may well be desirable to provide a certain degree of autonomy to each in setting the rules, or even contemplate political separation.

   The question of the boundaries of countries and the benefits of devolution of powers has long been a subject of inquiry among economists and political scientists. See, e.g., Alberto Alesina and Enrico Spolare, "On the Number and Size of Nations," *Quarterly Journal of Economics* 112, no. 4 (1997): 1027–56; and Joseph E. Stiglitz, "Devolution, Independence, and the Optimal Provision of Public Goods," *Economics of Transportation* 4 (2015): 82–94, written in the midst of Scotland's debate about independence.

4. See Adam Smith, *The Theory of Moral Sentiments*, III:V. This quotation may seem inconsistent with his better-known statement about the virtues of the pursuit of self-interest. Part of the resolution of the inconsistency lies in "reputation": it would not be in an individual's own self-interest to act in an untrustworthy way. But there is more to Smith's view than that: there are (to use current language) externalities associated with acting in an untrustworthy way, because it leads to a society in which trust is lacking, and this undermines a market economy. Smith emphasizes that in a good society, individuals have internalized this externality, and act accordingly. For an excellent discussion, see Jerry Evensky, "Adam Smith's Essentials: On Trust, Faith, and Free Markets," *Journal of the History of Economic Thought* 33, no. 2 (2011): 249–67.

5. Standard economics says that reputation mechanisms provide a check against such opportunistic behavior—but it is evident that such mechanisms provide only a partial check. The most important check against such aberrant behavior are, however, societal norms: We need to inculcate "decent" behavior. The criticism of current economic and societal arrangements is that they are poor in doing so.

6. In developing countries and emerging markets, matters are worse. As

discussed in chapter 12, under the influence of the IMF, countries have "liberalized" their capital markets, with adverse effects on their economy and democracy. Countries that have liberalized fear the loss of capital if they pursue policies that the international financial markets dislike— including reversing the policy of capital-market liberalization.

7. While there is a large literature consistent with this view, there are some among the Right who suggest the problem is that they don't have enough influence. If they did, Trump, a populist, would never have been elected. It is clear, however, that once elected, he directed policy in the interests of the very rich, as evidenced by the 2017 tax cut. See Greg Mankiw's blog, "Who Is the Prototypical Rich Person?" January 23, 2019, https:// gregmankiw.blogspot.com/2019/01/who-is-prototypical-rich-person .html.

8. In some ways, the extreme divisiveness is perhaps understandable: given that the Right's agenda was supported by a distinct minority, they had to do what they could while they were in power, and do what they could to make sure that their minority controlled the levers of power, at least as far into the future as they were able to.

9. Martin Wolf, *The Crisis of Democratic Capitalism* (New York: Penguin Press, 2023).

10. This is, of course, just one of many instances of the misreading of history. Hitler's rise is often attributed to inflation—and that "fact" is often given as an explanation for Germany's obsession with inflation. Hitler's rise has far more to do with unemployment and the Great Depression.

11. The fact that the survival of America's democracy has become such a concern, reflected in bestselling books like *How Democracies Die*, says a lot about where the US is today. See Steven Levitsky and Daniel Ziblatt, *How Democracies Die* (New York: Crown, 2019).